D0760610

CALGARY PUBLIC LIBRARY

FEB   2011

MONT BLANC WALKS

About the Author

Hilary Sharp is British, a qualified Accompagnateur en Montagne (Trekking Guide) and is based permanently in the village of Vallorcine near Chamonix Mont Blanc in the French Alps. She runs her own trekking business, Trekking in the Alps, guiding walks in winter, spring and summer. Her love of walking and climbing has taken her to many parts of Europe and further afield. Even after many years of exploring the Mont Blanc region she still discovers new walks every year.

Hilary is a contributor to several British walking magazines and is the author of *Trekking and Climbing in the Western Alps* published by New Holland in 2002 and *Snowshoeing: Mont Blanc and the Western Alps* (2002), *Tour of the Matterhorn* (2006) and *Tour of Monte Rosa* (2007) published by Cicerone Press.

Trekking in the Alps
Info@trekkinginthealps.com
www.trekkinginthealps.com

MONT BLANC WALKS

by
Hilary Sharp

CICERONE

2 POLICE SQUARE, MILNTHORPE, CUMBRIA LA7 7PY
www.cicerone.co.uk

© Hilary Sharp 2005, 2010

Second edition 2010
ISBN: 978 1 85284 597 1

First edition 2005
ISBN-13: 978 1 85284 414 1
ISBN-10: 1 85284 414 0

Photos: Hilary Sharp. Maps: Jon de Montjoye

A catalogue record for this book is available from the British Library.

Printed by MCC Graphics, Spain

Thanks

The following people have made writing this book much easier for me: Roger and Mu Portch, Des Clark, Patricia Loffi, Lucie Castell. I also want to thank Jean-Luc Lugon, for route advice and information; Nick Smith, for allowing me to write in the calm and pleasant surroundings of his house, away from the cold of home in the Haute Savoie; Mark Charlton, for vocabulary; and most of all Jon de Montjoye, for map drawing, proof reading and general support.

Advice to Readers

Readers are advised that, while every effort is made by our authors to ensure the accuracy of guidebooks as they go to print, changes can occur during the lifetime of an edition. Please check Updates on this book's page on the Cicerone website (**www.cicerone.co.uk**) before planning your trip. We would also advise that you check information about such things as transport, accommodation and shops locally. Even rights of way can be altered over time. We are always grateful for information about any discrepancies between a guidebook and the facts on the ground, sent by email to info@cicerone.co.uk or by post to Cicerone, 2 Police Square, Milnthorpe LA7 7PY, UK.

Front cover: On Mont de la Saxe above Courmayeur, looking across to the Mont Blanc massif from the south (walk 48)

CONTENTS

Mountain Warning
Mountain walking can be a dangerous activity, carrying a risk of personal injury or death. It should be undertaken only by those with a full understanding of the risks and with the training and/or experience to evaluate them. Whilst every care and effort has been taken in the preparation of this book, the user should be aware that conditions can be highly variable and can change quickly, thus materially affecting the seriousness of a mountain walk.

Therefore, except for any liability which cannot be excluded by law, neither Cicerone nor the author accept liability for damage of any nature (including damage to property, personal injury or death) arising directly or indirectly from the information in this book.

Map Key

～～	ridge
(glacier symbol)	glacier
～～～	walking route (various colours)
▲	mountain hut
～～～	road
～～	river/stream
⤨	col
▲	summits
+++++++++++++	railway lines
(lake symbol)	lake
....	road tunnel
(boundary symbol)	national boundary
P	parking
■■	buildings
├────────┤🚡	cableways
✝	church
→	direction of walk (various colours)
→	direction arrow
✳	place of interest

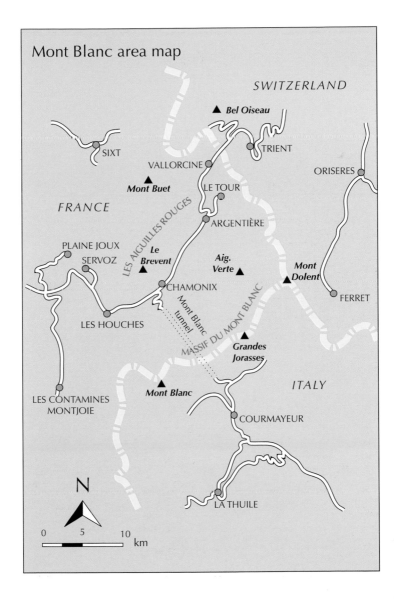

Mont Blanc area map

SWITZERLAND

▲ *Bel Oiseau*

SIXT

VALLORCINE

TRIENT

ORISERES

Mont Buet

LE TOUR

FRANCE

ARGENTIÈRE

PLAINE JOUX

SERVOZ

Le Brevent

LES AIGUILLES ROUGES

Aig. Verte ▲

Mont Dolent ▲

FERRET

CHAMONIX

Mont Blanc tunnel

MASSIF DU MONT BLANC

LES HOUCHES

▲ *Grandes Jorasses*

ITALY

LES CONTAMINES MONTJOIE

▲ *Mont Blanc*

COURMAYEUR

N

LA THUILE

0   5   10 km

The Mont Blanc massif is seen to full advantage from the Aiguilles Rouges (walk 20)

INTRODUCTION

Mont Blanc, at 4808m (or there-abouts, as they keep remeasuring it) is the highest mountain in Western Europe. No matter how many times I walk, run or bike the trails around the region, I can never ignore the sight of this huge peak and its equally spec-tacular neighbours. The major centres of Chamonix and Courmayeur are often busy, invaded by holidaymak-ers, not to mention the heavy goods traffic that has to come up the val-leys to get through the alpine chain. Some people claim the paths are too frequented, there is no wilderness anymore, there are cafés and lifts and signposts... but nothing changes the fact that these valleys have walks equal to anywhere for their views, terrain and variety.

I never fail to be moved by the sublime background of glaciers plunging towards the valleys, high snowy summits glinting in the sun, flower-bedecked slopes and rocky trails tempting me on towards new vistas and hidden valleys. Be it spring, summer or autumn, the sheer beauty and range of the walking here will satisfy any hiker – if it doesn't they're pursuing the wrong activity.

There are many famous trails that take hikers to wonderful viewpoints opposite the Mont Blanc massif. There

Mont Blanc massif seen at sunset from the Refuge de Bel Lachat (walk 19)

are also lesser-known paths and routes that lead to fairly remote areas where you will see few walkers even in the high season.

In really dry hot summers when the freezing level is fixed above 4000m for long periods, the glaciers melt, the crevasses become huge, and rocks fall down gullies and rock faces, the non-glaciated area of the mountains – the *moyenne montagne* as it is known in France – becomes particularly attractive. It is relatively unaffected by the objective dangers of the high mountains (the *haute montagne*). Many people enjoy walking on these high slopes way above the valley, with fantastic grandstand positions opposite the glaciated peaks, but with none of the attendant dangers associated with the high mountains.

THE REGION

The Mont Blanc massif straddles the frontier of three countries – France, Italy and Switzerland. Whilst Mont Blanc is the peak everyone has heard of, there are many other summits in the massif. It is said that this 25km-long range is made up of around 400 summits with at least 40 glaciers defining the valleys and faces.

The Chamonix valley runs northeast to southwest on the north side of the massif, while Courmayeur is situated in the Dora Baltea valley. This heads south from the long Veny and Ferret valleys which define the south side of the massif.

The Mont Blanc massif forms the east flank of the Chamonix valley, while the Aiguilles Rouges form the west side. Previously gouged out

Walking in the Aiguilles Rouges, with Mont Blanc behind (walk 23)

by the huge forces of the glaciers, the continuing slow erosion of the valley is now just due to the River Arve, with the additional force of the Arveyron from midway. The valley is headed by the village of Le Tour at its northern end. In descending order down the valley are the villages of Montroc, Argentière, Le Lavancher, Les Tines, Les Praz and the town of Chamonix. Continuing down the valley we then reach Les Houches and Servoz before the River Arve leaves the Chamonix valley for the flat plains of Le Fayet and Sallanches.

On the Italian side the Veny and Ferret valleys are much more sparsely populated, with Courmayeur being the real centre.

The Swiss part of the range is right on the northeastern edge, the nearest big town being Martigny, down on the flat plain of the Rhône valley.

For the purposes of this guidebook the region covered has been chosen for its proximity and views of the Mont Blanc massif, and its accessibility from the major resorts around the massif. The region extends slightly beyond the Chamonix valley on the French side: as far as the Contamines valley to the south, and to the Vallorcine valley to the north beyond the Col des Montets; then into Switzerland just above the Franco–Swiss border; and to the south of the Mont Blanc massif where the Ferret and Veny valleys converge just north of Courmayeur, as well as including the Colle San Carlo further south.

This gives an area that is easily visited by car during a week's holiday or longer. There is a wide range of walks, varied in both terrain and views. Within this relatively small area there are differences of nationality, language, food, farming, culture and, amongst other things, driving styles – there are plenty of opportunities to compare France with Switzerland and Italy on all these counts.

This book is biased to the French side of the massif. There are two reasons for this: firstly, this side has many of the most famous walks, such as the Lac Blanc walk and the Montagne de la Côte; secondly, I live there and consequently spend more time there. This in no way undermines the Italian or Swiss regions, where there is an equally fine number of superb walks. There is just no getting away from the fact that Chamonix is the place everyone has heard of, so it seems natural to give a certain predominance to that valley.

HOW IT ALL STARTED

Tucked away amongst the high mountains, cut off from the lower valleys by snow for a good six months of the year, the rest of the time struggling to scrape together some sort of existence, the inhabitants of the Mont Blanc valleys did not attract any attention for many centuries. Traditionally the peaks struck fear into the hearts of the locals: the source of violent storms, avalanches, mud slides, often wreathed in cloud and battered by winds, such places could only be the cursed home of dragons and evil spirits.

The glaciers themselves began to give cause for concern in the 18th century when, due to the so-called 'Little Ice Age', these frozen rivers increased in size almost daily and pushed down to the valley, threatening the villagers' meadows and dwellings. The local priest was called out frequently to exorcise the inexorable advance of these grotesque monsters.

However, not everyone shared this fear of the spectacular peaks. In 1741 a group of wealthy travellers, including the British Richard Pococke and William Wyndham, set out from Geneva to visit the glaciers they had seen glinting far away in the sun. Having made the difficult journey up into the Chamonix valley, rather to the surprise of the locals they continued up to a point level with the biggest glacier, the Mer de Glace. They were stunned by what they saw: 'like a huge river frozen in time' enthused Wyndham in his account of this visit.

Soon the glaciers of Chamonix became a must-do on any well-to-do traveller's list, and the next 50 years saw an increasing number of people make the pilgrimage to the mountains. The locals were quick to grab

The sign for the Gîte à Balmat on the trail up the Montagne de la Côte (walk 18)

the opportunity that this provided to make some cash guiding these travellers to the best viewpoints, and even setting foot on the ice itself.

The Genevan botanist Horace Bénédict de Saussure was the first to dream about standing on the top of the summits. The view of Mont Blanc that captivated him in 1760 when he climbed Le Brévent prompted him to offer a reward to the person who could find him a way to the top. It was to take 26 years before Jacques Balmat and Gabriel Paccard reached the summit on 8 August 1786, overcoming deep-set fears of the inherent dangers of venturing into these high, bewitched places. De Saussure made his ascent the following year. After that it was just a question of time before most of the peaks of the Alps were climbed, often by visiting alpinists accompanied by local guides.

Meanwhile, from the Italian side, Monte Bianco was not ascended until 1865 when a British team with Swiss guides climbed the Brenva spur route.

From then on no longer were the mountains a source of terror and inconvenience – on the contrary, it is thanks to the summits and glaciers that the alpine valleys now enjoy prosperity from tourism. In addition to the summer visitors, the huge and sudden growth of skiing in the early 20th century provided the 'white gold' required so that most alpine towns now rely almost totally on tourism for their living.

Today Chamonix sees its permanent population grow from 10,000 to 60,000 in the summer high season. On a good summer's day 200 people may stand on the summit of Mont Blanc.

GLACIERS

Glaciers and glaciated mountains are going to feature big-style in the views from most walks in the Mont Blanc region. The valleys have been carved by the ice and now what remains of these huge frozen rivers are what many people come to see.

Chamonix has about 40 glaciers – it is said that from La Flégère cable car you can see 14 all at once. There are two really well-known ones – the Bossons glacier and the Mer de Glace glacier. They are totally contrasting, the Bossons being very steep and the Mer de Glace pretty flat. Over in Courmayeur the Brenva glacier sweeps down from Monte Bianco in a chaotic mass of ice and rocks, whereas the Miage glacier is so flat that it looks like a river of scree, the ice in its lower part barely visible.

All glaciers have generally retreated for the past 120 years, although there have been mini cycles during that time. Previously the glaciers came all the way down to the Chamonix and Courmayeur valleys, and before that whole valleys were glaciated, the ice from the Chamonix valley going as far as Lyon – 15,000

15

years ago Chamonix was under 1000m of ice.

The Middle Ages were a time of relative warmth and many glaciers melted massively – artefacts found at now glaciated passes such as the Théodule Pass on the Italian–Swiss border attest to the fact that much of this terrain was ice-free for many centuries.

The Little Ice Age of 1550–1885 saw an impressive regain of territory by the glaciers. and gave rise to much fear and distrust of the glaciers among mountain people – the ice was literally pushing up against their front doors. Since this time there has been a general regression, with odd advances now and again. Whether we are now in a natural cycle, or whether the recent fast melting of the glaciers is due to the effects of modern civilisation, is still a moot point.

What is certain is that the glaciers add immensely to any walk in the mountains near Mont Blanc. They look their best after a light dusting of snow, giving them a fresh coat of paint. On sunny days the ice picks up the rays and throws them back, glinting and sparking; on cloudy days the glaciers reflect the grey, so pick your walks carefully and save those best glacier views for a perfect day.

VIA FERRATAS

Several of the walks described here feature via ferratas and since these are peculiar to Europe they need some explanation. The term is Italian and literally means 'iron way'. Via ferratas usually go up or along rocky faces or difficult terrain that would present an obstacle to most walkers. The addition of metal rungs, chains, cables and even ladders renders these sections accessible to the walker.

Via ferratas were built in the eastern Alps to facilitate mountain tourism in the 19th century, but played an important role in World War I when Italy and Austria were fighting there. The ground they were fighting on in the Dolomites was very mountainous and the conditions for the soldiers were extreme. To enable movement of the troops, sections of rock were often equipped with metal holds. After the war they returned to recreational use and many others have been built for this purpose since.

By far the greatest concentration of via ferratas remains in the Dolomites, but from time to time they are found on footpaths in the Mont Blanc region. Some long and impressive via ferratas require the use of ropes and harnesses to make them safe, but those on paths are always just to give some hand- and footholds for walkers. All those encountered in this guidebook can be done without equipment and only those afflicted with true vertigo would find them unpleasant. For everyone else they just add a little zest to the walk. Small children should, however, be roped up and dogs should not be taken at all on these routes, as a fall could be fatal and you don't want to put your beloved furry friend in such a position of danger.

Mention is made wherever via ferratas occur in these walks, and generally the route will be graded 3.

ANIMALS AND BIRDS

If you're lucky any alpine walk will not only be accompanied by exceptional views but also by sightings of alpine wildlife, or at least signs of their presence. It's handy to have an idea of what might be around: although sometimes from a distance identification can still be unsure it's nice to make an informed guess.

Cloven hoofprints can signify the presence of several different creatures – in the lower altitude forests there are various deer of different sizes. Chamois, the mountain deer, also frequent the wooded slopes in bad or cold weather, but otherwise they tend to stay higher up on the open slopes where there are also ibex, the hybrid mountain deer/goat. This latter is distinguishable from the chamois as the latter is more delicate in build and has a generally darker coat. The male ibex cannot be missed with its huge ridged horns and slow lazy gait.

A high-pitched shriek often has people looking to the sky for a bird, but this is most likely to be a marmot, warning his friends of danger nearby. This furry animal, when adult about the size of a big cat, lives underground in burrows and spends the summer months fattening up for the winter, when he will hibernate for seven months or so. Marmots have notoriously bad eyesight and hearing, but their sense of smell is phenomenal. If you come upon one and are downwind you have every

Wildlife is often seen if you're first on the trail in the morning

The north ridge of Mont Buet
provides a memorable route
to the summit (walk 43)

chance of sneaking up and getting a good view as he lazes in the sun or as the younger ones play-fight in front of their burrows.

There are hunting seasons in the Alps and culling of some animals is allowed, chamois being one of them. Ibex are totally protected, having been hunted to extinction everywhere except in parts of Italy from where they have now been reintroduced. Marmots are not generally hunted as they do not provide any suitable trophy to put on the wall and apparently their meat is not tasty.

Other creatures may make their presence known whilst you are walking – ermine are often to be seen scurrying around boulders, whereas lizards and more rarely snakes will certainly flick across the paths as you walk on sunny slopes.

In the sky, golden eagles are relatively common and are often seen playing on air currents in bad weather; lammergeier vultures have been reintroduced in the Mont Blanc region and are sometimes seen, but that is a real treat; the forests are home to any number of small birds, which will delight the birdwatcher.

Look out for tracks in the mud, droppings, chewed pine cones and nibbled tree branches – they all tell a story of what's around and this can be just as interesting as the views ahead.

FLOWERS AND TREES

One of the great things about walking in the Alps is the sheer variety of vegetation. In spring, summer or autumn there are always plants in flower, more or less abundant depending on the

The trumpet gentian is a sure sign of spring

altitude. Terrain is officially divided into different zones of vegetation, according to altitude, the main ones being colline, mountain, sub-alpine and alpine. What this means to the walker is that as height is gained, so the flowers and trees change. Chamonix and Courmayeur are at an altitude of 1000m–1200m and plants will begin to bloom on the slopes here around late April when the first trumpet gentians will be found on sunny aspects. Soon after, the alpenrose begins to flower. However, higher up at 1500m there is usually still snow so the flowers here will not bloom until late May, later still above 2000m.

July is absolutely prime time for flowery walking. From the meadows of vetch, orchids, bistort and globe flowers, to the slopes of pink alpenrose and yellow anemones, to the higher rocky slopes bejewelled with starry gentians, houseleeks and avens, this is almost flower-overload. Later in August there is not the wealth of blooms, but it only takes a little curiosity to find many small flowers above 2000m. Even in September the flowers are there, especially the late ones such as monkshood, which favours wet ground next to streams, rosebay willowherb, which so enhances those mountain shots, and the omnipresent wild pansies.

Many of the so-called alpine flowers are in fact smaller versions of valley plants. The growing season above 2000m is very short – just two months really. So these flowers have to be extremely efficient to flower and get pollinated in order to reproduce for the next year. They achieve this in part by being very small and intensely coloured so as to attract insects. Examples of this are the beautiful purple and orange toadflax, the rare deep blue King of the Alps and the cushions of bright pink rock jasmine.

Many of the alpine flowers are protected. This means they either should not be picked at all – the edelweiss being one example – or that it is forbidden to uproot the plant. In the past, a lot of plants were known for their medical properties; some remain popular and effective remedies – arnica extract, for example, is used to treat bumps and bruises. Others which relied on the root of the plant are usually no longer used, such as the yellow gentian whose root is effective in the treatment of certain cattle maladies.

In general flowers look a lot nicer where they are growing in the meadows or nestled among rocks than in a vase in the living room, where they will die very quickly. However, don't be surprised to see pots of gentians on the tables in the mountain huts!

Trees too employ various techniques to ensure their survival in a harsh environment. In the Mont Blanc region much of the forest is spruce and larch. The spruce is a shallow-rooted tree which takes advantage of the deep-rooted larch to give it protection from the wind. The larch itself

Houseleeks are able to grow on rocky ground with little earth

is at risk from the larva of the larch fly (strobilomyia) which eats its cones. So the larch varies production of cones from year to year – a year of many cones will be followed by a lean year, in the hope that the larvae will die off because of the paucity of cones. This is why larch trees only produce their beautiful pink flowers some years and not others. Unfortunately for the trees, the larvae seem to be perfecting the art of remaining dormant for a year, ready for a renewed attack when the larch produces a fresh crop of cones.

Many of the forested slopes in the Chamonix area have clear gaps where there are no mature trees. These are usually the slopes that avalanche every winter and so the larch and spruce never get a chance to grow

here. However, one tree does favour these slopes: the alder likes wet and mobile ground, and these bushes are able to survive avalanches as they bend under the weight of the snow. Once the alder colonise these gullies – providing there is no avalanche activity for some time – their roots stabilise the ground and other plants and trees will grow there.

It is interesting to look at old photos which show that a century ago the slopes above many villages were deforested to a much higher level than now, to allow as much cultivation of these difficult slopes as possible. Now that tourism provides most income and there is very little farming, the trees have been allowed to grow back with the benefit that the slopes are less prone to avalanches.

Marmots will accompany your walks

TRANSHUMANCE AND ALPAGES

Many of the tracks used for walking in the Alps are centuries-old access routes to the higher meadows above the treeline. In times past, the inhabitants of the alpine valleys lived by farming and raising cattle. This was a fairly precarious existence given that for six months or more of the year the valleys were snowbound. The cattle were kept indoors during those long winter months but, come the first days of spring, the cows would be put out to graze the valley fields.

As spring progressed the farmers would begin to herd the cattle upwards to higher ground where the grass was fresh and nutritious. They often had several summer farms, the main one being above the tree-line around 2000m altitude. These farms enjoyed good grazing, fresh cool air and plenty of running water for the animals. The meadows they occupied are known as

alpages, and although nowadays tourism has largely taken over from farming as the source of income for most alpine residents, alpage farms still exist and will be encountered on many walks. They often sell cheese, freshly made on the premises, and some also operate as huts and cafés.

Traditionally the cattle would be taken down to the valleys in early autumn to graze the valley fields for as long as the weather permitted. The descent of the herds was, and still is in some villages, reason for celebration, the cows being decked out with flowers and the villagers all coming out to welcome them back after a successful summer's farming.

This whole process of moving the animals up into the mountains is known as transhumance and still continues, albeit to a lesser extent than when farming was the source of survival for alpine people.

Even in a hot summer (such as 2003) you still have to be brave to take the plunge – here in the Lac Noir (walk 24)

WHEN TO GO

It can be fine and sunny at any time of year in the Alps, which is wonderful especially when sunshine is unexpected in the dark days of November. The downside of this, of course, is that it can also be rainy, snowy, stormy, and even tempestuous at any moment too: mountain weather does not respect the calendar.

Nonetheless, there are accepted times for walking in the mountains, and not only is the summer season the time when they tend to benefit from more stable weather conditions, it's also when the huts are open and the lifts working. So to have maximum choice of walks that's the time to come. This season extends from late June to mid-September. The real holiday period – which does create heaving crowds in towns and at honeypot areas – is 14 July (Bastille Day in France) to 15 August (Assumption).

Outside this time-frame you can still expect to get some fantastic

23

Enjoying high pastures between the Croix de Fer and the Tête de Balme (walk 32)

walking conditions: earlier, in June the weather is often hot and sunny and the days are long. Nevertheless, despite the heat in the valley, névé often remains above 2000m or lower, and can seriously interrupt a high level walk (see Névé and snow level, in Safety section below). Early on the huts and mountain cafés will usually not be open, nor the cable cars. Many hotels take a break in May and June so accommodation options are limited.

Later, in September and October the same applies as far as lodging is concerned. The chance of névé is far less, but fresh snow is likely to fall sometime early autumn and the shorter days and lower sun ensure that above a certain altitude on shady slopes this doesn't melt. The upside is that in autumn the light can be magnificent, with wonderful sunsets at the end of the afternoon, and there's

nothing more beautiful than walking the hills alone, with a fresh sprinkling of snow all around and the smell of autumn in the air.

An informed choice is necessary, and if you choose to come on the edge of the summer season be prepared to adapt your walks according to the conditions.

GETTING THERE

When the famous British 19th-century alpinists set off for the Alps it was a huge undertaking that would last months. First, they had to travel by coach all the way to the foothills, then onwards on foot into the alpine valleys, which was not only arduous but also risky and at times very difficult. Edward Whymper, the English mountaineer known best for being in the first ascent party on the Matterhorn, used to routinely walk to Chamonix from Geneva – about an hour in a fast car!

Nowadays there are plenty of quicker options, and from Britain it's even feasible to envisage a long weekend visit to the Alps.

Air

With the advent of cheap flights in the last few years, travel to the Alps could not be easier, at least from Britain. Geneva is the nearest airport, but Lyon and Milan are not too far away. Geneva airport can be found on the internet on www.gva.ch tel: +41 22 717 71 11 info@gva.ch

Many airlines fly into Geneva:

- From Britain, British Airways www.ba.com tel: 0845 722 2111; Easyjet www.easyjet.com tel: 0870 600 0000; jet2 www. jet2.com tel: 0870 737 8282; Swiss (previously Crossair), www.swiss.com tel: 0845 601 0956; BmiBaby www.bmibaby. com tel: 0870 264 2229
- From America, Swiss (sharing with American Airlines), Continental and Lufthansa (sharing with United Airlines)
- From Ireland, Aer Lingus www. aerlingus.com tel: +353 1 886 8844.

Onward travel from Geneva airport to Chamonix can be by train, bus or shuttle taxi. A regular bus service runs twice a day, operated by SAT in Chamonix, tel: 04 50 53 01 15. The French SNCF train runs from the airport to St Gervais via Geneva town centre, or you can choose to take a Swiss train via Martigny and Vallorcine/Argentière. Alternatively there are plenty of taxis serving the airport (Airport Transfer Services, tel: +33 450 53 63 97).

Rail

The train is a viable option from Britain now, especially from the south where Eurostar provides a high-speed service from London to Paris, from where the TGV goes on to St Gervais. From here there is a regular service up to Chamonix and onwards to Vallorcine and then Martigny in Switzerland. The French railways can be found on www.sncf.com; Eurostar: www. eurostar.com; Swiss railways on www. sbb.ch tel: 0900 300 300.

Bus

Eurolines offer a regular service from Britain and Ireland to Chamonix and Courmayeur. Whilst the journey is long the price is competitive: www. eurolines.com, tel: 020 7730 8235.

Getting around by road

Once in the Alps there are various options for making the most of your visit. The Chamonix valley has a very good bus service, named appropriately **Chamonix Bus**. This serves the whole of the valley from Les Houches to Le Tour and the Col des Montets. It does not go as far as Servoz or Vallorcine, but these villages are both on the **SNCF railway** from St Gervais

The full-grown male ibex cannot be mistaken for anything else!

Le Fayet to Martigny. In the summer anyone staying in hotel/gîte accommodation in the Chamonix valley is entitled to a *Carte d'Hôte* which, among other benefits, allows free travel on the Chamonix Bus.

St Gervais (which, despite the name, is not where the railway goes, this being down in the valley at Le Fayet) and Les Contamines can be reached by bus from Le Fayet. There is a twice-daily SAVDA Italian bus service between Chamonix and Courmayeur.

Each walk has details of public transport if it exists, but the nature of walks is that they do not always start at the nearest village or bus/train station. Some of the walks would be difficult to reach by public transport, or you may end up adding on a few kilometres of road walking at the beginning or end of the day. The ideal would be to rent a car, at least for part of a walking holiday.

There are plenty of car hire companies operating out of Geneva airport. There is also one company based in Chamonix: Europcar, tel: 04 50 53 63 40, fax: 04 50 53 91 32, email: autolux1@wanadoo.fr. In Courmayeur the tourist office has details of several hire car possibilities.

There is a host of possibilities, ranging from hotels of all standards to gîtes to huts to campsites. In the summer season – July and August – there is a huge demand for accommodation; advance booking is highly recommended.

Hotels

These range from 4-star luxury to no-star basic. Major towns such as Chamonix and Courmayeur have many to choose from, whereas the small villages will just have a handful, usually in the 2-star or below category. The local tourist offices will provide a list of hotels and may even make bookings for you.

The Refuge de Platé is a typical moyenne montagne hut, providing midday refreshments and overnight accommodation (walk 9)

Gîtes

There are two types of *gîte* available: a regular gîte is a house available for rent for self-catering accommodation – these will often be big enough for several families. More appropriate for holidaying walkers are the *gîtes d'etape* which offer basic lodging, usually in shared rooms, with dinner and breakfast. These can be very good value and also a good way to sample local food and culture. They exist in many villages, especially where a major long-distance trek such as the Tour du Mont Blanc passes through. Again the tourist office will have details of gîtes and gîtes d'etapes.

Campsites

There are many sites in Chamonix and around Courmayeur, as well as sites in the neighbouring villages. Camping is generally not allowed in the valley outside of campsites. Ask the tourist office for details.

Huts or refuges

It can be very pleasant to spend a couple of nights in mountain huts when exploring the area. These vary greatly in the facilities they offer, from quite luxurious with showers and even rooms, to the most basic with just a dormitory and a dining room. There are always toilets, and running cold water is almost guaranteed (although the exceptionally hot summer of 2003 did see isolated cases of dried-up water supplies).

Most huts are open from mid-June to mid-September, and there will be a guardian in residence. Usually the guardian cooks an evening meal and also provides breakfast. At a few huts you can take your own food, but you must make sure the guardian is happy with this. It is hardly worth the effort of carrying up food when a very good meal will be on offer for a reasonable price. Drinks – alcoholic and otherwise – are also sold.

On the Office de la Haute Montagne website (www.ohm-chamonix.com) you can find a list of all huts in the Mont Blanc massif with the dates they are open and wardened, as well as contact telephone numbers during and out of season, and a list of tariffs.

LANGUAGE

The Mont Blanc massif straddles the frontiers of three countries: France, Italy and Switzerland. In the not-so-distant past all these areas formed the Kingdom of Savoy, thus sharing a common link in culture and language.

The different regions were annexed more or less to the countries to which they now belong during the 19th century. The Aosta region of Italy enjoys a status of limited autonomy, and there almost everyone speaks both Italian and French. Although the Haute Savoie only became French in 1860, French has been spoken here as long as records exist. In Switzerland three

Reflections in Lac du Vieux Emosson (walk 43)

languages are spoken, French being that of the Valais canton which borders the Mont Blanc region.

Wherever you go in the Mont Blanc region, French will be understood and spoken. The major centres of Chamonix and Courmayeur are inundated with foreign visitors during the holiday seasons and you will hear a great variety of languages being spoken in town, English being predominant. The shopkeepers and hoteliers have realised that it serves them well to speak English and most do to some extent. Notwithstanding this, it is worth making the effort to learn a few basic words and there is a lot of pleasure to be gained by communicating in the local language as far as you are able. Generally people will meet you halfway and will respect your endeavours in the realm of international relations!

Some useful words are noted in the Useful Terms and Glossary, and those relative to the weather can be especially helpful if you do not manage to find a forecast in English.

CURRENCY

With the Euro it has become very easy to travel around Europe, although some consider it a bit dull – gone are the heady days when you could go armed with millions of Italian lire to buy a loaf of bread! In Switzerland, however, the Swiss franc remains the currency but some cafés and supermarkets will accept Euros if that's all you have. The same applies to Swiss mountain huts, but don't expect to get a good rate of exchange. Change will generally be given in francs.

29

MAPS

The best-scale maps available for summer walking in the Mont Blanc region are the 1:25,000 (4cm:1km) and four of the French Institut Géographique Nationale (IGN) Top 25 series cover nearly all the walks featured here. They are:

- IGN Top 25 3630 OT *Chamonix Massif du Mont Blanc* for all walks in the Chamonix valley from Chamonix northwards

OBTAINING MAPS

Maps are available from newsagents – presse in France – and bookshops. The most extensive selection in Chamonix is at the Maison de la Presse, on the main street Rue Docteur Paccard opposite Snell Sports; in Courmayeur, La Stampa has a very good selection and is on the main street near the church.

Maps are also available from:

- **The Map Shop**
  Freephone: 0800 085 40 80;
  tel: 01684 593146;
  fax: 01684 594559;
  e-mail: themapshop@
  btinternet.com;
  www.themapshop.co.uk
- **Stanfords**
  Tel: 020 7836 1321;
  fax: 020 7836 0189;
  e-mail: customer.services@
  stanfords.co.uk;
  www.stanfords.co.uk

- IGN Top 25 3530 ET *Samoëns Haut Giffre* for all walks west of Chamonix
- IGN Top 25 3531 ET *St-Gervais-les-Bains Massif du Mont Blanc* and IGN Top 25 3531 OT *Megève Col des Aravis* for those walks to the south of the Chamonix valley.

In addition to these, the north end of Lac d'Emosson is covered by the 1:25,000 map Carte Nationale de la Suisse 1324 *Barberine*.

The walks around Courmayeur are on the Italian 1:25,000 Istituto Geografico Centrale (IGC) 107 *Monte Bianco Courmayeur La Tuile Chamonix Mont Blanc*. Some are also on the IGN Top 25 3531 ET *St-Gervais-les-Bains Massif du Mont Blanc*.

A 1:50,000 (2cm:1km) map is useful to get an overview of the region. The whole area is covered by the IGN Rando Editions map A1 *Alpes Pays du Mont Blanc*. (NB This map uses French names for all places, including those in Italy. These names may be in Italian on the 1:25,000 map but will still be recognisable.)

SAFETY

Whilst walking on non-glaciated alpine terrain does not involve the dangers of high mountaineering, there are nevertheless hazards that must be taken into account. It's therefore important to be equipped accordingly, both in terms of actual gear

Signposts sometimes give safety information –
this one is near the Croix de Fer (walk 32)

carried and also as regards information acquired beforehand.

Equipment

In addition to the first-aid equipment detailed in the Security and Rescue section below there are certain essentials to carry for summer day walks in the Alps (in addition to personal items):

- waterproofs – jacket and trousers
- map and compass
- whistle
- warm sweater/fleece
- fleece hat and gloves
- sunhat and sunglasses
- suncream – body and lips
- water and food
- headtorch if walking late in the season when the days are short

- mobile phone
- first-aid kit
- bivvy bag/space blanket.

On overnight trips you need to add in gear for the hut. When open, with a resident warden, alpine huts provide bedding and meals. The only extra gear needed is a minimal change of clothes, a toothbrush and money to pay for the night. The only huts described in this guide are those that are open usually from late June to late September and during that time are wardened. An unwardened hut does not necessarily have bedding or cooking facilities. Some huts leave a room open when they are officially closed, but be sure to check on facilities before heading up.

If you need extra gear, there is a multitude of gear shops in Chamonix

31

and a couple of Courmayeur, as well as in Argentière and Les Houches.

Alpine weather

From deep snow in mid-August, to hot sun and green hillsides in mid-December, the weather in the Alps can do anything, anytime. Whilst it is accepted that the summer season begins late June and finishes mid-September it would be a mistake to expect warm temperatures throughout this period. At some stage during the summer it always snows below 2000m.

The mountains create their own weather, as the airflow is forced up and over the peaks, becoming colder and thus forming water vapour which falls as precipitation.

There are several relatively common effects that it's worth bearing in mind when coming to the Alps to walk:

The foehn effect

Take the example of a southerly foehn: a frontal system approaching the Alps from the southwest carries air laden with moisture from the sea. When it hits the Alps the air cools and deposits precipitation on the slopes exposed to the southwesterly flow. The air then flows down the northwesterly slopes, warming as it descends (due to the fact that dry air warms more quickly), hence leaving this side of the Alps in a warm dry airflow. So, for example, it can be sunny in Chamonix but

pouring with rain in Courmayeur on the other side of the Mont Blanc massif, and vice versa.

Lapse rate and wind-chill

It may be a pleasant 20°C in the valley, but as you go to higher altitudes it will certainly get colder. This temperature drop is known as the lapse rate, and technically 0.65°C is lost for every 100m of ascent. However, this rate is also affected by humidity – the drier the air, the higher the lapse rate. Temperatures drop noticeably in the shade, at night and during storms. The wind also has a dramatic effect on perceived temperature and the effect of wind combined with air temperature is known as wind-chill. For example, air temperature of 0°C combined with a 40kph wind will feel like -13°C.

Afternoon storms

Afternoon storms are common throughout the Alps in summer. They are the result of very hot air and the storm build-up is usually rapid, preceded by the formation of huge anvil-shaped cumulus clouds. The storms are commonly violent, with spectacular lightning and heavy precipitation, often hail and snow. They will usually abate as fast as they came, but during such storms it is very unwise to be out on exposed summits or ridges.

Cloud inversion

High-pressure weather can result in inversion cloud in the valleys, the

*Lenticular clouds over the
Chamonix Aiguilles*

result of the air being held down at lower altitude by the anticyclone. In winter this can result in freezing fog filling the valleys, whilst in summer it can be seen as a build-up of pollution lower down. Hence the Geneva and Annecy valleys may be gloomy all day whilst it's perfectly sunny higher up.

Weather forecasts

It is vital to check the weather forecast before setting out on a committing walk – one where bad weather would cause problems of navigation, cold, or danger. However, it should be remembered that the weather in the mountains does not always follow the general meteorological trend and can vary locally. Do not take the forecast as gospel – if they forecast *beau et chaud* but the grey clouds are building

and the wind howling, consider an alternative such as the museum or the swimming pool.

In Chamonix the weather forecast is displayed on a printout and a television screen in the window of the pharmacy. This is situated at the crossroads with the bell tower, next to the road that goes up to the church and tourist office.

Weather forecast numbers

The weather forecast is provided at tourist offices in the summer season. There will usually be an English translation and, if not, the staff can translate. Nevertheless it's worth having some rudimentary knowledge of weather vocabulary – see Appendix 2: Useful Terms and Glossary.

For those reasonably fluent in French or Italian the forecast is available by recorded telephone message, updated several times daily:

- France – tel: 08 92 68 02 74, www.chamonix.com
- Switzerland – tel: 848 800 162, www.meteosuisse.ch/fr
- Italy – tel: 0165 44 113, www.regione.vda.it/protezione_civile/meteo/

Sometimes the Chamonix forecast is available by phone in English but this service is not consistent. The best source of information in Chamonix on the weather and conditions is the Office de la Haute Montagne. This can be visited during office hours in the Maison de la Montagne in Chamonix, next to the church in the centre of town; tel: 04 50 53 22 08, fax: 04 50 53 27 74, e-mail: ohm-info@chamonix.co. The OHM website www.ohm-chamonix.com has lots of very useful information including current conditions of non-glaciated terrain (moyenne montagne). The website is not in English but the staff at the office are fluent.

For Courmayeur try the Courmayeur tourist office, www.courmayeur.net. The Guides' Office in town is also a good source of mountain information.

Névé and snow level

When planning summer walks in the Alps it's important to take into consideration the fact that snow that fell in the winter can remain until well into the summer months. This old snow is known as *névé*. The level at which it remains, and the length of time, depend on several factors:

- The amount of snow that fell during the winter

The Maison de la Montagne in Chamonix is a valuable source of information for walkers and climbers

- The amount of snow that fell late winter/early spring
- The weather during May and June
- The aspect of the slope
- The altitude of the slope.

The reason most alpine huts do not open until late June is that many slopes are not snowfree until then. This can be dangerous for walking. Watch out for gullies that may not receive much sun, and north- and west-facing slopes. Generally, after a 'normal' winter and spring, by the end of June most slopes are snowfree below 2000m. This doesn't mean, however, that there won't be the odd patch of névé which could make a normally easy footpath quite a challenging proposition. Traversing even a short section of névé can be very dangerous – if the slope is long and steep a fall could have extremely serious consequences. Similarly descents can be difficult if snow remains.

When considering a walk early in the season ask for advice at the huts; also consider which slopes may still be snowy and whether your walk will take you to these places early morning (when the snow may be frozen) or later in the day. Whilst still not always to be recommended, slushy melting snow is generally easier to walk on than the hard icy version.

Carrying an ice axe does not ensure safe passage across névé. Firstly, you need to know how to use it, both to cut steps efficiently and also to self arrest in case of a fall; should

such a fall occur, you need to have the presence of mind, the time, and the luck to do this. A long axe does serve as a walking stick which can be very useful on snowy slopes, but trekking poles are just as effective.

I recommend extreme prudence on névé wherever it is encountered, and if in any doubt do not venture on to it – change your route.

SECURITY AND RESCUE

Whilst walking in the non-glaciated mountains of the Alps is becoming increasingly popular, so are the incidences of accidents. These apparently innocuous hillsides, criss-crossed with trails and scattered with mountain huts and cafés, can be the scene of all sorts of problems, ranging from the most banal to the most serious. When walking in the Alps you need to be prepared and therefore avoid, or at least know how to deal with, most situations.

First aid
All walkers should routinely carry a basic first-aid kit in their rucksacks. However, the walks described here are generally just day walks and this – as well as the fact that there is a good and reliable rescue service in the Chamonix and Courmayeur valleys – means that the first-aid kit can be kept to the bare essentials:
- plasters
- painkillers
- aspirin

- antiseptic cream
- crêpe bandage
- fly repellent
- antihistamine cream
- scissors
- tweezers
- antiseptic wipes
- wound dressing
- latex gloves
- triangular bandage – can be substituted by a scarf or bandana
- bivvy bag or space blanket (shiny foil).

This kit allows treatment of any emergency encountered during a day walk. Resourcefulness is most useful – for example, a trekking pole can be used to splint an injured arm or leg.

Potential problems

As well as carrying the gear it's also crucial to know what to do in the event of possible incidents during mountain walks:

Heart attack

Everyone should have basic first-aid knowledge. Treatment of a heart attack victim goes beyond the scope of this guide but should be learned regularly at a first-aid centre. Hopefully this knowledge is never used, hence the need for regular refresher courses.

Hypothermia

Walking in the summer months you would not expect to be at risk of hypothermia which is generally associated with winter expeditions and high-altitude mountaineering. However, there are a surprising number of incidences of hypothermia each summer in the non-glaciated Alps. Classically the victim has been very hot and consequently sweaty whilst walking uphill, then cools very quickly, exacerbated by wind-chill and tiredness. The same situation can arise during bad weather when above 2000m snow is frequent even in the summer. The victim's core body temperature drops slightly and the body's response is to cut off circulation to the outer extremities. Hands and feet become very cold; the victim starts to shiver and to become irrational, unable to make basic decisions such as stopping to eat and put on warm clothes. Eventually a comatose state is reached and death will follow quickly.

The best action to take against hypothermia is to avoid it in the first place. When the top is reached or the wind gets up, put on an extra layer straight away; don't hesitate to change your planned route if necessary. The symptoms of impending hypothermia (sometimes referred to as exposure at the early stages) should be recognised and dealt with as soon as possible: give the victim warm drinks and food and put on clothing – a hat will prevent considerable heat loss. If feasible the walk should be cut short to get the victim down to the valley for warmth and rest. If the situation has already become more serious, with the victim displaying irrational and aggressive behaviour, it is imperative to act quickly. Once the stage of coma

The end of a good day, near the Loriaz alpages (walk 41)

is reached the rescue service must be called as the group cannot move the victim themselves. At this stage the victim must be kept warm, insulated from the ground as well as from the elements and not moved at all.

Altitude sickness

It is extremely unlikely that true altitude sickness will be encountered on any of the walks in this guide since generally they all remain well under 3000m. Whilst people may sometimes think they are feeling the effects of high altitude, altitude sickness is really only encountered above 3000m. However, those coming from sea level will certainly feel breathless the first day or so hiking in the Alps. To what extent this is due to the thinner

air and to what extent the inclines is a moot issue. When going high be sure to drink plenty of water and, if necessary, take small doses of aspirin for headaches. Stick to lower altitudes for the first days of a holiday.

Falls

The outcome of a fall can range from minor scrapes and grazes to sprained and broken limbs, or worse. The former are easily treated with dressings and antiseptic creams. Sprains can be strapped up effectively and the victim can usually make his way down with help. Broken limbs can be splinted using a trekking pole, but whether the victim can walk down depends on where the break is and the severity of it: if in doubt call the rescue service.

37

EMERGENCY ACTION

In the case of a genuine need for rescue this is the procedure:

- Call the rescue services:
  France – 112 Chamonix PGHM, tel: 04 50 53 16 89
  Italy – Aosta Valley 118. 112 also works in Italy
  Switzerland – Valais 144

- Have the following information ready for the rescue service:
  1 Your name and your mobile phone number
  2 The nature of the accident
  3 The number of victims
  4 The seriousness of the victim's injuries – is he conscious?
  5 Your position, your itinerary, your altitude
  6 The time of the accident
  7 The current weather conditions – wind and visibility

- Prepare for the arrival of the helicopter team by putting the injured person in an accessible place – this will not always be possible but, if feasible, find a flat place where the helicopter can land. Do not move an unconscious patient or one who may have back injuries. In all events secure the victim and also all equipment. Keep everyone else away from this area – the helicopter will generate a lot of wind when it arrives.

- Make your position visible, by using brightly coloured items such as a bivvy bag or rucksacks

- When the helicopter appears use your arms in the air to make a Y symbol to indicate that you are the people who called for rescue.

One arm raised diagonally, one arm down diagonally:
- help not needed
- do not land here
- NO (to pilot's questions).

Both arms raised diagonally:
- help needed
- land here
- YES (to pilot's questions).

Anything worse requires help from professionals – back and head injuries are potentially very serious so the victim should not be moved (unless by staying where they are further injury is likely) and the rescue service should be called immediately.

Rescue

Should the unthinkable happen and you do have to call the rescue services, it's reassuring to know that, compared to many mountain areas, the Alps are relatively friendly in an accident situation. Given good weather, you can expect the mountain rescue to arrive within a short time of your call.

The Chamonix valley has a headquarters of the Peleton de la Gendarmerie de la Haute Montagne (PGHM). This is a professional rescue service, using trained rescue personnel, doctors and guides (a similar set-up exists in Courmayeur). They generally operate with helicopters from a base very near town. Only in bad weather will the helicopter not be able to fly, in which case a rescue party might be sent on foot and this could take a lot longer.

However, calling the rescue should be seen as a last resort. Since mobile phones have become part of the walker's kit list, the PGHM get called out for the most trivial of reasons, ranging from tiredness to being late for a restaurant reservation. It should be remembered that having the back-up of such a service is a privilege not to be abused.

Once the team have arrived they will take over. The rescue services in the Alps speak English so this is not the time to try out those new French/Italian phrases.

It is recommended that in the Alps walkers carry a mobile phone, but only to be used to call the rescue when it is truly necessary. There is telephone network cover almost everywhere. It is vital to know your own number as the rescue service will ask for it.

NB Rescue and medical costs are charged in Europe so be sure to have insurance for this before coming out, or buy a Carte Neige from the tourist office in Chamonix. (French Alpine and Austrian Alpine Club memberships include this insurance.)

GUIDED WALKING

You may decide that rather than organise your walking holiday yourself you'd prefer to join an organised holiday, or hire a trekking guide.

Many companies offer guided walking holidays in the Mont Blanc region. When making your choice check that your guide has got the appropriate qualification to lead in the mountains. In both France and Italy it is a legal requirement that to guide on non-glaciated terrain the person holds the Accompagnateur en Montagne (France)/Accompagnatore di Montagna (Italy) diploma. This qualification exists in Switzerland too, but is not yet legally required. An unqualified person will not have liability insurance.

These guides are not only well qualified in navigation skills and the techniques for walking and leading groups, they are also a mine of information about the region, the flora, fauna, geology, history and culture. A day out with such a guide should enhance your visit even if you can perfectly well find the path yourself.

The British qualification European Mountain Leader has equivalence with the European qualifications, but generally a person resident in the Alps will be the most informed about the area and conditions.

WALKING WITH DOGS

In the reserves and national parks it is generally the rule that dogs are allowed if kept on the lead, although in some places they are not allowed at all. Where there are cattle or sheep, the dog should be restrained.

It's worth thinking hard before taking old Fido out in the Alps as his presence will ensure you see very little wildlife. The canine scent tends to warn the chamois, ibex, marmots, deer and so on of your approach long before they might otherwise clock you. Also don't forget that any difficult sections of paths – rocky scrambles, via ferratas, wobbly bridges – can prove not only problematical but also dangerous for your canine friend – there are often impressive voids below the paths.

MOUNTAIN BIKING

I have nothing at all against mountain biking, or the people that do it. On the contrary I think it's great fun and good training for hiking. However, there is a history of problems on some of the paths around Chamonix with the result that there are restrictions on where bikes can go, and a map of permitted trails is available from the Chamonix tourist office. In spite of this, following problems between walkers and bikers on the Chamonix trails in recent years, bikes have now been banned from many paths.

The problems mainly arise on narrow paths which traverse or zig-zag. The slopes taken by these paths are often very steep, and any deviation from the trail will result in rolling down the precipice. Walkers can stop to let each other pass, and so can bikers if they go slowly, but unfortunately that isn't always the case. The trend for bikers is to do fast descents (having taken a cable car or chairlift up) which require incredible skill and instant reactions. But when confronted by a walker – who may not know the biker is coming up behind, or may panic in trying to get out of the way – the result is often disaster. The bikers are generally helmeted and padded at all joints, so they will probably not fare too badly from a tumble (and falling is part of their game), but since the average walker is not equipped in this way it's easy to see who loses out in any collision.

Be aware that bikers may be present on some of the tracks described on walks in this book – tyre tracks in the dust are a sure indicator of popular routes. On these tracks it is perfectly feasible for walkers and bikers to share the route harmoniously. If you see the biker coming, step aside to let him pass without having to stop. However, if a biker intimidates you on a narrow path there's nothing wrong in showing your displeasure by suggesting he slow down, or go to a more appropriate area. Permitted mountain bike trails in the Chamonix valley are signed with a coloured triangle with two dots next to it. Similar restrictions exist elsewhere.

Mountain-biking trails are now regulated, and indicated by this sign

TRAIL RUNNING

It is ever more common to be walking along a footpath and hear the huff-puffing of a runner coming up behind you. Trail running has taken off in the last few years, and many of the walks in this guide are also good for running. Unlike Britain, for example, where much of the fell running is on muddy grassy terrain, here the ground tends to be rocky or, in the forests, composed largely of tree roots and pine needles. A good pair of shoes with a high traction sole is essential, but beyond that the sky's the limit. The best trails are those that do not climb too steeply, otherwise, for most people, the 'run' becomes a fast walk, so the walks graded 1 or 2 are probably best. However, beware of going too far and getting cold if the weather changes. Consider the change in temperature, as well as the chill of the wind, as altitude is gained – it's always advisable to take a windproof. In hot weather for a run of more than an hour it's also recommended to carry water. Clearly running can be dangerous: it's all too easy, for example, to turn an ankle, so a mobile phone is a good idea.

There are lots of mountain race events in the summer in the Alps. The event in Chamonix is the Chamonix Marathon and Chamonix Cross (the latter a shorter version, which was the original event), which take a course with some of the most beautiful running you'll ever do. This normally takes place the last Sunday of June (details from Chamonix tourist office). Walkers beware: this is not the day to walk the Grand Balcon Sud from Planpraz to La Flégère (Walk 20). (For details www.sports. chamonix.org)

For those with obscene amounts of energy, or a very optimistic nature, the Ultra trail is a 166km run around Mont Blanc on the TMB trail, which takes place over the last weekend in August, with a time limit of about 48hr; for details go to www. ultratrailmb.com.

THINGS NOT TO BE MISSED

One of the most pleasurable aspects of a walking holiday is being able to explore a different culture, be it from the point of view of the language, the way of life, the food or the environment. In the Mont Blanc Alps there is a wealth of variety and peculiarity that the walker has a unique opportunity to discover.

Firstly there are the obvious differences between France, Switzerland and Italy, which are in many respects quite pronounced (even though their borders are so close). Then there are also all the little aspects of life here that you will not come across elsewhere.

Gastronomically the list is endless, but to give a few specialities: everyone, at least once during a visit, has to try a tarte aux myrtilles (blueberry tart), available in all the patisseries in the Chamonix valley, as well as many alpine huts; over in Courmayeur the gelati (ice cream) is a must; Switzerland is, of course, renowned

for its chocolate, and none better than that made from alpine cows' milk. On the alcoholic front any evening meal should be followed by a génépy, a digestif available in France and Italy, made from the génépy flowers found on the highest slopes. Any alpine cheese will be worth trying, especially when you come across an alpage where they are making and selling it on site. Other classic gastronomic specialities are fondu and raclette, both melted-cheese based; and charcuterie – dried meats.

Apart from eating there are clearly other activities not to be missed. In the Chamonix valley, if you have a day when walking doesn't appeal, then a trip up the Aiguille du Midi cable car will not disappoint – but be sure to pick a fine day. At 3842m this is the highest cable car in Europe and the views from the top are truly spectacular. From Courmayeur similar views are to be had from the Helbronner cable car. Some rather pretty red gondolas join these two cable cars and if you have plenty of time you can make a round trip, using the bus service to rejoin the valley you started from.

Walking in the rain can only be done for so long, so if you end up with several bad weather days then a visit to Chamonix Alpine Museum is an interesting diversion; art fans will enjoy the Fondation Pierre Gianadda in Martigny, and it's worth going there on the mountain railway which is pretty steep in places; and, bad weather or not, a trip to Chamonix

Reflections at the Col des Montets (walk 50)

would not be complete without at least one descent on the summer luge! (See also Appendix 4.)

Finally the Reserve Naturel des Col des Montets has a very informative centre on the col and would-be flower experts can test themselves on the *Sentier Botanique*.

HOW TO USE THIS GUIDE

The walks

The 50-plus walks in this guide are organised according to the nearest town base. In each area there is a collection of walks of all difficulties. In addition to the high-level walks there is often a valley walk that can be done whatever the weather, or on 'tired' days, with dogs, children or by bike, or as a run.

There are also four multi-day treks which are briefly detailed. They all use parts of other walks already described in the book.

Grades and times

It is always hard to grade walks as difficulty can vary immensely depending on the weather conditions. However, grades are given as a guideline and the factors taken into account are:

- length of walk
- ascent and descent
- type of terrain
- presence and nature of trails
- need to navigate.

Further important points regarding any of these factors are noted in the route description and the grade and difficulties section. Walks have been graded from 1–3 (see box overleaf).

43

WALK GRADES

- **Grade 1:** These walks are of a standard that any reasonably fit person can manage. The paths are all good and usually waymarked. The walks do not involve more than about 500m of ascent and/or descent. Whilst it's always important to be able to read the map and navigate, grade 1 walks will not call for more than basic map-reading skills. They are good for the first day of a holiday, or a half day, possibly bad weather days (depending on the route and the type of bad weather), and for people who don't want to go too far.

- **Grade 2:** These walks are usually quite long and involve up to about 1000m ascent and/or descent. The terrain can be quite rough, but there are always paths which are often quite good and waymarked. These walks take a full day, up to about 8hr.

- **Grade 3:** These are the tough ones. The routes are long, often going through some terrain where there is no trail or where the path is difficult to find; navigation may be difficult and there could also be some scrambling; there is considerable height gain and loss. Whatever makes these walks difficult will be noted in the grade and difficulties section. These walks should only be undertaken by experienced walkers who have already hiked in the Alps

Timings are given solely as a guideline; they are not intended as a challenge, and certainly should not be treated as such. If you find your time to be faster or slower than those in the book then adjust your expectations accordingly. Timings are based on ideal conditions and many factors can affect how long a walk takes, not least that of taking time to enjoy it. There is no 'right' time for a walk so long as it is undertaken safely and you don't get caught out in the dark (unless you had planned for that), or miss the last bus back.

You will see timings on many of the signposts that are increasingly being put up on popular trails. They give an indication, but you can work out your anticipated time yourself after you've done a couple of walks. The essential element in any alpine walk is ascent. There are few flat trails of any length so really what counts is the rate of ascent per hour. I have calculated the walk times on a conservative rate of 300m of ascent an hour; unless the descents are particularly long and difficult these usually take about half the time of the ascent, so where the walk is a simple ascent/descent this is how it is calculated. If there is some flat distance involved too then the rate of 4kmph is used for those stretches.

These times do not include time spent resting, taking photos, eating or any of the other things that can make a walk that much longer. Do allow time to enjoy yourself.

Waymarks

Many trails in the Mont Blanc region are waymarked. These signs vary from paint flashes and spots on the rocks and trees to full-blown signposts with destination and estimated time to reach it. The major trails, such as the Tour du Mont Blanc (TMB) and

Signposts often give timing as well as direction

INFORMATION GIVEN FOR EACH ROUTE

Each route description includes a box that summarises useful information about the walk.

- Details regarding the car park. This is according to common usage, but clearly if the parking area is full you will have to find another suitable spot that doesn't interfere with private property or parking areas for local people.
- Starting and finishing points are noted, as is the highpoint and approximate altitude gain for the walk. Altitude loss is not given, not because I consider this unimportant but because it's less of a factor in planning a walk than the altitude that must be climbed. However, where rapid altitude loss is significant, for example where there is a stretch of very steep descent, it has been noted.
- The appropriate 1:25 000 map is noted, and is an essential item in your rucksack – the sketch maps in the guide are not intended to be adequate for navigation.
- The approximate distance of the walk is given.
- Brief details of any public transport to reach the start and finish from the nearest centres.
- Where appropriate, any accommodation is noted along with telephone numbers.

The 'Tip' box notes any interesting extensions or variations to the walk, or any important advice.

the Grande Randonnée (GR) trails in France are marked by red and white paint flashes. Local trails can be marked in any colour – often yellow in France and Switzerland.

Where trails are less obvious or go across scree slopes there will often be cairns. For most of the walks in this book I have tried to note whether there are waymarks of some kind or not. However, waymarks do get changed, and even removed from time to time. Where there is no trail you will sometimes be following your nose or the compass, so it's crucial to use the map and not to venture off good paths if the visibility is very poor.

As for cairns, whether or not you think they are a 'Good Thing', please leave them where they are. They may be there for a reason that is not initially apparent – walkers share the hills with many other people, for recreation or otherwise – and usually a cairn has been erected for a purpose.

On or off piste?

Most of the walks described in this guidebook follow some sort of path. Occasionally a section is included where there is no path, but this is unusual. In general in the Alps it is very difficult to walk on the terrain off the trail. There may be boulders, loose scree, very steep ground... basically a path, however small, is usually needed to make progress here. Mostly the paths are well maintained – in France by the FFRP (Féderation Française de la Randonnée Pédestre)

or the local commune, elsewhere by local towns and huts – and are way-marked or signed. However, these can be difficult to follow in anything but good weather – snow, fog or heavy rain all mean that it's easy to miss the path and then life becomes very difficult. Whilst not being on the path does not mean you are lost, it does mean that you need to find it again otherwise it may be impossible to go up, down or across the slope.

It's also important to understand why there are waymarks, for example on terrain where a path will never form, such as boulders. The idea is that everyone follows the same route so that the terrain stabilises and becomes safer and easier to cross. Walkers should respect the paths and not short-cut – even when other people have – as this causes erosion. Experience has shown that a good well-made path is actually less intrusive than widespread erosion where there is no official path.

I have nevertheless included some selected walks where there is a pathless section that does not run the risk of erosion, as there is no denying the pleasure of walking across apparently untouched ground, making your way into the wilderness.

Telephone numbers

Telephone numbers are given for mountain huts, and for weather forecasts and rescue purposes. Telephone numbers are quoted for phoning from their own country. To call a Swiss

Not far from the Refuge de Bel Lachat with Mont Blanc as backdrop (walk 9)

number from abroad dial 00 41, and miss out the first 0 of the phone number; for France dial 00 33, and miss out the first 0 of the phone number; for Italy dial 00 39, then all the telephone number. Information numbers, such as the weather forecast, often only work when called from that country.

ABBREVIATIONS USED

Several abbreviations have been used throughout this guide:

- **SNCF** Société des Chemins de Fer – French Railways
- **TMB** Tour du Mont Blanc – this, the best known long-distance trek in Europe, is a circumnavigation of the Mont Blanc massif and hence our walks quite often coincide with parts of this
- **GR** Grande Randonnée

Place names

Despite an effort to be consistent with place names throughout this book, there will certainly be inconsistencies. One problem is that in the Aosta region of Italy French is almost an equal first language with Italian, a result of the many years' existence of the Kingdom of Savoy, grouping what is now Savoie, Valais and Aosta. The Italians themselves cannot seem to decide which language to use as can be seen from their maps, where the place names vary from French to Italian.

Actual place names do not always correspond to the French IGN 1:50 000 map. Place names generally correspond to either the 1:25 000 map (mentioned in the walk details), or just to common usage. However, since the names are similar in each language it's just a question of being prepared to find differences.

CHAPTER 1

ST GERVAIS LES BAINS AND
LES CONTAMINES-MONTJOIE

The Bon Nant torrent has its source way up towards the Col du Bonhomme ridge and is fed by the huge glaciers of Tré-la-Tête and Miage, as well as tributaries of rainwater and snowmelt. At certain times it truly lives up to it name, and the steepness of some of its rapids creates impressive waterfalls on

Valley walking, here near the village of Champel, provides a welcome respite from the mountains

its route down to join the River Arve at Le Fayet.

The river forms the Montjoie valley which is relatively flat and hospitable from St Gervais les Bains (which guards the entrance to the valley and overlooks the Arve) all the way to the steepening at Notre Dame de la Gorge. Hence there are hamlets and villages all along its length, but the main town in the valley is Les Contamines-Montjoie.

The valley has been much frequented since Roman times when it was a key route through from Aosta; the name 'Montjoie' comes from the old Celtic word for a military outpost. Later the Château de Montjoie was constructed in Les Contamines to guard against intruders coming through the neighbouring cols. In the 14th century, Les Contamines lost its strategic position to St Gervais, which became the administrative capital of the region. Béatrix de Faucigny, daughter of the Compte de Savoie, favoured St Gervais as a place of residence, doubtless because of its privileged position high above the Arve valley, safe against any surprise attack.

Les Contamines-Montjoie was, for centuries, a collection of farms, but is well known for the sacred place of Notre Dame de la Gorge. The Baroque church, much restored in recent times, was built and consecrated in 1701, but was a place of pilgrimage long before that, and now sees annual pilgrimages, especially on 15 August (Assumption).

Nowadays both St Gervais and Les Contamines prosper mainly from tourism. The whole area provides fine walking possibilities, and a base in either of these towns would be perfect. There is a regular bus service from St Gervais up to Les Contamines, with frequent stops along the valley. Cable cars and chairlifts operate throughout the summer in both towns, giving access for walkers to the higher slopes above the valley.

Both towns have all necessary facilities and are popular holiday resorts, somewhat less fervent than their more renowned neighbours.

THERMAL SPRINGS

St Gervais owes its fame to its thermal springs which were only discovered in 1806 when a miner from Servoz noticed thick steam when fishing. He carried out a little excavation and found hot water seeping out. In 1815 the two main thermal baths were established, and with them the success of St Gervais was assured. In 1892 a huge flood streaming down from the high slopes wiped out one of the main thermal stations, killing more than 200 people, but even so the crowds still came.

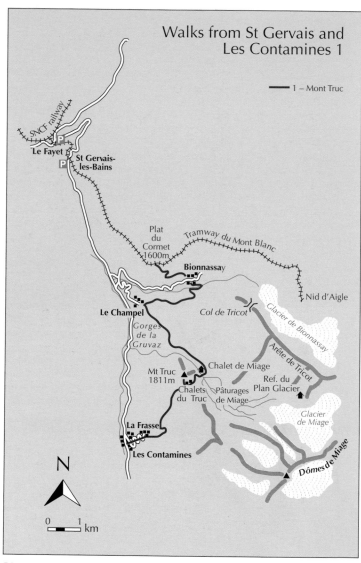

Walks from St Gervais and
Les Contamines 1

1 – Mont Truc

SNCF railway

P
Le Fayet

P
**St Gervais-
les-Bains**

Plat
du
Cormet
1600m

Tramway du Mont Blanc

Bionnassay

Nid d'Aigle

Col de Tricot

Glacier de Bionnassay

Le Champel

Gorges
de la
Gruvaz

Arête de Tricot

Chalet de Miage

Mt Truc
1811m

Ref. du
Plan Glacier

**Chalets
du Truc**

Pâturages
de Miage

Glacier
de Miage

La Frasse

Les Contamines

N

Dômes de Miage

0   1 km

Walks from St Gervais and Les Contaminès 2

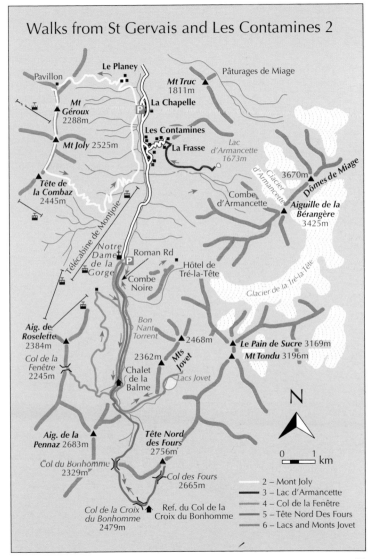

Pavillon

Le Planey

Pâturages de Miage

Mt Truc
1811m

Mt
Géroux
2288m

La Chapelle

Les Contamines

La Frasse

Mt Joly 2525m

Lac
d'Armancette
1673m

Tête de
la Combaz
2445m

Glacier
d'Armancette

3670m

Dômes de Miage

Combe
d'Armancette

Aiguille de la
Bérangère
3425m

Télécabine de Montjoie

Notre
Dame
de la
Gorge

Roman Rd

Hôtel de
Tré-la-Tête

Glacier de la Tré-la-Tête

Combe
Noire

Bon
Nant
Torrent

Aig. de
Roselette
2384m

▲ 2468m

2362m

Le Pain de Sucre 3169m

Mts
Jovet

Mt Tondu 3196m

Col de la
Fenêtre
2245m

Chalet
de la
Balme

Lacs Jovet

N

Aig. de la
Pennaz 2683m

Tête Nord
des Fours
2756m

0   1
km

Col du Bonhomme
2329m

Col des Fours
2665m

Col de la Croix
du Bonhomme
2479m

Ref. du Col de la
Croix du Bonhomme

2 – Mont Joly
3 – Lac d'Armancette
4 – Col de la Fenêtre
5 – Tête Nord Des Fours
6 – Lacs and Monts Jovet

WALK 1
Mont Truc

Small it may be, insignificant in the scheme of things, but Mont Truc is still a summit, and the views are definitely worth it.

Mont Truc cannot be considered a major summit – it might be if it was situated somewhere flat like Holland, but here in the Alps it is somewhat swamped by almost everything around it. I've always had a bit of a soft spot for it, especially as for many years I translated its name as 'Mount Thingy' (*truc* in French is a 'thing'). However, I was eventually put right – *truc* is local dialect for a rounded dome, which suits Mont Truc admirably.

An adventurous – and unusual – walk can be had by beginning in St Gervais and taking the rickety Tramway du Mont Blanc as far as the Plat du Cormet stop. Be sure to get off here, otherwise you'll end up at the Nid d'Aigle at lot further up the hill. This tramway has an interesting history: at its conception in 1912 it was envisaged to go right to the summit of Mont Blanc, forging its way through the glaciers! World War I put paid to all such extravagant projects, but it's fascinating to wonder how far they might have got.

From here the walk goes through the charming villages of Bionnassay, and Le Champel, then all the way round the hillside above the Gorges de Gruvaz to reach the Chalet de Miage in time for lunch. What a place for it, with the leaning seracs and glistening ice of the northwest face of the Dômes de Miage right in front of you

A CHOICE OF CAFÉS

This dome happens to be right next to the TMB trail, but most TMBers are on a mission to reach their next stopping place and to veer off the trail, even when tempted by a summit like this, will probably mean losing a valuable half hour. So most don't. Mont Truc is also right next to a delightful café, the Chalet du Truc, the only downside of which is that it has no licence to sell beer. It tends not to be too crowded, as just over the hill is the Chalet de Miage which does have a licence. Clearly the answer is to visit both cafés and enjoy the best of both worlds.

Somehow the drinks always taste that much better when you've walked uphill for them!

and the roar of the glacier melt filling your ears. Regional specialities abound here, so be sure to arrive hungry and try everything. The chalet is also a refuge, and you may well be tempted to spend a night here.

A short climb leads to the Truc alpage just above and, suitably restored after lunch, you'll be able to tackle Mont Truc.

A good track leads down to Les Contamines, from where there is a regular bus service back to St Gervais.

Car park	St Gervais station
Starting point	Plat du Cormet 1600m
Finishing point	Les Contamines 1150m
Highpoint	Mont Truc 1811m
Altitude gain	400m
Map	IGN Top 25 3531 ET St Gervais-les-Bains Massif du Mont Blanc
Distance	12km (7.5 miles)
Time	5hr
Grade/difficulties	1/2. Good paths all the way
Public transport	Tramway du Mont Blanc Le Fayet–St Gervais–Plat du Cormet; bus Les Contamines–St Gervais
Tip	This is a good walk for early in the season when the higher slopes might be snowy. It is also flatter then many alpine hikes, so may be a welcome alternative after lots of uphill days.

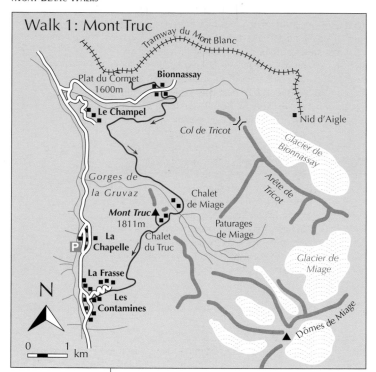

Walk 1: Mont Truc

Tramway du Mont Blanc

Plat du Cormet
1600m

Bionnassay

Le Champel

Nid d'Aigle

Col de Tricot

Glacier de
Bionnassay

*Gorges de
la Gruvaz*

Chalet
de Miage

*Arête de
Tricot*

Mont Truc
1811m

Chalet
du Truc

*Paturages
de Miage*

P
**La
Chapelle**

La Frasse

*Glacier de
Miage*

N

**Les
Contamines**

Dômes de Miage

0   1
⊢――――⊣ km

Route

From the tramway stop take the signed path to **Bionnassay** village. Follow the road through the village, past the Auberge de Bionnassay. The path leaves the village just beyond on the right, heading down across the river then up onto a track and into **Le Champel**.

Just on the outskirts of the village a path goes off left, signed to Miage. This traverses sparse woodland across the hillside, above the deep Gruvaz gorge, to then meet gentler terrain as it enters the **Paturages de Miage** (Miage meadows). This is a haven in all ways – postcard surroundings and a great café. But be warned: arrive here in the height of summer at lunchtime and you could be in for a long wait ---if it's heaving enjoy the view but save your appetite for the Chalet du Truc half an hour away.

Cross the little footbridge and follow the winding trail through alder bushes to reach the flat Truc alpage and the café at the far side of the meadows, in the shadow of our objective, **Mont Truc**. A little path goes straight up to the top and doesn't take very long at all. From the summit the Dômes de Miage dominate the view, along with the Aiguille de Bionnassay and the long ridge of the Arête de Tricot. With binoculars you may well spot chamois and ibex roaming these slopes – the number of chamois trophies displayed on the walls of the Chalet de Miage attests to their profusion in this region.

Return to the **Chalet du Truc**, and follow the track which disappears south into the forest. It is signed all the way to **Les Contamines**, cutting the road as it reaches the outskirts of town, and comes out by the church near the centre. Turn right along the main street to get to the bus station and the shops.

WALK 2

Mont Joly

Seen from Megève, the summit of Mont Joly may appear to be an easily attained objective, but don't be fooled – whilst the ascent has a gentle pastoral start, the summit ridge bears a certain resemblance to the hautes montagnes, exposed and buffeted by winds.

The summit can be ascended and descended by the same route from Les Contamines, and this is a fine outing. However, once at the top your eye will be drawn to the long, narrow ridge snaking away south past several smaller tops. What a shame, having made such an effort to gain the altitude, not to continue along this delightful and unusual route – and so we shall. The walk onwards to the next peak, the Tête de la Combaz, provides a wonderful continuation before having to leave this unique position to return to the valley depths.

Since the summit of Mont Joly will give you the 'Rolls Royce' of views, save this walk for that perfect day.

VIEWS FROM THE TOP

Mont Joly is seen from so many places down in the Arve valley that it goes without question that it must be a good viewpoint. It is actually one of the best belvederes from which to view the Mont Blanc region – an orientation table helps you to identify the many peaks which greet your arrival. Straddled between the Arve valley and the Contamines valley, it's almost true to say that what you can't see from here isn't worth seeing! Close up are the Dômes de Miage and the Aiguilles de Tré-la-Tête, de Bionnassay, du Goûter and des Glaciers; beyond Mont Blanc are the Vanoise and Ecrins massifs, their distant misty summits seeming to stretch away forever. Slightly nearer, the Beaufortain can be recognised by the pronounced tooth of the Pierra Menta, whereas the limestone massifs of Belledonne, Les Bauges and the Jura present more gentle profiles. Further east the Swiss Diablerets is recognisable by its flat plateau-like summit.

Car park	La Chapelle, 2.5km north of Les Contamines
Starting point	La Chapelle 1050m
Finishing point	La Chapelle 1050m
Highpoint	Mont Joly 2525m
Altitude gain	1475m
Map	IGN Top 25 3531 OT Megève Col des Aravis
Distance	15km (9.3 miles)
Time	8hr
Grade/difficulties	2/3, for the amount of ascent and also for the terrain which is rough, steep in ascent and descent, and in bad visibility to be avoided. Early in the season *névé* will probably remain on shady slopes so this walk should not be attempted until well into the summer season
Public transport	Bus Les Contamines–St Gervais
Tip	You will probably look at the ridge running on southwards beyond the Tête de la Combaz and wonder if it's an option. The answer is yes, but not only is this very long but it also has some precipitous sections around the Aiguille Croche. This can be done in a day but to do it north to south from Les Contamines would be a very demanding expedition. Taking the chairlift from Les Contamines to Le Signal allows the whole ridge to be traversed from south to north, but it cannot be overemphasised that this ridge is airy and exposed and a fall would have bad consequences.

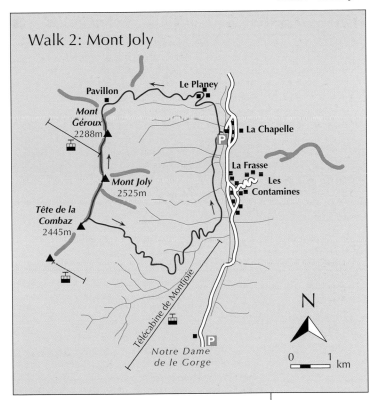

This walk should be avoided in anything but good stable weather. In fog and rain it would be easy to become disorientated, especially on the eastern slopes of Mont Joly itself; the ridge, whilst not too difficult in dry conditions, quickly becomes slippery and treacherous when wet.

Route

Walk out of **La Chapelle** on the small back road that heads south and then turns over the Bon Nant river to gently descend north into the hamlet of Les Hoches. Here, just after a hairpin over a stream, find a path on

57

If you're lucky you might glimpse chamois on the trail

the left and take this alongside the stream until it swings right to the buildings of Le Carteyron. Continue along the small road until a path goes off to the left, up the hill and left again, zigzagging up though the forest.

At a track near Porcherey go straight on, above the tree-line now, heading for a group of chalets prominently perched on the skyline above. Once round this shoulder the café of **Le Pavillon du Mont Joly** (2002m) is a welcome sight not far away, and a drink stop here allows the next part of the walk to be contemplated.

The ridge ahead is steep as it approaches the precipitous slopes of **Mont Géroux**, but once this has been passed on its west side things do ease off temporarily, although if you look up at this stage it's fairly clear that steep is not finished for the day as **Mont Joly** looms ahead. This summit is crowned with a large cairn, as well as solar panels, a transmitter and a viewing table. There is a final stiff pull to reach the top, but hopefully as you regain your breath and gaze around your general feeling will be that it was worth it. Prepare to be impressed!

Once you have recovered, the onward route is not so demanding, but still requires care, especially at the start of the descent where the huge cleft of the source of the Nant de la Chovettaz stream forms an interesting obstacle. This is avoided on the right (west) to then take the ridge downwards.

Ahead is the **Tête de la Combaz** (2445m), and this cairn can be reached to make for a two-summit day, before retracing your steps for 200m to the path that plunges off to the east towards the Contamines valley.

The path winds down past the old buildings at La Combaz, to pick up a steeper trail near to the stream valley of the Ruisseau du Ty. Easier ground then goes down to the jeep track at Colombaz. Turn left and follow this to Le Baptieu and then along the back road staying to the west of the Bon Nant torrent all the way into **La Chapelle**. This last part of the walk coincides with the TMB trek so you may suddenly find there are other weary hikers around.

Wet weather encourages fungi and mushrooms in the woods

WALK 3
Lac d'Armancette

A delightful place to spend an hour or so. Enjoy a picnic in the wild surroundings of this mountain lake, with its beautiful views of the Mont Joly ridge.

The Lac d'Armancette is situated in a wonderful wild cwm, surrounded by rocky peaks and very close to the high mountains. Opposite is the Mont Joly ridge which looks exceptional from this vantage point.

The lake can be reached easily from Les Contamines by a fairly steep but non-technical path through the forest. This itself is pleasant but the final part above the tree-line is really stunning.

Previously there was a trail on the far side of the cwm which was described in earlier editions of this guidebook as a much longer route coming from the Hotel Trè-la-Tête. This path at the far side of the lake was always to be avoided in rainy weather, but it is now closed following landslides caused by very heavy storms in the last few years.

Notre Dame de la Gorge, a site of pilgrimage for many centuries

It is still possible to make a much longer outing by going up to Notre Dame de la Gorge at the head of the Contamines Valley, then taking the steep trail up to the

Car park	Les Contamines La Frasse. Take the road to La Frasse and continue to the end of the road where there is a small parking place on the left.
Starting point	La Frasse end of the village 1263m
Finishing point	La Frasse end of the village 1263m
Highpoint	Lac d'Armancette 1673m
Altitude gain	450m
Map	IGN Top 25 3531 ET St Gervais-les-Bains Massif du Mont Blanc
Time	3hr
Distance	5km (3 miles)
Grade/difficulties	1. Good paths
Public transport	Bus service from the Arve valley to Les Contamines
Tip	If you want a longer walk it's definitely worth going up to the Hotel Trè-la-Tête which is in a superb situation. The topographical meaning of its name is 'beyond a rocky summit'. Alternatively if you decide to start the walk in Les Contamines itself, rather than driving up to La Frasse, you could vary the descent by returning to Cugnon via Les Feugiers.

Hotel Tré-la-Tête and taking the high balcony trail around the hillside, but instead of heading on the upper trail under Mont Freugé, you would stay lower and join the trail described here coming up from Les Contamines.

However, I prefer to describe this as a much shorter walk, one that most people could manage and which will provide great views and a lovely foray into the Combe d'Armancette.

Route

From the parking go right at a junction up a steep jeep track in the forest. Go past an isolated house and continue leftwards at the next junction. Higher up, after two switchbacks, at a small oratory and a fountain, leave the track which is a dead end, and take a trail on the right.

This forest ascent is very agreeable on a hot day as the spruce trees give welcome shade and soon the trail follows a small stream, adding to the cool fresh ambience.

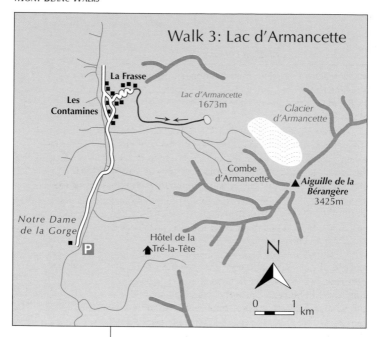

Walk 3: Lac d'Armancette

La Frasse

Les
Contamines

Lac d'Armancette
1673m

Glacier
d'Armancette

Combe
d'Armancette

Aiguille de la
Bérangère
3425m

Notre Dame
de la Gorge

P

Hôtel de la
Tré-la-Tête

N

0   1
━━━━━━━ km

Eventually the treeline is reached and you'll enter
the **Combe d'Armancette**. If you're there in the first
half of the summer these meadows will be carpeted in
alpine flowers, notably globe flowers and the exceptional
Martagon lily. To the right small rocky summits stretch
along the ridge of the Têtes de Tré-la-Tête while to the
left are tantalising views of the Dômes de Miage and the
Aiguille de la Bérangère, testifying the nearby presence of
the glaciated massif.

The **Lac d'Armancette** itself is not far away, situated
in a hollow surrounded by vegetation. Despite its modest
size, it is a popular place to come notably for the views
and the unusual, if somewhat dangerous, surroundings.
The old path on the far side of the cwm is quite obvious –
but don't be tempted to go there.

Return by the same route.

WALK 4
Col de la Fenêtre

Many walks are possible from the upper Contamines-Montjoie valley – some described in this book – and the TMB and GR5 trek also use it to access the southern side of the region.

Its history goes way back into the mists of time; certainly the Romans came over this way from the Aosta valley. History records that the Col du Bonhomme, at the head of the valley, was a hazardous passage for travellers for whom the associated dangers of bad weather and difficult terrain made this a major undertaking. Stories abound of victims of hypothermia, avalanche and exhaustion, even during the summer months when trying to travel from one valley to another.

Nowadays you will hardly be alone as you head up past the Chalets of Nant Borrant and La Balme, but the track is wide enough to accommodate plenty of people, and most will be heading south, their sights set on the cols up ahead. This is why our route heads west instead, with the rocky Col de la Fenêtre (2245m) as objective. The col is situated on the western boundary ridge of the Contamines valley, and the views afforded from this spot more than reward the effort put in to get there. To the east is Mont Blanc, shadowing the Tré-la-Tête glacier and Monts Jovet below, whilst to the west and north and south a whole new vista opens up, stretching far away towards Beaufort and the Aravis.

Beyond the col the path continues – it is part of the Tour du Pays du Mont Blanc (a relatively low-level trek exploring the French side of the Mont Blanc region), and this could be followed to the lift system of Les Contamines – but if you wish to return to the startpoint it's better to descend a little from the col and take a high-level path that traverses across the hillside above the treeline through lovely alpages to return to Notre Dame de la Gorge.

The upper part of the Contamines-Montjoie valley is very popular hiking ground, partly for its beauty and partly because it provides an accessible way into high mountain scenery.

Car park	Notre Dame de la Gorge
Starting point	Notre Dame de la Gorge 1210m
Finishing point	Notre Dame de la Gorge 1210m
Highpoint	Col de la Fenêtre 2245m
Altitude gain	1035m
Map	IGN Top 25 3531 0T Megève Col des Aravis
Distance	13km (8.1 miles)
Time	6hr
Grade/difficulties	2. Good paths, some wider than others. The slopes below the col often hold snow well into the summer and should be avoided when this is the case
Public transport	Bus from Les Contamines to Notre Dame de la Gorge
Tip	From the Col de la Fenêtre there is a vague path that cuts down east to the flatter Plan de la Fenêtre then northeast across the hillside to descend to the Chalets des Prés just above the forest. If the visibility is good this is a good route, but you have to keep your eyes open for the intermittent path. The route described here is easier and the path is good.

Route

From Notre Dame take the very obvious **Roman road.** Walking up this, straight out of the car, is a good wake-up call. After the **Nant Borrant** gîte on the right the track levels a bit and soon enters the beautiful open valley which leads to La Balme.

At the **Chalet de La Balme** (just after a bridge over the river) the track steepens noticeably, and soon after there is a junction: the TMB goes straight on to the Col du Bonhomme and the right (west) fork is signed to the Col de la Fenêtre. The track passes a huge limestone boulder and at the next junction goes right to reach a small

NOTRE DAME DE LA GORGE

It's worth taking the time to stroll round Notre Dame: the chapel has been restored, but there has been a sanctuary on this site for many centuries and this is still the site of pilgrimages, especially on 15 August (Assumption).

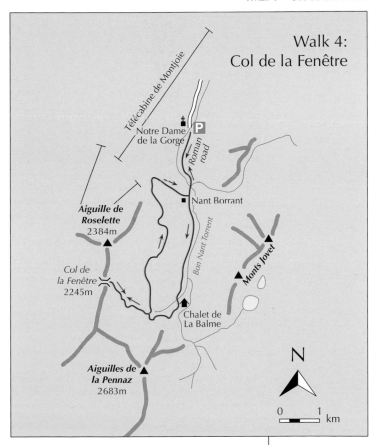

Walk 4:
Col de la Fenêtre

reservoir. Here we take the path on the left, signed to the Col de la Fenêtre and the Col de Cicle (the path to the right being for the return).

The trail winds uphill through stubby grass and stony pastures. It levels at the Plan de la Fenêtre, a good place to take a break and check out the view behind: the Aiguille du Goûter, Mont Blanc and the Aiguille de Bionnassay. Ahead the **Col de la Fenêtre** stays hidden

The sunny southern slopes provide perfect conditions for flowers and butterflies

until the last minute, and the rocks look dauntingly impenetrable, but all will be revealed. After a dismantled pylon, the trail goes left, and cairns lead onwards to the north to the final rocky scramble to the col.

For the easiest way down, retrace your steps to the reservoir and then take the clear path which undulates northwards, staying above the forest with electricity cables paralleling to the right. After going under the cables you reach the Chalets des Prés and the path narrows to head around Les Rosières des Prés, cables now on the left. Go right to Les Chenalettaz, then take the right turn, but not the sharp right that crosses the hillside, rather the right that goes downhill (southeast). There is a path off left soon after, but don't take this: continue onwards across two streambeds and emerge at Nant Borrant. Have a drink in the garden there before continuing down the Roman road to the car park.

WALK 5
Tête Nord des Fours

Non-glaciated summits often give fantastic panoramas, and the Tête Nord des Fours is certainly no exception.

From the summit of Tête Nord des Fours on a really clear day you can see Mont Blanc, the Grand Combin and the Matterhorn. Most days, of course, are not crystal clear, but even so you'll probably get to see some nearby snowy mountains. Even if it's cloudy it's worth the effort as this little peak is accessed by a beautiful walk.

Quite apart from the peak, the rest of the walk is really a delight, starting with the Roman road which took the Romans from the Tarentaise valleys over towards the Arve and onto what is now Valais in Switzerland. This cobbled track heads steeply up from Notre Dame de la Gorge alongside the Bon Nant torrent, past the lovely traditional gîte at Nant Borrant – for an early start this is definitely the place to stay.

The Tête Nord des Fours is a small summit with a big view

Continue up into the pastoral meadows of La Balme. En route to the Col du Bonhomme a huge pile of stones is passed – a logical place to rest after the first steep climb. Known as the Plan des Dames, legend has it that a travelling lady dropped dead here and that this is her burial pile, along with her maid in waiting. It is thought much more likely to be a monument to Jupiter dating from

TOUR OF MONT BLANC TRAIL

The whole of this hike follows the Tour du Mont Blanc trail, although from the Col de la Croix du Bonhomme it is a high variant. In the main summer season there will be quite a lot of folk toiling along under huge sacs. You, however, will just have a daypack and can trot past them. I've been on this trail many times and even on the busiest day the summit will be a pleasure. Most TMB candidates stop at the Col des Fours and picnic – few go up to the summit.

Car park	Notre Dame de la Gorge – the parking is about 300m before the chapel
Starting point	Notre Dame de la Gorge 1210m
Finishing point	Notre Dame de la Gorge 1210m
Highpoint	Tête Nord des Fours 2756m
Altitude gain	1550m
Maps	IGN Top 25 3531 ET St Gervais-les-Bains Massif du Mont Blanc
Distance	20km (12.4 miles)
Time	8–9hr
Grade/difficulties	2/3. Paths are good all the way to the Col des Fours; then cairns and a vague path lead up to the summit. Depending on the previous winter, snow can remain in places throughout the route after the Chalet de la Balme. Whilst this is not dangerous it can make route-finding a bit more difficult
Public transport	Bus from the centre of Les Contamines to Notre Dame de la Gorge
Tip	This walk is quite long for one day – and it is possible to stay somewhere along the way. Nant Borrant or the Chalet de la Balme will give a head start in the morning; the Refuge Col de la Croix de Bonhomme allows the summit day to be shortened, giving more time to enjoy it. If this option is chosen then it would be possible to include the Lacs and Monts Jovet (Walk 6) on the first day.

Roman times – especially with Monts Jovet so close (see Walk 6). This pass has been used to cross from one valley to the other since time began. Traditionally travellers would lay a stone on a cairn as they passed, symbolically laying down their fatigue. Whatever you believe, it's a good picnic place.

There is a tiny emergency shelter at the Col du Bonhomme, usually occupied by lunching TMBers when it's windy. At the second col, the Croix du Bonhomme, there is big renovated hut where you can get refreshments before tackling the final part of the route to the Col des Fours and the summit.

Unless you can organise transport from the rather inaccessible village of Les Chapieux, accessed by car via

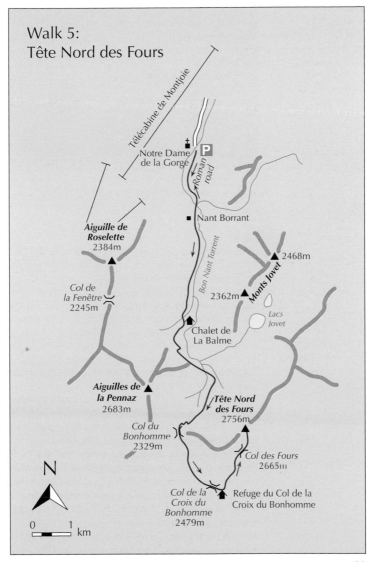

Walk 5:
Tête Nord des Fours

Télécabine de Montjoie

Notre Dame
de la Gorge

P

Roman road

Nant Borrant

**Aiguille de
Roselette**
2384m

Bon Nant Torrent

▲ 2468m

Monts Jovet

2362m ▲

*Col de
la Fenêtre*
2245m

Chalet de
La Balme

*Lacs
Jovet*

**Aiguilles de
la Pennaz**
2683m

*Tête Nord
des Fours*
2756m

*Col du
Bonhomme*
2329m

Col des Fours
2665m

N

*Col de la
Croix du
Bonhomme*
2479m

Refuge du Col de la
Croix du Bonhomme

0   1
———————— km

*En route to the
Col du Bonhomme*

Beaufort or Bourg St Maurice, return from the summit is by the same route.

Route
From Notre Dame the way is pretty obvious – up the very steep cobbled road. After 30min you'll see **Nant Borrant** on the right. Another hour brings you to the **Chalet de La Balme**. Here the wide track becomes a footpath and heads up past very obvious pylons. The steep parts are interspersed with flat sections. At the first of these the path to the Lacs and Monts Jovet heads off left, whilst our track continues heading south. The path zigzags up to reach the flat of the Plan des Dames and its huge cairn, followed by another climb to the **Col du Bonhomme** (2329m) – seen from afar the rocks to the left of the col are said to represent the *bonhomme* (gentleman), and to his left the smaller figure of his lady. Once at the pass the vista to the south opens up – the Beaufortain, and far away the Vanoise.

A rising rocky traverse leads rapidly to the next col, the **Croix du Bonhomme** (2479m) and the hut is just 5min along the path from the col to the right. It's worth making the detour for a cold beer or hot chocolate depending on the conditions. Now follow the signs to the **Col des Fours** (2665m), which just happens to be along the line of pylons heading northeast. From the col small cairns and an intermittent path take you around to the north to reach the summit. Return by the same route.

WALK 6

Lacs and Monts Jovet

We know that the Romans came through the Tarentaise valley en route from Italy to the Valais region. They came down to what is now the Contamines valley, before continuing their descent to the Arve valley. Many Roman artefacts and villa ruins have been found on the sunny hillside now occupied by the village of Passy.

Monts Jovet is a great objective for a walk, but even if the summit is not reached the Lacs Jovet below make for a pleasant outing. The walk up the valley from Notre Dame de la Gorge is beautiful, past traditional farms and grazing cows. The scenery is impressive, and as height is gained towards the lakes the high peaks start to make their appearance.

Monts Jovet forms a cirque with Mont Tondu and the Pain de Sucre, and the two main lakes are nestled into this. There is no path marked on the IGN map to the summits of Monts Jovet but an easy ridge leads to the south summit (2362m) and is well travelled. From here you can just see Mont Blanc far away.

Throughout the Alps the names *Jovet* or *Joux* crop up frequently. These seem to date back to Roman times and are derivatives of the Roman name for Jupiter, whom they worshipped.

Car park	Notre Dame de la Gorge
Starting point	Notre Dame de la Gorge 1210m
Finishing point	Notre Dame de la Gorge 1210m
Highpoint	Monts Jovets Pointe Sud 2362m
Altitude gain	1152m
Map	1:25 000 IGN Top 25 3531 ET St Gervais-les-Bains Massif du Mont Blanc
Distance	14.5km (9 miles)
Time	7hr
Grade/difficulties	1/2 to the lakes, 2/3 to the summit. Good path all the way to the lakes but then smaller trail up the ridge to the top
Pubic transport	Bus from Les Contamines to Notre Dame de la Gorge
Tip	Allow plenty of time if you plan to go right to the summit since the return is by the same route and it's a long way back down the Borrant valley.

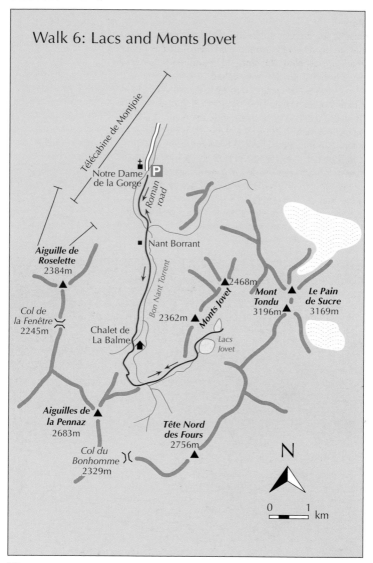

Walk 6: Lacs and Monts Jovet

Télécabine de Montjoie

Notre Dame de la Gorge

P

Roman road

Nant Borrant

Aiguille de Roselette
2384m

Bon Nant Torrent

▲2468m

Mont Tondu
3196m

Le Pain de Sucre
3169m

Col de la Fenêtre
2245m

2362m ▲ **Monts Jovet**

Chalet de La Balme

Lacs Jovet

Aiguilles de la Pennaz
2683m

Tête Nord des Fours
2756m

Col du Bonhomme
2329m

N

0   1 km

Route

First be sure to have a look round Notre Dame – the chapel has been beautifully renovated. Take the steep Roman road up past **Nant Borrant** and continue up the much flatter valley to **Chalet de La Balme**.

The track gives way to a rocky footpath, signed to the Col du Bonhomme and the Lacs Jovet. A short climb eases at a very obvious huge pylon right overhead. Continue along this main path until a flat area, where there are often marmots playing in the boulders. Here the direction is east, and you leave the TMB trail (which continues south). Past the Chalets de Jovet, gently ascend pleasant slopes, up a steeper section and suddenly there they are, those beautiful **Lacs Jovet**.

For those wishing to go on to the summit take the south ridge and follow it to the top.

Return by the same route.

CHAPTER 2

SERVOZ AND THE PLATEAU D'ASSY

Among the attractions of Servoz are interesting sites, not too many visitors, and great views. It's a lively place; lots of families with children live here, and there is a lot going on. The perfect-sized village, it has all necessary facilities as well as a very sunny aspect.

The name 'Servoz' comes from the Latin serva meaning 'little lake'. This dates from the landslide in 1471 down the Dérochoir, which forms part of the Rochers des Fiz, the rocky barrier high above the village. The huge rockfall cut the River Arve and flooded the area, leaving behind a lake (where the village is now) and also Lac Vert, which is above Servoz (Walk 7). Another landslide in 1751 exacerbated this damage, sending down huge boulders that now litter the hillside.

The lower lake has gone, but that part of the village has kept the name Le Lac. Strangely, Le Lac is in a different commune from the rest of Servoz, being part of Les Houches. In times past this area was owned by the Comtes de Genève, who became the Seigneurs of the Chamonix valley from Diosaz to La Balme on the Swiss frontier.

THE CHÂTEAU OF SAINT MICHEL

This was built in the late 13th century to protect the Chamonix valley, and the ruins of the towers provide the focus for a very short but interesting walk from Le Lac. The outlook is now dominated by the Autoroute Blanche motorway and its constant stream of trucks and cars, but it's fascinating to imagine how it was hundreds of years ago when the sentries would be looking out for invaders. The views of the Aiguilles de Bionnassay and du Goûter and the Dômes de Miage, as well as the Pointe Percée in the Aravis, would have been the same. This fortress captured the imagination of many visitors to Chamonix in times past, and it often features in engravings and descriptions, such as those by De Saussure and Victor Hugo.

To reach the ruins, locate the start of the path which is signed to the Tour St Michel: it goes from the Route du Lac, near the chapel on the rock, taking about 20min to reach the ruins by a pleasant path in oak and beech forest. Coming back, take the path left from near the bench, and then left again at the junction.

Walks from Servoz and Plateau d'Assy

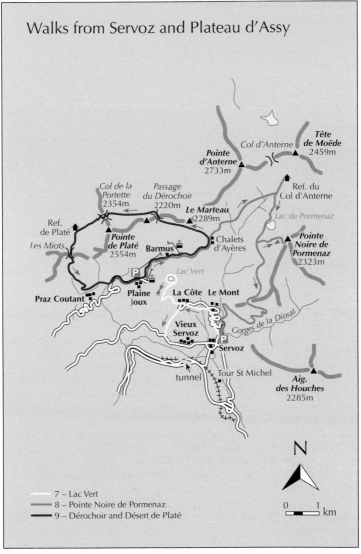

Tête de Moëde 2459m

Col d'Anterne

Pointe d'Anterne 2733m

Ref. du Col d'Anterne

Lac de Pormenaz

Col de la Portette 2354m

Passage du Dérochoir 2220m

Le Marteau 2289m

Ref. de Platé

Pointe de Platé 2554m

Les Miots

Barmus

Chalets d'Ayères

Pointe Noire de Pormenaz 2323m

P

Plaine Joux

Lac Vert

La Côte

Le Mont

Praz Coutant

Vieux Servoz

Gorges de la Diosaz

P

Servoz

tunnel

Tour St Michel

Aig. des Houches 2285m

N

—— 7 – Lac Vert
—— 8 – Pointe Noire de Pormenaz
—— 9 – Dérochoir and Désert de Platé

0   1
km

The village of Servoz with the Rocher des Fiz behind and the Dérochoir

The main attraction in Servoz is the Diosaz gorge which is a conservation area and has an entrance fee. It's worth the visit for the many waterfalls to be seen on the 1.6km, 300m ascent. The Diosaz river comes down from the slopes of Mont Buet, the highest peak in the Aiguilles Rouges range, and the force of the water has carved this deep chasm into the limestone.

The Plateau d'Assy is situated way above the Arve valley, under huge limestone cliffs and summits which form the southern extremity of the Désert de Platé. Famous for its relatively modern church, Notre Dame de Toute Grace, the Plateau d'Assy is also home to several large convalescence hospitals and sanatoriums,

dating from the days when TB victims were brought to the Alps for the clean air. These buildings are now used as hospitals for physiotherapy for accident victims and terminal care for the sick.

Just 5km further northeast is the resort of Plaine Joux, popular for skiing in winter and a departure point for many walks in summer. The calm and isolation here gives a sense of being far away from Chamonix, yet it enjoys superlative views of the Mont Blanc massif and allows easy access into the neighbouring non-glaciated mountains. There is little accommodation, and not much at all except a few cafés and lots of car parking space. Plateau d'Assy has all facilities.

WALK 7
Lac Vert

You can, of course, drive up to Lac Vert (albeit not from Servoz), get out of your car, and there it is. But this is a guide for walking, not car touring, and it makes for a good outing to go from Servoz to Lac Vert on foot.

Leaving the village of Servoz, a good track leads steeply through the hamlets of Le Mont and La Côte, where the old farms attest to a history of cultivation on these sunny slopes. This is charming terrain where more than once you'll be happy to take a break from the fairly relentless climb to savour the surroundings. A good path goes on through forest to emerge right at the lake.

There are likely to be lots of people there, mostly accompanied by their cars, but you can always find somewhere quiet to sit. It's worth taking some time to enjoy – look up at the impressive rocky slopes high above and you'll see the Dérochoir, scene of a rockslide which took place in 1471. Many huge boulders will be seen on the ascent to Lac Vert, vestiges of this landslide and one in 1751.

The return can either be by the same path or via a rather unusual variant from the car park at La Côte which follows a tenuous path in beech forest all the way down fairly directly to the outskirts of Servoz.

A varied, pretty and interesting walking route; the lake seems much more impressive when you've put in some effort to get there.

A MAGICAL PLACE

At first glance Lac Vert does not seem special at all – just a lake surrounded by trees. However, once you walk round to the far side the views are really something. The name 'Lac Vert' comes from the reflections of the green spruce, and on a clear, calm day this image is enhanced by the snowy summits of Mont Blanc and Bionnassay mirrored in the still waters. Prepare to be surprised and moved.

Car park	Servoz – in the centre of the village near the post office – named Le Bouchet on the map
Starting point	Servoz post office 814m
Finishing point	Servoz post office 814m
Highpoint	Lac Vert 1266m
Altitude gain	452m
Maps	IGN Top 25 3530 ET Samoëns Haut Giffre
Distance	7.5km (4.6 miles)
Time	3hr 30min
Grade/difficulties	1 if done there and back on ascent path; 2 if done as described. The tracks for the ascent are all good and signposted. The descent path in the woods is very indistinct in places, but is waymarked with small orange dots. Although you may feel lost if you miss the path, heading south would bring you to the road so it's not a problem
Public transport	None available
Tip	There's plenty in Servoz to fill a day. Combine this walk with a visit to the ruined Tour St Michel and the Diosaz gorge.

Route

From the post office take the road north which is signed to Le Mont. After about 200m don't miss a narrow steep road going off left which is signed to Lac Vert. Take this and keep going uphill. Any junctions are signed, and the track crosses the main road several times as it makes its way through authentic alpine farms and meadows.

After about 30min the old fountain is reached at **Le Mont**. Here the way is indicated to the left and then right at the next junction. Soon after, a sign points right and uphill again to finally emerge on the road with a car park on the left (this car park is the dividing point of routes for the descent). Many people walk to the lake from here. Be sure to take time to look around – views behind of the Mont Blanc massif are opening up and above, to the right, are the complex slopes of the Pointe Noire de Pormenaz.

From the car park a wide track leads onwards and it's best to stay on this all the way to **Lac Vert**. Just before you

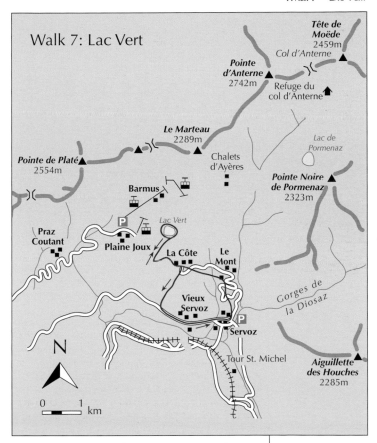

reach the lake the track joins the old road and this takes you past limestone boulders on an interesting route.

There is a botanical path around the lake, and it's important to stay on this when strolling around as erosion is killing off the trees, hence the many young saplings planted in an effort to save the site. Once on the far side of the water it's impossible not to linger with such a splendid vista.

The reflections of the spruce trees in Lac Vert give the lake its name

Return can be by the same route, and if it's raining (or has done recently) this may be the best option. Similarly if your knees don't appreciate steep terrain don't do the alternative descent.

But for those who'd like to get away from the crowds and feel just a little bit isolated there is an option. Take the path back down to the car park near **La Côte**, noted on the ascent. Instead of following the road out of this area, locate the wide track that goes directly south into the forest – there will be pink or orange marks on the trees. Very soon, turn left – again there are orange dots on the trees. There may also be a wooden sign with a snow-shoe on it. The dots mark the path all the way but are often quite discreet; they are also quite high up as they mark the path for the winter snow when this is a popular route on snowshoes. The path basically heads south, but it weaves all over the place and it is advisable to stay on it. Just don't get too distracted by the distant views of the Aravis range.

Frequented by locals, this is known as the 'Chemin des 3 Gouilles', a *gouille* being a pond (but you'll be doing well if you find them all). The shade of the beech forest is welcome on a hot day, and this is certainly not your usual Chamonix valley terrain. The first pond is really well hidden, but the second is more obvious and is turned on the right by a very muddy path. Soon after you'll find a wobbly log bridge over the river, then just keep following the dots and heading downhill. Just beyond a narrow passage between two big rocks – which have come all the way from the Dérochoir (the third goulllle is near here) – there is a short moment when the dots seems to disappear, but keep going down and right. There are a few red marks on trees before the regular orange ones appear again and you soon pop out onto the road that leads left back into town. It's possible that by taking a different turn you'll come out parallel to this road, in the old part of town, but it's easy to get back to the centre of **Servoz**.

WALK 8
Pointe Noire de Pormenaz

As well as giving great views of the Mont Blanc massif very close by, the ascent of the Pointe Noire de Pormenaz is also a superb and varied walk. It can be approached from the village of Plaine Joux or from the top of the Brévent lift via the Refuge du Col d'Anterne. Either way is excellent. Whilst its north slopes are short, the other faces are intricate and, isolated as it is, it's a summit to be treated with respect.

The walk to the Refuge du Col d'Anterne from the Brévent is described in Walks 22 and 23, so here the

The Pointe Noire de Pormenaz is a considerable summit, standing alone, separated from the neighbouring Aiguilles Rouges and Rochers des Fiz.

OPTIONS

On a hot day, plan a dip in the lake on the way up. Consider making it a two-day trek, staying the night at the Refuge Col d'Anterne – your knees will thank you during the descent to Servoz.

Note: The Refuge du Col d'Anterne is more commonly known as the Refuge Chalet Moëde d'Anterne, but the map refers to it as the Refuge du Col d'Anterne.

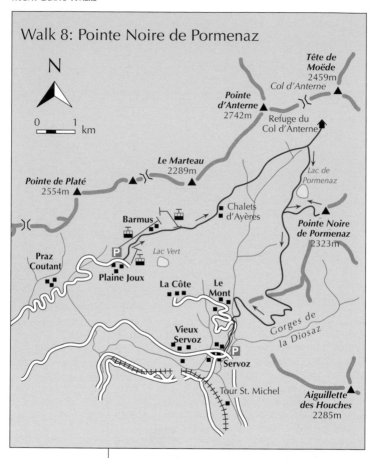

Walk 8: Pointe Noire de Pormenaz

N

0   1 km

Tête de Moëde
2459m
Col d'Anterne

Pointe d'Anterne
2742m

Refuge du Col d'Anterne

Le Marteau
2289m

Lac de Pormenaz

Pointe de Platé
2554m

Chalets d'Ayères

Pointe Noire de Pormenaz
2323m

Barmus

Lac Vert

Praz Coutant

Plaine Joux

La Côte

Le Mont

Gorges de la Diosaz

Vieux Servoz

Servoz

Tour St. Michel

Aiguillette des Houches
2285m

ascent of the Pointe Noire de Pormenaz is detailed from Plaine Joux. Even though this route is perfectly feasible in the day, a night spent at the hut will allow another walk to be envisaged the next day – for example the Col d'Anterne and the Tête de Villy – so this is worth considering if time permits.

Car park	Plaine Joux
Starting point	Plaine Joux 1337m
Finishing point	Servoz 814m
Highpoint	Pointe Noire de Pormenaz 2323m
Altitude gain	990m
Maps	IGN Top 25 3530 ET Samoëns Haut Giffre
Distance	16.5km (10.2 miles)
Time	7hr+
Grade/difficulties	2/3. This walk is quite long, but mainly the paths are good except for the summit path itself where the way is a little vague
Public transport	SNCF train Chamonix–Le Fayet, then local SAT bus to Plaine Joux via Passy; SNCF train Servoz–Chamonix
Accommodation	Refuge du Col d'Anterne, 04 50 93 60 43
Tip	The path from the Lac de Pormenaz to the summit isn't on the map, but is on the ground. However it is a small path marked by cairns and there are several possibilities to choose from; this would not be a good place to be in bad visibility, so if the mist comes down miss out the summit and go on down to Servoz.

Route

From Plaine Joux find the track that leads uphill to the hamlets of Ayères. This is a driveable track, reserved for motorists going to these hamlets, and is signed. Be sure to go uphill to Barmus and not to follow the road to Lac Vert. From **Barmus** the track pleasantly traverses the hillside. Views of the Mont Blanc massif are already good and get better as you approach the hamlet of Ayères des Rocs, followed by Ayères des Pierrières (**Chalets d'Ayères**). In the summer season there is often a café open here which gives a pleasant break as the old chalets against the distant hazy snowy peaks make an attractive backdrop.

The main trail is followed around the hillside, ignoring the marked path off left to the Dérochoir. The slopes above coming down from the huge Rochers des Fiz are most impressive. Eventually a junction gives left to the Col d'Anterne, right to the **Refuge du Col d'Anterne**: take the right and go and have a beer at the hut whilst considering the next stage. (It is possible to take the trail via the Chalets du Souay which cuts up directly to the Lac de Pormenaz, but I can think of no good reason to avoid visiting the hut.)

The path saunters its way towards the slopes of the **Pointe Noire de Pormenaz**, gently ambling up, in and out of small bumps and dips, amongst clumps of fluffy white cotton grass, to the **lake.** It's very tempting to take a break here and swim out to the island in the middle. Check the time first, though, as the descent to Servoz usually takes longer than expected. From the lake to the summit is another 350m. If in doubt – regarding time or energy levels – don't hesitate to leave the summit for another day. The lake is a great objective in itself and it's better to have time for a leisurely descent than to be stumbling down exhausted as darkness falls.

Continue along the path to the end of the lake where there is a signpost (the sign was missing in summer 2004). Straight ahead is the path down to Les Ayères. Go left (yellow and white waymarks) away from the lake and around the hillside. (This path eventually goes down to Servoz and will be your descent later.)

A bit further along than you expect you'll find a red arrow on a rock pointing left. This is the summit path. It is quite vague in places but there are cairns (lots of them) and the odd red flash. The path crosses the junction between limestone and granite at a stream. I usually lose the red marks about here but following the cairns always leads to the summit. There are several small paths – choose one but be sure not to go too far over to the left (northeast). Basically the route is up the west slopes of the mountain. Finally a large cairn marks the main top with a short airy ridge nearby to the true highpoint. Views are magnificent.

Coming down you may well lose the path you took up but follow cairns – if anything staying further to the west – until you hit the trail that goes down to Servoz. It will take you via the Chalets de Chavanne Neuve – be careful on the initial descent from the summit in bad visibility.

From here the path continues contouring to the Chalets de Pormenaz from where begins the long descent towards the forest. Servoz is at 814m so it doesn't take a rocket scientist to figure out that this is some serious 'down', which at the end of the day is pretty tiring (this is where the wisdom of a two-day trek becomes apparent so as to be on the summit well before lunchtime, with plenty of time to enjoy the descent). Servoz is reached eventually – when you come out on the road at **Le Mont** just keep following your nose downhill into the town. There is a welcome bar en route to the train station.

Mont Blanc seen from the summit of the Pointe Noire de Pormenaz

WALK 9
The Dérochoir and the Désert de Platé

The name 'Dérochoir' comes from the French word *dérocher*, meaning to scour or to clear of rocks.

Looking up from the Arve valley, the Rochers des Fiz present a huge and apparently impenetrable bastion. It's impossible to see any way through, and yet one does exist. The Dérochoir is graphically named as this landslide channel is the only weakness in this formidable wall of rock. Even so, this passage is steep and requires a via ferrata (no equipment necessary) to overcome the final rock face.

The reason to go up here is to gain the fabulous limestone plateau of the Désert de Platé from the Arve valley side instead of going all the way round to the Giffre valley and coming up from Flaine. Also, of course, for the challenge of finding the way through and the pleasure of the steep climb. Needless to say, situated as it is right opposite the Mont Blanc massif, views are great.

The circuit described here is very varied and is done by going up from Plaine Joux to the Dérochoir then continuing over to the Chalets de Platé where the French

Car park	Plaine Joux
Starting point	Plaine Joux 1337m
Finishing point	Plaine Joux 1337m
Highpoint	Col de la Portette 2354m
Altitude gain	1020m
Map	IGN Top 25 3530 ET Samoëns Haut Giffre
Distance	11.7km (7.3 miles)
Time	6hr 30min
Grade/difficulties	3. The paths are all good but the aided section to the Dérochoir is relatively long. The descent is relentless but the trail is well made. This route does require the paths to be snowfree
Public transport	SNCF train Chamonix–Le Fayet then local SAT bus to Plaine Joux via Passy
Accommodation	Refuge de Platé, 04 50 93 11 07
Tip	Be sure that the slopes up to the Dérochoir and beyond are snowfree before embarking on this hike.

Alpine Club refuge provides welcome drinks and even a bed for the night if further exploration of this area is envisaged. The descent is by the Egratz couloir, another steep and improbable way (slightly less rocky than the Dérochoir), to return to Plaine Joux.

Once attained the Dérochoir is a great vantage point

Route

Starting from the Plaine Joux car park, it's not immediately obvious where the footpath goes. There are several false tracks which are ski pistes. Head around right to the cafés and a sign indicates all paths up and left. (The road goes on round to Lac Vert.) Going up the track there is the odd sign to Les Ayères and the Col d'Anterne – this is the right direction. This driveable track goes all the way to beautiful old chalets, first **Barmus** and then the various Ayères hamlets (**Chalets d'Ayères**). There is often a café open in Ayères des Pierrières in high summer, and this forms a justifiably popular outing in its own right.

Just after these chalets look out for a path going left, signed to the Dérochoir. This is waymarked in red and rises gently at first. It is signed as a 'dangerous path', probably because of the rocky nature and also because in snowy conditions it could be quite difficult.

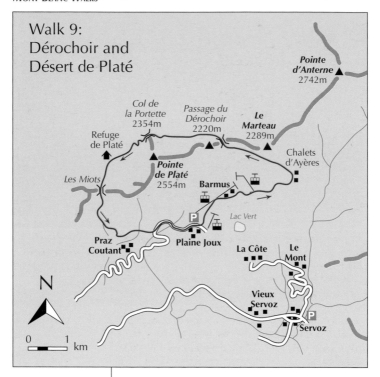

Walk 9:
Dérochoir and
Désert de Platé

This short aided
section needs no
equipment and should
present no difficulty
for most walkers.
Small children and
those with severe
vertigo may be safer
roped up.

As it gains height the path becomes more and more rocky and plunges through boulderfields higher up, until the way is barred by a cliff. Cables and chains, with the odd metal footstep and ladder, make this barrier surmountable ◀ and afterwards a path leads quickly to the col, the **Passage du Dérochoir** (2220m). Behind, the Mont Blanc massif presents its full glory, whilst ahead a whole new vista opens up: the limestone pavement of Platé, with its characteristic crevasses and huge waves of grey rock. Beyond, the rock gives way to grassy meadows where the Chalets de Sales enjoy an idyllic position and the dinging of cowbells drifts up to the col.

In the distance the top of the Flaine ski lift system can just be seen, explaining why this area can become quite crowded on holiday weekends.

Descending from the Désert de Platé meadows

Whilst it is tempting to descend to the alpage and visit the Refuge de Sales, if the route is to be completed in the day this variation is a little too long. The next objective is the **Col de la Portette**, seen not too far away to the left (west). It's further than it looks as the terrain is bouldery in places. Beware early in the season as this slope can hold névé for some time and in such conditions this traverse could be quite dangerous, or at least scary.

The col (2354m) is a lovely place to stand and stare. Now the views include the Chalets de Platé, just below, and to the west the whole of the Arve valley spread out thousands of metres below. Beyond is Mont Joly and behind again the Aravis chain. To the north the glaciers of Mont Ruan can be seen at the far end of the Sixt valley.

A good path invites you to scurry down the hillside quickly to reach the welcome refreshments of the **Refuge de Platé**. A night spent here would allow the ascent of the Tête du Colonney (2692m) the next day, to get a full 360-degree panorama of the region.

Onwards from the hut to the south, a nice flat grassy wander suddenly ends at the head of an unlikely couloir

On the via ferrata which allows the improbable passage through the Dérochoir

– unlikely in the sense that there is a regular path descending it. I'm not sure I'd like to ascend this but plenty of people do. Here the zigzag is king – there are hundreds of them. At first, views down are almost giddy, so steep is the drop – one slip and you feel you'll be down on the Autoroute Blanche! However, the trail is excellent and the grade perfect.

The knees may groan so speed is of the essence down here. Once down at the tree-line a flat track is reached; on hot days you will not be tempted to linger as this hillside is a suntrap and shade is rare. The presence of many alder bushes attests to the frequent avalanches in this channel, which prevents other trees or bushes getting a hold.

Once on the track follow it left. It goes up rather more than you expect, or desire, at this stage. Don't miss a little path on the left near the end signed 'Plaine Joux 20min'. This emerges on the road just near the Colonie de Vacances at Guébriant, and 10min on the road is enough to reach **Plaine Joux** and a welcome beer.

CHAPTER 3

LES HOUCHES

Les Houches is situated just after a bend in the River Arve at the western end of the Chamonix valley. It is generally regarded as the first village you reach on entering the valley, and nestles under the sombre slopes of the Aiguille du Goûter. The word 'Houches' (spelt with or without an 'H') apparently comes from the Celtic term *olca*, meaning the first cultivated ground.

In winter Les Houches is famous for its shady aspect, when for several months the centre of the town only gets to see the sun tantalisingly close on the nearby slopes. However, in summer it is a pleasant town, surrounded by flowery meadows. TMB aspirants often start from there and any day in the season will see many hikers strolling down the high street stocking up on hill food for the day. Many trails head out from the centre, usually signed, and there are also two cable cars functioning in summer to allow the climb out of town to be avoided, thus making it an ideal base for walkers. Monday is market day, a good source for local specialities.

Les Houches is served by both the Chamonix Bus and the SNCF Martigny–Le Fayet train.

AN INSPIRATIONAL SPOT

Les Houches has become *the* place for British to buy houses, and if you want to get as close as possible to the massif this is the place to be. Its proximity gives it unusual views – not the wide-reaching panoramas so typical of the other side of the valley, but neck-craning, breathtaking glimpses of steep crevasse-ridden glaciers and impossibly high rocky buttresses. This is a place where mountaineering dreams are born.

From higher up on the outskirts of town, the Aiguille Verte is seen for the hugely impressive summit that it is, and to the north the western peaks of the Aiguilles Rouges along with the impenetrable barrier of the Fiz.

Walks from Les Houches

N

0 —— 1 km

Pierre
Blanche

Aig.
des Houches
2285m

Le Plan de la Cry

La Flatière   Le Bettey

Chalets de Chailloux

Le Coupeau

P

Tête
Noire
1746m

Charousse

SNCF railway line

Col de la
Forclaz
1533m

La Côte

Les Chavants

Le Prarion
1969m

P

Télécabine Prarion

P

Les Houches

Tramway du Mont Blanc

Col de
Voza
1653m

Téléphérique Bellevue

Mt Lachat
2115m

Les Bettières

Le Planet

Chalets
de Tricot
(ruins)

←tunnel

Glacier
de Tête
Rousse

Glacier de la Bourgeat

Mt Vorassay
2303m

Nid d'Aigle

Glacier de Bionnassay

Col de
Tricot
2120m

Arête de Tricot

10 – Le Prarion

11 – Mont Vorassay

12 – Aiguillette des Houches

WALK 10
Le Prarion

Le Prarion is a peak which does not come close to attaining even half the height of most of the lofty summits that surround it. A bit of a nonentity perhaps in this, the Mecca of high mountains? No, not at all. As is so often the case these relatively small non-glaciated hills occupy a privileged position on the edge of the massif that means they offer superlative belvederes: from these summits you get to see everything else. Le Prarion has to be one of the best.

But, I hear you say, there's a lift called Le Prarion from Les Houches – surely this goes to the top of it? Not quite, although it does provide a nice gentle descent option for those with knee issues. However, it would be a crime to miss out on the wonderful and unlikely route to the summit, and since you only see the lift after reaching the top it's not really a temptation.

Starting in Les Chavants, the route takes you through the unique hamlet of Charousse. Later the Col de la Forclaz provides a lovely shady resting place, complete with picnic table, before the rigours of the summit ridge. From the top it's not far to the Prarion lift. If you want a longer walk, or the lift isn't functioning, there is a good path back down to Les Chavants.

Le Prarion is the very last summit at the western end of the Chamonix valley.

Heading along the summit of Le Prarion

CHAROUSSE

Although there are lots of *alpages* in the Chamonix region with old farms and the like, this one is really exceptional as it's so unspoilt. It's easy to see why this cluster of buildings has been used many times for films – emerging from the forest on the ancient track you can feel yourself stepping back several centuries, and almost expect milkmaids to come out of the old larch-and-stone houses. As for the views, they are something else – the summits of the Mont Blanc massif (although not Mont Blanc itself), the Arve valley, the Aiguilles Rouges...

Car park	Just beyond Les Chavants at La Côte
Starting point	La Côte 1131m
Finishing point	La Côte 1131m
Highpoint	Le Prarion 1969m
Altitude gain	850m
Map	IGN Top 25 3531 ET St Gervais-les-Bains Massif du Mont Blanc
Distance	9km (5.6 miles)
Time	5hr 30min–6hr
Grade/difficulties	2. Good paths
Public transport	SNCF train or Chamonix Bus to Les Houches
Tip	If you do not have transport then you will want to start this walk in Les Houches at the Prarion lift car park. Similarly, if you plan to take the Prarion cable car down, then start at the car park and follow the Route des Chavants from town up through Les Chavants. Follow signs to Charousse, past the Amis de la Nature building to La Côte. Add on another 45min–1hr for the extra ascent.

Route

From La Côte take the track into the beech forest and follow it to **Charousse**. A sign points the way onwards (this is also the Tour du Pays du Mont Blanc, TPMB) around the hillside under the shaly slopes of Le Prarion.

The path leaves Charousse, descending slightly into the woods, and turns left over a stream to hit a track. This track eventually doubles back and shortly after that there

Walk 10: Le Prarion

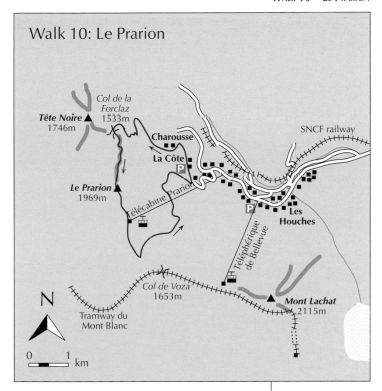

is a signposted turning (TPMB Col de la Forclaz) onto a beautiful path on the right. This path (not marked on the 1998 map) takes you quite steeply in woods via multiple zigzags to emerge onto a track which leads quickly up to the **Col de la Forclaz** (1533m).

Here again the way is signed directly up the broad north ridge of **Le Prarion** and this track, recently improved, is a real pleasure. At first views are tantalisingly brief as the path winds through forest, but once above the tree-line the panorama is superb, alternately of Mont Blanc, the Chamonix Aiguilles and the Aiguilles Rouges on the left, or the Arve valley and the Aravis to the right. This excellent trail continues (occasionally protected by hand-line cables) through a carpet of alpenrose, past a small col, to reach the top, a rounded ridge several hundred metres long, where early in the summer flora enthusiasts will be thrilled by this rather unexpected haven of wild-flowers. The highest point on the ridge is marked by a small cairn.

The descent path, clearly marked continuing along the ridge heading south, winds its way down a rounded, bushy shoulder through rocks and shrubs to the top of the **Prarion cable car**. Either get in this, or continue beyond to the Prarion hotel/restaurant for a drink.

Two options for descent on foot

The easiest option is to continue southeast along the signed trail to the **Col de Voza** and to take the well-signed track down – preferably the one going towards Maison Neuve if you want to return to La Côte.

More direct (but less knee-friendly) is to descend under the ski drag lift which is between the Prarion cable car and the Prarion hotel/restaurant. Follow these grassy slopes all the way down to the bottom of the lift where you'll join the track coming down from the Col de Voza. Turn left on the track. This leads all the way down to **Les Houches**, but to return to La Côte it's best to take a path that soon goes off left, signed to 'Les Baux/Charousse'. This descends diagonally and very pleasantly through the woods to an unsigned junction, with a mountain bike symbol for the right-hand way. Both ways lead into Charousse from where you take the ascent route back to **La Côte**. To go on down to the cable car car park, go along the Route des Chavants, then for a direct descent go left down the Chemin de Bovresse, then continue along the Chemin des S'Nailles to meet the Route des Chavants above the lake. Turn right to get to the parking area.

WALK 11

Mont Vorassay

Any walk within sight of the major peaks of the Mont Blanc massif is going to benefit from exceptional views. Mont Vorassay has the additional advantage of being right on the edge of the southern extremity of the range, very close to the sweeping Bionnassay glacier and the snowy crests of the Dômes de Miage.

Our route follows the TMB so there will be plenty of people around, but the TMB candidates will generally be toiling along under large rucksacks whereas you should be skipping by. We briefly leave the main trail to ascend Mont Vorassey and this route takes us onto a delightful ridge from where we'll have all-round views – not only of the glaciated peaks nearby but also towards the far-off Aravis.

Unless you can arrange transport back from Les Contamines, the return is more or less by the same route, with a variant at the end to go up to the Col de Voza and then descend on foot to Les Houches. For this reason I suggest that the initial uplift is gained by taking the cable car out of town.

The very small summit of Mont Vorassay guards the Col de Tricot, an important passage on the TMB. This saddle gives access to the southern part of the route as it heads towards Italy.

Crossing the footbridge en route to the Col du Tricot

Car park	Bellevue cable car, Les Houches
Starting point	Top of Bellevue cable car 1801m
Finishing point	Bellevue car park 993m
Highpoint	Mont Vorassay 2303m
Altitude gain	900m
Map	IGN Top 25 3531 ET St Gervais-les-Bains Massif du Mont Blanc
Distance	15km (9.3 miles)
Time	6hr+
Grade/difficulties	2/3. Good paths all the way along the TMB, but the path is smaller to the summit and then down to the col
Public transport	Chamonix Bus or SNCF train to Les Houches
Tip	Once at the Col de Tricot it's certainly very tempting to go on down to the Miage *alpage* where the Refuge de Miage offers rest and refreshment in a fine wild setting. You could then continue up to the Truc *alpage* and finish in Les Contamines (Walk 1) by using the local bus service to return to Les Houches.

Route

Coming out of the lift, turn right and go along next to the **Mont Blanc tramway** to a crossing over it, which leads to a path across a meadow and down towards the sparsely forested Bionnassay valley. The trail takes a descending traverse all the way down to the valley floor where several streams are crossed before the big glacial torrent pouring down from the Bionnassay glacier. A rather smart suspension bridge crosses this river; less sturdy bridges have, in the past, submitted to the forces of nature, notably avalanches or floods.

After the bridge the path rises to a junction. Stay left in the direction of the Col de Tricot and follow the path on surprisingly stable moraine alongside the dirty grey snout of the glacier. You have to look closely to even see that this is ice as it carries layers of silt ground up by the endless action of the glacier.

Now we enter the Tricot valley, and the trail meanders most pleasantly between limestone boulders and alpenrose. Keep your eyes open at about 2000m for a red

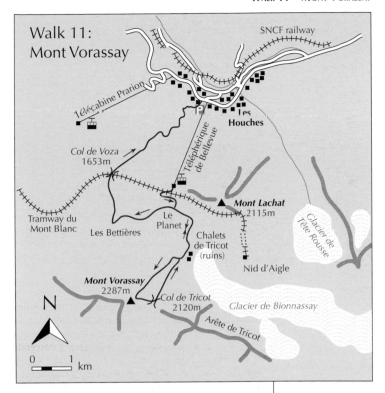

Walk 11:
Mont Vorassay

SNCF railway

Télécabine Prarion

Les
Houches

Col de Voza
1653m

Téléphérique
de Bellevue

Tramway du
Mont Blanc

Les Bettières

Le
Planet

Mont Lachat
2115m

Glacier de Tête Rousse

Chalets
de Tricot
(ruins)

Nid d'Aigle

Mont Vorassay
2287m

Col de Tricot
2120m

Glacier de Bionnassay

N

Arête de Tricot

0   1 km

marker on a boulder pointing rightwards, as this is where
we leave the main trail. The path is indistinct at first, but
heads north through alder bushes to the end of the ridge
above, and arrives at a perfect picnic spot. Opposite is
the hugely impressive Aiguille de Bionnassay, and to its
left the Aiguille du Goûter. Look closely and you might
see the Goûter hut, its metal sides gleaming in the sun.
Look even more closely – we're talking binoculars now
– and there may be tiny moving specks around the hut,
mountaineers returning from the summit of Mont Blanc.

The way on is a little overgrown as the bushes are
succumbing to gravity and falling down the slope. Push

past and the trail traverses along towards the Col de Tricot. At various points you can regain the ridge, so do so as soon as you like and follow this to the summit of **Mont Vorassay**.

Descend by the easiest route to the **Col de Tricot** (2120m), then take the TMB route down the Tricot valley and retrace your steps all the way down, over the bridge and up to the path junction from where we came in from the right earlier (Les Vrets). Turn left and go along a wide track to **Le Planet**, then onwards to the big car park at **Les Bettières**. We rejoin the TMB here, this time the regular route which goes to the Col de Voza.

A jeep track climbs at a reasonable angle in open country and once again the Aiguilles du Goûter and de Bionnassay dominate the views. At the **Col de Voza** (1653m) there is a café nearby for a cooling ice cream before you tackle the descent into town. Take the time to savour the fine vista of the Chamonix Aiguilles and beyond before you stroll on over the tramline and along a track which, after a brief rise, descends rightwards and down to town. You pass several houses and ski-tows before hitting a metalled road at La Maison Neuve. After several hairpins at a junction go right, over a stream then along a no-through road to join a track that leads all the way down into the town. Turn right to reach the Bellevue car park.

WALK 12
Aiguillette des Houches

The Aiguillette des Houches is geologically interesting as here the granite of the Mont Blanc massif gives way to the limestone of the northern ranges, starting with the imposing barrier of the Rochers des Fiz.

The Aiguillette des Houches is a delightful peak which defines the southern end of the Aiguilles Rouge range before it descends into the deep ravine of the Diosaz gorge.

There are various routes to reach the summit and the one chosen here is reasonably arduous as it traverses the summit without taking advantage of the relatively nearby Brévent lift system. The advantage of this route is that it takes in the wonderfully airy Pierre Blanche ridge which adds a certain zest to the hike.

The imposing Mont Blanc massif from beneath the Aiguillette des Houches

Car park	Le Bettey, on the road from Le Coupeau to La Flatière
Starting point	Le Bettey 1352m
Finishing point	Le Bettey 1352m
Highpoint	Aiguillette des Houches 2285m
Altitude gain	950m
Map	IGN Top 25 3530 ET Samoëns Haut-Giffre
Distance	8km (5 miles)
Time	5hr 30min–6hr
Grade/difficulties	2. The paths are all good but the ridge is airy and the descent is steep at the start
Public transport	There is no bus service from Les Houches to Le Coupeau or La Flatière
Tip	The Aiguillette des Houches can be climbed from the Brévent cable car via the Tête de Bel Lachat and the path which goes west from here. An airy circuit can be had by continuing on over the Aiguillette du Brévent.

Situated as it is at the far end of the Chamonix valley it goes without saying that from here you can see quite a lot: not only the Mont Blanc massif from end to end but also the Aravis, dominated by the soaring summit of the

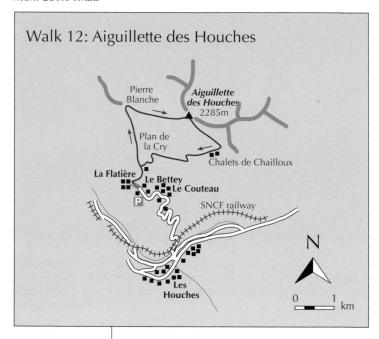

Walk 12: Aiguillette des Houches

Pierre Blanche

Aiguillette des Houches
▲ 2285m

Plan de la Cry

Chalets de Chailloux

La Flatière

Le Bettey
Le Couteau

P

SNCF railway

Les Houches

N

0   1 km

Pointe Percée, and to the north the deep dark depths of the Diosaz gorge with the intriguing slopes of the Pointe Noire de Pormenaz behind. Beyond is Mont Buet and the distant hazy Diosaz valley.

Route

From **Le Bettey** go along the road to the religious centre of **La Flatière** and be sure to look at the view from this idyllic spot. A path heads off east to **Plan de la Cry** where there are several paths – ours is the one to the left and left again which goes north across the wooded hillside in a rising traverse. At a junction a path left is signed to Montvauthier but we go straight ahead to reach the **Pierre Blanche** ridge at Pt 1687.

Now the shoulder is followed, with extensive views down to the Diosaz gorge on one side and towards the

Mont Blanc massif on the other. Underfoot are alpenrose and bilberries, while up ahead can be seen a subsidiary summit (not the Aiguillette, which is just behind). Keep to the crest of the ridge throughout this ascent, except for one deviation to the right (southern slopes) under the first highpoint on the ridge.

Once on the **summit** your efforts are well rewarded with an unbeatable panorama. The Bossons glacier looks especially close from here and this is a superb vantage point for glacier enthusiasts or those studying glaciology.

The descent route leaves from the summit, heading south in a series of tight, steep zigzags which soon lead down to easier ground. Pleasant high meadows are descended to a sharp turn right (west) to the **Chalets de Chaillouz** *alpage*. This is classic high grazing terrain, just above the treeline. Enjoy the views for a final time before plunging into the forest, which offers welcome shade in hot weather. At the path junction at 1782m choose the right option to Plan de la Cry (the left one going to Merlet animal park), and follow it down through the forest and back to the hamlet. A quick descent past the houses and you're back at the car.

Enjoying a spectacular sea of cloud on the ridge of the Aiguillette des Houches

CHAPTER 4

CHAMONIX

Known the world over, the name 'Chamonix' inspires dreams and desires: it is, quite simply, the Mecca of mountaineering. Live here and you see it all the time. People go to Chamonix as if on a pilgrimage, to see Mont Blanc, to climb it, to see the glaciers. Nowadays a big source of tourism is skiing – whilst Chamonix does not have the most extensive ski pistes, its couloirs and steep faces attract the best, and those with the biggest ambitions.

It was not always so, for the early inhabitants of this deep, cold and hostile valley eked out a precarious existence in a country where more months of the year were spent under snow than not, and where the ground provided little in the way of sustenance. The name Chamonix could have its origins in champs de neige, or nid de chamois for example, but it is now thought that it dervies from the Roman Campus Munitus – 'area closed on all sides by steep hillsides'.

Whilst there have been signs of life since before the Bronze Age – and later the Romans – the history of Chamonix really starts with the establishment of the Priory in 1091. Led by the prior, the monks and locals exploited the land and lived a relatively harmonious communal life until ceding authority to greater bodies in the 16th century.

The year 1860 heralded the end of the Kingdom of Savoy with the

THE ADVENT OF TOURISM

The Chamonix people were known for their rebellious nature, preferring to make their living from smuggling and illegal trading than working the land. All this was to change with the visit of Wyndham and Pococke in 1741 (see Introduction, How it all Started), which heralded a new era: tourism, which was to change Chamonix from a modest town into the mountaineering metropolis of today. Hotels soon sprang up, mostly named for the British at first since they formed the majority of visitors. In 1830 one was moved to write: 'Before, Chamonix was a valley, today it's a hotel.'

In 1786 the first ascent of Mont Blanc guaranteed the future of Chamonix as a mountain centre, and the following years saw tourism rise exponentially.

The steep rocky walls of Les Drus turn a magical orange at sunset. (This photo was taken before several major rockfalls in the last few years.)

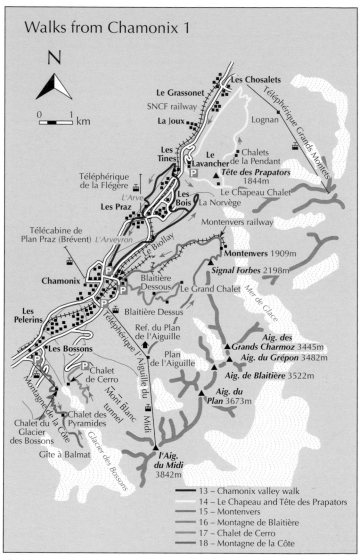

Walks from Chamonix 1

N

0   1
═══════ km

Les Chosalets

Le Grassonet

SNCF railway

Téléphérique Grands Montets

La Joux

Lognan

Les
Tines

Le
Lavancher

Chalets
de la Pendant

Téléphérique
de la Flégère

P

▲ *Tête des Prapators*
1844m

L'Arve

Les Praz

Les
Bois

Le Chapeau Chalet

La Norvège

Montenvers railway

Télécabine de
Plan Praz (Brévent)

L'Arveyron

Le Biollay

Montenvers 1909m

Chamonix

Blaitière
Dessous

Signal Forbes 2198m

P

Le Grand Chalet

P

Mer de Glace

P

Blaitière Dessous

Les
Pelerins

Ref. du Plan
de l'Aiguille

Téléphérique l'Aiguille du Midi

Plan
de l'Aiguille

Aig. des
▲ *Grands Charmoz* 3445m
  ▲ *Aig. du Grépon* 3482m

Les Bossons

P

P

Chalet
de Cerro

Montagne de la Côte

Mont Blanc tunnel

Aig. de Blaitière 3522m

Chalet du
Glacier
des Bossons

Chalet des
Pyramides

▲ *Aig. du
Plan* 3673m

Gîte à Balmat

Glacier des Bossons

▲ *l'Aig.
du Midi*
3842m

13 – Chamonix valley walk
14 – Le Chapeau and Tête des Prapators
15 – Montenvers
16 – Montagne de Blaitière
17 – Chalet de Cerro
18 – Montagne de la Côte

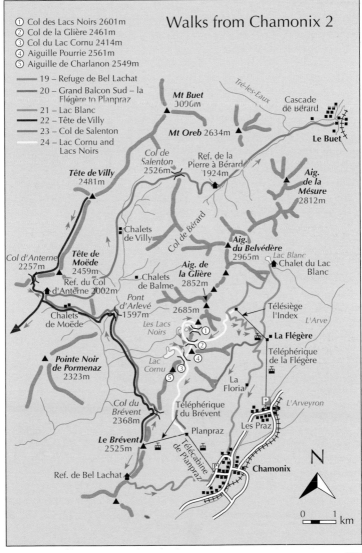

① Col des Lacs Noirs 2601m
② Col de la Glière 2461m
③ Col du Lac Cornu 2414m
④ Aiguille Pourrie 2561m
⑤ Aiguille de Charlanon 2549m

— 19 – Refuge de Bel Lachat
— 20 – Grand Balcon Sud – la Flégère to Planpraz
— 21 – Lac Blanc
— 22 – Tête de Villy
— 23 – Col de Salenton
— 24 – Lac Cornu and Lacs Noirs

Walks from Chamonix 2

Tré-les-Eaux

Cascade de Bérard

Mt Buet 3096m

Le Buet

Mt Oreb 2634m

Col de Salenton 2526m

Ref. de la Pierre à Bérard 1924m

Tête de Villy 2481m

Aig. de la Mésure 2812m

Col de Bérard

Chalets de Villy

Aig. du Belvédère 2965m

Lac Blanc

Chalet du Lac Blanc

Col d'Anterne 2257m

Tête de Moëde 2459m

Ref. du Col d'Anterne 2002m

Chalets de Balme

Aig. de la Glière 2852m

2685m

Télésiège l'Index

L'Arve

Pont d'Arlevé 1597m

Les Lacs Noirs

La Flégère

Téléphérique de la Flégère

Chalets de Moëde

Lac Cornu

④

Pointe Noir de Pormenaz 2323m

La Floria

L'Arveyron

Col du Brévent 2368m

Téléphérique du Brévent

Les Praz

Planpraz

Télécabine de Planpraz

Chamonix

Le Brévent 2525m

N

Ref. de Bel Lachat

0   1 km

Chamonix is centred on its church, with the Brévent behind

annexation to France of the region of Haute Savoie, of which Chamonix is part.

Nowadays Chamonix bears very little resemblance to its former self, and the rate of change continues unabated. The Mont Blanc tunnel, opened in 1965, provides transalpine passage and hence the presence of heavy goods traffic on the outskirts of town; the Aiguille du Midi cable car is, at 3842m, the highest in Europe, and attracts thousands of visitors a year; the old buildings have either been destroyed or swamped by the endless construction of new hotels and apartments. For some Chamonix no longer has any appeal but it does have its views; Mont Blanc, despite being raped and pillaged, is still there and if you take the time to look around town there is a certain charm to be found.

This is certainly the place to stay if you want all services, and it also provides a mid-point between all the walks in the book – the perfect location. To find a link to the past it's definitely worth visiting the Alpine Museum in the centre of town. Just be prepared: it has been said 'in Chamonix the tourist no longer conquers, he dominates'.

WALK 13
Chamonix Valley Walk

There is bound to be one day during a holiday in Chamonix when the idea of walking uphill just doesn't appeal – maybe the weather is not so good, fatigue has set in, you want to visit Chamonix market on the Saturday morning...

Much of the Chamonix valley is forested, and this makes for very pleasant walking as mostly it is not too dense and every so often there are tantalising views of the surrounding summits. This is certainly the case in the Bois du Bouchet and Les Bois, where the shade of the trees is welcome on hot days.

Tracks and footpaths abound throughout this walk, the valley being popular for family strolls, trail running, biking and cross-country skiing. The route described is just one option and if you choose to revisit the Bois du Bouchet you'll find other variants easily. The views are superb whichever way you go: the huge rocky spire of Les Drus dominates and is seen in all its glory, especially late on an autumn day when it captures the sun's last rays for a fiery spectacle.

Later, the village of Les Bois gives a chance to check out some of the finest old chalets in the area, before the Paradis des Praz reveals its delightful waterside setting.

Don't feel that you always have to make for the mountains: the Chamonix valley has its own delights and it's a shame not to spend time discovering them.

Car park	Chamonix, Place du Mont Blanc – the car park by the roundabout next to the fire station
Starting point	Chamonix, Place du Mont Blanc 1037m
Finishing point	Chamonix, Place du Mont Blanc 1037m
Highpoint	La Norvège in the Bois du Bouchet 1150m
Altitude gain	120m
Maps	IGN Top 25 3630 OT Chamonix Massif du Mont Blanc
Distance	10.8km (6.7 miles)
Time	3–4hr
Grade/difficulties	1
Public transport	SNCF train stations at Chamonix, Les Praz and Les Tines
Tip	This route can be cycled easily. It also makes a good running circuit.

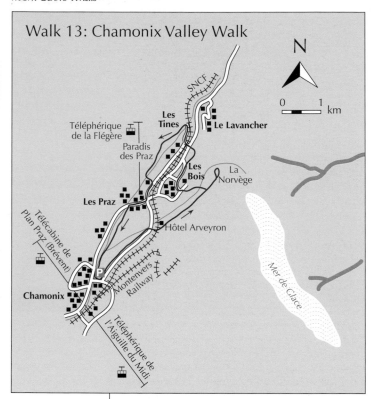

Walk 13: Chamonix Valley Walk

N

0   1 km

SNCF

Les Tines

Le Lavancher

Téléphérique
de la Flégère

Paradis
des Praz

**Les
Bois**

La
Norvège

Les Praz

Télécabine de
Plan Praz (Brévent)

Hôtel Arveyron

P

Montenvers Railway

Mer de Glace

Chamonix

Téléphérique de
l'Aiguille du Midi

Route

Walk out of town from the Place du Mont Blanc along the
main road towards Argentière/La Suisse as far as the Foyer
du Ski de Fond. Cross the side road and take the good
track which runs along parallel to the road, in sparse forest. It crosses several side roads and goes past the landing
area for the *parapentes* (paragliders). Follow it under the
road to the **Hôtel Arveyron** and continue, staying on the
true left bank of the Arveyron, ignoring a bridge over this
river. You will see on the right the famous Pierre d'Orthaz,
very popular with climbers. A working farm is passed and

The Pierre d'Orthaz has long been much-loved by boulderers

you'll reach another bridge on the left where a sign points to Les Bois and Les Praz, part of our route.

However, a nice loop is to continue along the left bank on a rising track which goes up to **La Norvège**. Here continue along the track which loops back on itself coming out eventually at the bridge seen earlier; cross this and go straight ahead to a sign *Retour des Fatigués* (for cross-country skiing). Go straight on along a smaller path which pops out on a road. Left here, then right at the dustbins into the charming village of **Les Bois** and follow signs through the village to **Les Tines** (don't miss the best ever view of Les Drus from just by the restaurant Le Sarpé). Stay on the small road which goes right (Chemin des Lanchettes), then left and right again, past the Hotel Le Prairie, to become a forest track. Continue on this – don't go left – and pass a forest barrier to another small road. A left turn leads down to the main road. Cross the **level crossing** and turn right to go parallel to the railway. At the end a left turn and we're onto the Petit Balcon Sud. Remember to look around as the views are superb – from Les Drus to Mont Blanc to the Aiguilles Rouges leftwards the footpath leads along to **Paradis des Praz** where there may be quite a festive atmosphere depending on the season – in summer a café is open and there are donkeys.

The wide track goes along next to the river to the golf course – one of the most sought-after due to its rather special backdrop. Don't even think about venturing on to the grass – stay on the path, protected by a sort of roof, until you reach the Hotel Labrador and the golfers' car park. Just at the road there is a path that runs right next to the road going right, next to a hedge. This brings you out at the La Flégère *téléphérique* car park. Continue down the road past the Hotel les Lanchers to where it crosses the river. Just before the river there is a good wide track that leads all the way back to **Chamonix** along the left bank of the Arve.

WALK 14
Le Chapeau and Tête des Prapators

Le Chapeau has been visited for centuries for its fantastic views of the surrounding mountains and the Mer de Glace. This is a magnificent hike.

Long before the cable cars were built this was a must-do walk. In those days the Mer de Glace was a rather bigger glacier but even now, in these days of receding ice, this walk is a classic. As far as the viewpoint just beyond the Chalet du Chapeau the path is completely dog- and child-friendly and this in itself is a perfectly good objective, returning by the same route.

For a longer walk, and a very varied circuit, the route can be continued up and around the Tête des Prapators, which is a ridge running down from the Aiguille à

UNWELCOME INTRUSIONS

The only flaw is the presence of the chairlift construction of La Pendant. Whilst this is very welcome for winter skiers, in summer it can only really be described as an eyesore. For sure there are all the other lifts of the Lognan Grand Montets system just a little way across the mountain side, and the Lognan cable car can be used as part of this walk. However, since I do not describe the walk using this lift I feel free to criticise the pylons at La Pendant. So in this area, just for a short section, wear blinkers and concentrate on the beauty of this cwm. The remainder of the walk well makes up for this in scenery and variety of terrain.

Car park	At the top of the village of Le Lavancher
Starting point	The top of the village of Le Lavancher 1250m
Finishing point	Le Lavancher 1250m
Highpoint	Tête des Prapators 1844m
Altitude gain	600m
Map	IGN Top 25 3630 OT Chamonix Massif du Mont Blanc
Distance	9.4km (5,8 miles)
Time	4hr 30min–5hr
Grade/difficulties	2/3. The path is good and even the short section of cables is very easy
Public transport	Chamonix Bus to Le Lavancher
Tip	To make a shorter hike, the Grand Balcon Nord can be taken from La Pendant down to Le Lavancher. Alternatively, to save knees, continue to the Lognan cable car and take this down. Then you can walk along the Petit Balcon Nord back to Le Lavancher.

Bochard, and into the Pendant cwm. From here several alternatives present themselves, depending on where the finish is envisaged.

Route

The track is well signed to Le Chapeau and it leaves the road immediately for the forest. As it climbs up there are frequent gaps in the trees allowing glimpses of the Aiguilles de Chamonix, the Dôme de Goûter and Chamonix itself stretched out far below, the silver gash of the Arve running through the middle.

After about 50min of very pleasant walking the chalet café of **Le Chapeau** (1550m) is reached. This is in a peculiar location, just 10min from the real belvedere, but handy for a drink. The path goes on rightwards and there is a junction signed to Lognan and Prapators. This is for later. Meanwhile go to the end of the main path to a superb open area from where the Mer de Glace can be seen, including the relatively recently formed emerald glacial pools at its snout. Behind is the Dent du Géant, very prominent in profile, and the adjoining Rochefort Arête. The Aiguilles

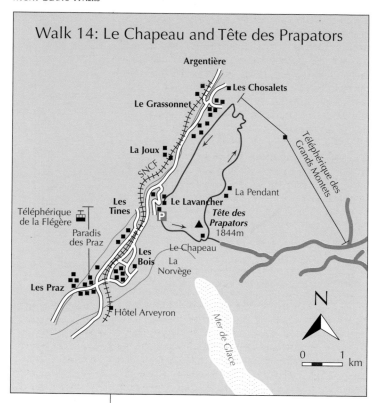

Walk 14: Le Chapeau and Tête des Prapators

de Chamonix are silhouetted, with the Aiguille de la République particularly striking.

Returning towards the café, either take the path back down or go on up towards **Prapators**. The sign warns that the trail is *escarpé* (precipitous) but it isn't bad at all. It does go up for 300m though, rather steeply, and there is a short section of ladder and cable. Seen from this path, the Mer de Glace is even more impressive.

Finally, after quite a lot of hairpins, the path suddenly flattens and turns the ridge at 1844m to descend into **La Pendant**. There is a very tempting flat glade just as the cwm is reached and if you sit here and face left you don't see the chairlift. A short climb leads out of the cwm and onto the main track towards Lognan. Follow this for some way until a footpath off left. Those wishing to take the lift should stay on the track. However, to descend on foot it's best to take the footpath which is signed to **Les Chosalets**. Note the large number of tyre tracks in the dust on this path – mountain bikes. They generally take the cable car up to Lognan then go for max on the descent – so watch your back!

The path winds nicely through the forest and every now and again Argentière is to be seen below through the trees. Eventually you pop out onto a wide track where a left turn brings you to the Petit Balcon Nord which goes from Argentière to Chamonix, very conveniently via **Le Lavancher**. A really nice grassy section brings you into the village where you turn left and walk up the road to the car.

WALK 15
Montenvers

In the 18th century the Mer de Glace glacier was far bigger than it is today. It descended all the way to the Chamonix valley and was hugely, massively deep, riven by gaping crevasses and leaning seracs. In those days the local farmers walked their cows up to Montenvers, then across the glacier (with woolly socks on their feet to give traction) to graze the slopes under Les Drus, a feat which seems incredible now.

A visit to Montenvers is obviously not to be missed. The train goes there and it's a nice journey, so that's a possibility on a non-walking day; otherwise the route described here is pretty good. Taking the Aiguille du Midi cable car to the midway station means that 1200m altitude is gained in the blink of an eye. Afterwards, the trail across the hillside is easy on the lungs and the feet, giving a chance to enjoy the views.

However, a walk isn't quite right without some 'up', so a quick climb to the Signal Forbes (named after James Forbes, a 19th-century Scottish geologist who was very

'Montenvers' clearly refers to the 'back side of the mountain' (in this case behind the Charmoz), but has also been written as 'Montanvert', possibly a reference to the greenness of this area.

THE GROWTH OF TOURISM

This is where tourism really began in the Chamonix area, following the visit of Wyndham and Pococke (see Introduction, How it all Started). Their glowing and excited reports of the Mer de Glace, sent back to England, inspired many thousands of wealthy tourists to follow their example. After the first ascent of Mont Blanc in 1786, climbing summits became increasingly popular and Montenvers quickly became the starting point for mountain ascents as well as a place of inspiration for artists and literary notables such as Wordsworth, Shelley, Byron and Ruskin.

The construction of the Montenvers railway in 1908 was greeted by the locals with hostility and suspicion. Their mule-guiding business taking people up the trail to the viewpoint was threatened, and they saw this as the end of a productive trade. Little did they know that it would only add to the success of Chamonix.

Car park	Aiguille du Midi cable car
Starting point	Plan de l'Aiguille 2310m
Finishing point	Chamonix 1037m
Highpoint	Plan de l'Aiguille 2310m
Altitude gain	120m
Maps	IGN Top 25 3630 OT Chamonix Massif du Mont Blanc
Distance	10km (6.2 miles)
Time	4hr (not including time to visit the sites at Montenvers)
Grade/difficulties	1/2. Good paths all the way but in very bad weather the traverse from the Plan de l'Aiguille to Montenvers can require a little concentration, and should not be done when there is still *névé*
Public transport	SNCF train to Chamonix train station, just next to the Montenvers station
Tip	Clearly this route could be done the other way round using the Montenvers train, then walking down from the Plan de l'Aiguille, but this path is fairly unrelenting and not very knee-friendly. Alternatively, an almost totally flat day could be had (almost unheard of in the Alps) by using both the cable car and the train. What decadence!

active in the Alps) is recommended for the fantastic view of the Grandes Jorasses (amongst others) before heading

down to the station café or the Montenvers hotel restaurant (depending on the state of your wallet) for lunch. Take time to visit the crystal museum, the wildlife exhibition, which is excellent, and the Grotte de Glace (if that's your thing), before following the old mule track all the way down to Chamonix.

The Montenvers is a great place from which to look at Les Drus. This photo was taken before the huge rockfall (July 2005) on the West face.

Route

Leave the cable car station and descend to the **Chalet du Plan de l'Aiguille**. The path onwards is clearly signed and it traverses across the hillside, around shoulders and across gullies, always at around the 2100m mark. Less than 1hr from the chalet a path heads off right to the Signal Forbes. ▶ Take this and climb up to a place where it looks like there's been a cairn-building workshop. This is the **Signal** (2198m). A very good paved trail leads down to **Montenvers**, arriving behind the Temple de la Nature, one of the first buildings to be constructed here in the 19th century, which now houses the museum. Just below is the wildlife exhibition. The hotel is worth a visit as it has maintained an aura of the dignity and adventure of early mountaineering.

James Forbes first described the alternating bands of light and dark ice which form on glaciers, usually found down-glacier from steep narrow icefalls, which are considered to be the result of different flow and ablation rates in summer and winter. These are now named Forbes Bands.

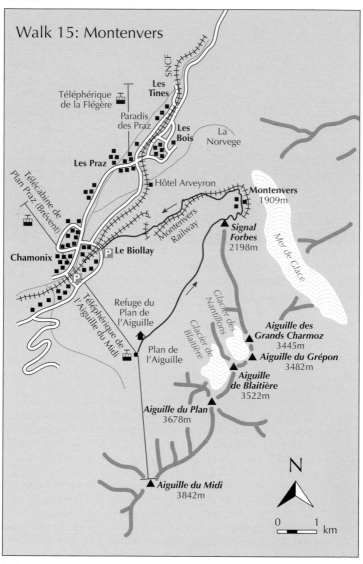

Walk 15: Montenvers

Téléphérique de la Flégère

Les Tines

SNCF

Paradis des Praz

Les Bois

La Norvege

Les Praz

Hôtel Arveyron

Télécabine de Plan Praz (Brévent)

Montenvers Railway

Montenvers 1909m

Mer de Glace

Signal Forbes 2198m

Chamonix

P Le Biollay

P

Téléphérique de l'Aiguille du Midi

Refuge du Plan de l'Aiguille

Glacier des Nantillons

Glacier de Blaitière

Aiguille des Grands Charmoz 3445m

Aiguille du Grépon 3482m

Plan de l'Aiguille

Aiguille de Blaitière 3522m

Aiguille du Plan 3678m

Aiguille du Midi 3842m

N

0   1 km

The descent path starts just next to the hotel and there are two options, the original way (the Chemin du Montenvers on the map) being the best past the Buvette Caillet and exits the forest at Les Planards. If you feel inclined you can do the last few metres of descent on the summer luge to arrive in Chamonix in style!

The Montenvers train and hotel

WALK 16
Montagne de Blaitière

Whilst there are lots of walks on the northern (south-facing) slopes of the Chamonix valley, there are fewer options on the south side. Obviously, from the north side the Mont Blanc massif views are exceptional, but the other side should not be discounted. From Montagne de Blaitière not only will you have a great vantage point for the Aiguilles Rouges but also the Chamonix Aiguilles present a very dramatic profile with their soaring, jagged summits piercing the skyline.

This walk takes us into the alpages of Blaitière past three old summer farms. One of these is now just a ruin

From the north side of the Chamonix valley views of the Mont Blanc massif views are superb, as might be expected – but the south side should not be ignored, as proved by this route.

Car park	Big car park, next to the cemetery in Chamonix, opposite Montenvers station
Starting point	Le Biollay 1046m
Finishing point	Le Biollay 1046m
Highpoint	Blaitière Dessus 1926m
Altitude gain	900m
Map	IGN Top 25 3630 OT Chamonix Massif du Mont Blanc
Distance	6km (3.7 miles)
Time	5hr 30min
Grade/difficulties	2. Good paths in general, but quite rough between the Blaitière and Grand Chalet farms
Public transport	SNCF train or Chamonix Bus
Tip	From Blaitière Dessus a path leads up to the Grand Balcon Nord which could be followed either northeast to Montenvers or southwest to the Plan de l'Aiguille.

but the others are still working farms in the summer, and one has recently been renovated. This is surprising in view of the relatively limited farming that takes place in Chamonix now that tourism brings in by far the most income.

These slopes offer good rough walking above the tree-line and this circuit is wilder than some of the more famous hikes in the valley since it is not on a major trail, even though the Grand Balcon Nord is just above.

The northwest-facing slopes between the Blaitière farms and the Grand Chalet are riven by the Grépon torrent whose shady depths tend to hold névé well into the summer season. Given the steepness of this hillside it is not recommended to venture up here too early in the season, and if you meet hard icy slopes then turn back.

Route
The path takes off from behind the houses of **Le Biollay**, up a small road from the far right-hand corner of the car park, and signed to the 'Alpages de Blaitière'. After 100m take the left-hand path (not the Cascade de Blaitière path) which immediately enters sombre spruce forest and zig-zags up amongst moss and lichen. Some way up at a left

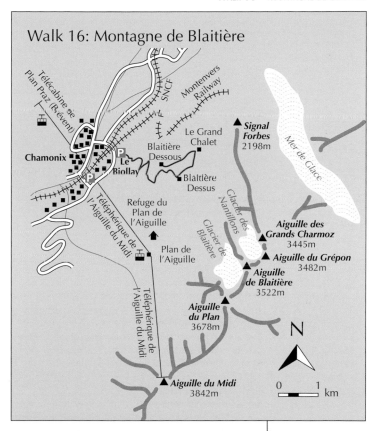

Walk 16: Montagne de Blaitière

bend, a path leads off right (west) to the cascade, and it's worth going for a look.

Onwards and upwards to the top of the forest where the Blaitière torrent is reached, cutting into the hillside. A left turn here heads across quickly to the first farm, **Blaitière Dessus** (1708m). Already the views are exciting across the valley to the southern end of the Aiguilles Rouges. A rough path leads on from this alpage eastwards. It crosses various streams, including the deep cleft of the Grépon torrent, before ascending to the rather finely positioned **Grand Chalet** ruins (1910m). From here there is a superb panorama which includes all the red-tinged rocky summits opposite, as well as the darker grey needles behind.

To reach Blaitière Dessous we must recross the Grépon torrent, but this time on a path higher up (not shown on 1:25,000 map), heading south. We go back into the trees for the short distance to the rather more substantial buildings of this last farm (1926m). Just before reaching the farm, a path is crossed which heads up east. This is the way up to the Grand Balcon Nord, easily attained from here, which allows an variation of the route is wished. If not, then take this path downwards (west) back to Blaitière Dessous and retrace the ascent route.

WALK 17
Chalet de Cerro

Compared to the longer walk up the Montagne de la Côte (Walk 18), on the other side of the Bossons glacier, this is an easier option but the glacial views are equally fine.

The Chalet de Cerro is, like many in this area, a café, or crémerie, on a site where there has been a shelter and viewing point since tourists started to show an interest in the glaciers. When the Bosson glacier was much deeper it was very popular to hire a guide for a crossing. Whilst this outing is still offered, it is far less in demand these days; people usually want to go up things rather than across them, and the glacier in its diminished form is not so pleasant to walk on as it was in its glory days.

Nevertheless, the Chalet de Cerro is certainly worth a visit, and if you make the effort to climb the extra 500m up to the glacial moraine, this is one of the best vantage points for viewing the glacier and is particularly useful for those studying glacial geography.

Route
A trail leaves the far end of the car park, signed to the Chalet de Cerro, and heads up through the forest. Soon it takes a footbridge over the Crosette torrent and continues up in zigzags, now joined by a path coming up from the valley.

The impressive flame at the entrance to the Mont Blanc tunnel

Car park	On the right just before the Mont Blanc tunnel entrance
Starting point	Mont Blanc tunnel car park 1270m
Finishing point	Mont Blanc tunnel car park 1270m
Highpoint	Cerro 1358m; moraine/glacier junction 1850m
Altitude gain	To Cerro 88m; to moraine/glacier junction 580m
Map	IGN Top 25 3630 OT Chamonix Massif du Mont Blanc
Distance	4km (2.5 miles)
Time	Cerro Chalet walk 1hr; full hike 3hr
Grade/difficulties	1. Good path all the way. although it is far less frequented beyond the Chalet de Cerro
Public transport	SNCF train or Chamonix Bus to the outskirts of Chamonix, nothing up to the Mont Blanc tunnel
Tip	If you do not have a car then this walk can still be done in a longer version by taking the path from the bottom of the Mont Blanc tunnel road that cuts straight up the hillside, past the Cascade des Dards, where there is a small café. There is then a trail up to the tunnel entrance. Add on another 45min or so for this extra ascent.

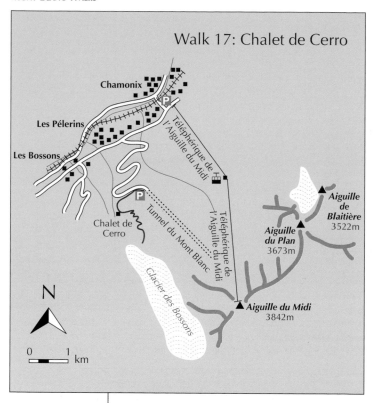

Walk 17: Chalet de Cerro

Chamonix

Les Pélerins

Les Bossons

Téléphérique de l'Aiguille du Midi

Téléphérique de l'Aiguille du Midi

Chalet de Cerro

Tunnel du Mont Blanc

Glacier des Bossons

N

0   1 km

Aiguille
de
Blaitière
3522m

Aiguille
du Plan
3673m

▲ Aiguille du Midi
3842m

Once at the **Chalet de Cerro** you will doubtless be surprised at how impressive the views of the glacier are from here. If you only go this far it's certainly very rewarding.

For those with extra energy the path continues upwards, back into the forest, and back over the stream. The terrain in the woods is pleasant, but once you emerge onto the moraine it's rather rougher underfoot. Finally you reach the **glacier** and can go no further. This is one of the best viewpoints in the Chamonix valley for seracs and crevasses and should be enjoyed to the full before taking the same path for the return.

WALK 18
Montagne de la Côte

The Bossons glacier – 7.8km long, with an average slope of 45°, from its source near the summit of Mont Blanc – snakes down to the Chamonix valley, allegedly making the biggest vertical drop (3500m) of any glacier in the world. This frozen river of ice moves at around 250m a year and if you fall in a crevasse at the top it will take about 25 to 40 years for any remains to appear at the bottom.

The Montagne de la Côte is the name given to the ridge that separates the Bossons glacier from the Iaconnaz which parallels its fall line. When Jacques Balmat and Gabriel Paccard made the first ascent of Mont Blanc in 1786 they climbed first up this ridge to gain maximum height before setting foot on the glacier. At the top of the ridge are two huge boulders where the pair bivouacked – known as the Gîte à Balmat. This is a poignant reminder of how bold and daring such a venture was in those days when the mountains were believed to be cursed, the home of dragons and the like. It's hard to imagine how they might have felt, dining on their bread and red wine and wondering what the next day held in store for them.

Even though the Bossons glacier (like most others) has regressed markedly in recent years, it is still one of the most eye-catching features in the Chamonix valley.

The big boulders of the Gîte à Balmat where the first ascentionists of Mont Blanc sheltered for the night

THE BOSSONS GLACIER

From the Montagne de la Côte the views of the Bossons glacier are really spectacular. Because the glacier is so steep it moves very fast – compare its 250m a year flow rate with the much flatter Mer de Glace which churns along at 70m a year. The Bossons forms huge spectacular seracs which regularly break off, and the ice is particularly white as it forms very high up and doesn't have time to melt during its journey to the valley. This ice scenery is seen at its best from about half way up the Montagne de la Côte at Les Pyramides, named after the leaning seracs far below.

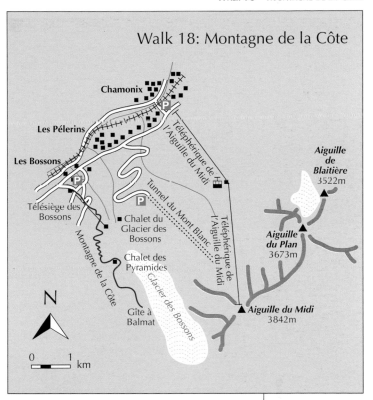

Walk 18: Montagne de la Côte

At the end of the ridge you are stopped by a sea of ice – La Jonction – a chaos of crevasses where the Bossons and Taconnaz glaciers go their separate ways. This is definitely a place to linger – the panorama is splendid. Up above, perched on a rocky ridge, the Grands Mulets hut is just visible, whilst beyond are the seemingly interminable slopes leading to Mont Blanc. Incredibly, some intrepid mountaineers still use this route to ascend Mont Blanc, foregoing the luxury of the Aiguille du Midi cable car to gain height. As the French would say, 'Chapeau!'

Car park	Near Le Mont at the base of the chairlift going up to the Chalet du Glacier des Bossons
Starting point	Chalet du Glacier des Bossons 1350m
Finishing point	Bottom of the chairlift 1020m
Highpoint	Junction of Montagne de la Côte and Bossons glacier 2589m
Altitude gain	1240m
Maps	IGN Top 25 3531 ET St Gervais Massif du Mont Blanc
Distance	9.25km (5.7 miles)
Time	6hr 30min–7hr
Grade/difficulties	2/3. Good path all the way, but can remain snowy higher up. There are a couple of sections of very easy scrambling
Public transport	SNCF train or Chamonix Bus to Les Bossons
Tip	The route described here uses the ascent path for descent. An alternative, less well used route splits off at 2200m to come down very steeply under the Taconnaz glacier.

Route

You have the option of taking the little chairlift up to the **Chalet du Glacier des Bossons**; add 45min to the time if you don't. Be sure to check out the view from the chalet, already quite impressive, and also the artefacts found after the two Air India crashes that have occurred on the summit of Mont Blanc. There is an interesting exhibition of photos of the glacier and its regression, just behind the café.

The trail is wide and obvious going up to the **Chalet des Pyramides** (1895m) and takes about 1hr. Just before the café there is a fine viewpoint of the seracs far below. Beyond, the Aiguille Verte looks particularly imposing. After a coffee break it's time to head on up again. The path is not so wide now but always well marked, snaking up from one side of the ridge to the other: one minute you're enjoying views of Taconnaz glacier and Mont Blanc, the next you're looking up the Chamonix valley towards the Col de Balme.

A couple of hours after Les Pyramides you reach the boulders of the **Gîte à Balmat** (2530m), and then it's a short 50m climb to the end of the ridge, up against the ice.

Descend by the same route – it looks quite different on the way down as your gaze is drawn to the valley and the Aiguilles Rouges on the other side.

WALK 19

Refuge de Bel Lachat and Le Brévent

There are many different reasons for visiting a refuge, or mountain hut. There are:

- those that are crucially placed for climbing nearby summits
- those that provide essential information for the continuation of a trek
- those that provide local specialities
- those that serve lunch at just the right time on a day walk
- those that provide fantastic views
- those that have no particular charm, but provide the only accommodation on a multi-day trek
- those where, as soon as you walk through the door, it's like coming home.

The Bel Lachat hut falls into this last (as well as the views) category. Often there is no need to stay there – it's only a couple of hours or so of descent to Chamonix. However, think about the position of this hut, perched

As long as Madame Balmat is running the Bel Lachat hut I recommend a visit, be it for lunch or an overnight stay.

The Refuge Bel Lachat with the Aiguille Verte behind

on the southern side of the Aiguilles Rouges massif right opposite Mont Blanc. From the Bel Lachat terrace you feel as though you are almost at the same height as Mont Blanc; the Bossons glacier can be seen all the way from its smooth snowy top to the chaos of crevasses and seracs in the middle, right down to the rather sad grey ice of its snout. Far below, the traffic churns along the Autoroute Blanche whilst all around are summits and, way beyond, the misty outlines of other ranges.

Given good weather this is mighty impressive in the day time, but stay here for the night and the experience just gets better and better. As the sun sets and the valley falls into deep shade the summits of the massif are kissed by pink and orange rays: the Aiguille Verte, the rocky spire of Les Drus, the Chamonix needles; Mont Blanc de Tacul, Mont Maudit and Mont Blanc, not to mention the Dôme du Goûter and the Aiguille de Bionnassay. From this amazing vantage point you can savour this magnificent scene until the very last rays dwindle – expect to go into overload on photos.

The morning brings its own delights as the sun rises, on a different side of Mont Blanc this time, and you have to be up early to catch it before it heads around to the southern side of the massif.

Of course all this splendour depends on the weather being perfect. I've stayed at Bel Lachat many times and seen absolutely nothing of the view. Which brings me to the other reason to visit here: as far as hut welcomes go Bel Lachat is up there with the best. Madame Balmat and her team will make you so at home you'll feel like you belong. So whether it's for a cup of tea or the full overnight stay this hut will not disappoint.

There are lots of ways to make this day longer or shorter. Described here is a route from the middle station of the Brévent lift system, descending to Chamonix afterwards, a route which can be done in reverse. It's also feasible to add in an ascent of the Aiguillettes du Brévent and des Houches, or a visit to the Lac du Brévent. Alternatively take the lift to the top of Le Brévent, and do the whole route in descent.

Car park	Le Brévent cable car station
Starting point	Planpraz 2000m
Finishing point	Le Brévent car park, Chamonix 1087m
Highpoint	Le Brévent 2525m
Altitude gain	550m
Maps	IGN Top 25 3530 ET Samoëns Haut Giffre
Distance	7.75km (4.8 miles)
Time	5hr 30min–6hr
Grade/difficulties	2. The paths are all good and waymarked. However, *névé* can remain well into the summer on the slopes leading from the Col du Brévent to Le Brévent
Public transport	Chamonix Bus to Le Brévent car park
Accommodation	Refuge de Bel Lachat, 04 50 53 43 23
Tip	Instead of descending steeply to Chamonix, it is pleasant to take the Tour du Mont Blanc trail down past the Merlet animal park to Les Houches. Return to Chamonix by train.

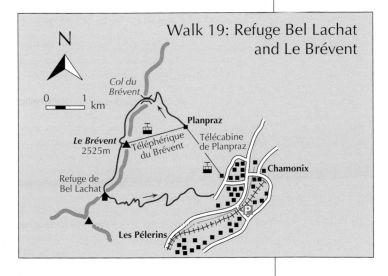

Walk 19: Refuge Bel Lachat and Le Brévent

Route

From **Planpraz** head up the wide track to the flat area at 2000m, by the chairlifts. This is the take-off point for the

131

parapentes and it's worth waiting to watch if one is about to launch. Just beyond is a junction of footpaths, all of which are signed: take the highest one going rightwards to the **Col du Brévent**. This zigzags up pleasantly to arrive in about 1hr at the col (2368m). The views open up to the north and west, with the huge bastion of the Rochers des Fiz taking prime position. The Plateau d'Anterne and the Refuge du Col d'Anterne (Moëde d'Anterne) can be easily distinguished, guarded to the south by the huge bulk of the Pointe Noire de Pormenaz. Be sure to turn around to see the Mont Blanc massif summits behind you.

The route from here is delightfully intricate, heading left, southwest, from the col up slightly rocky ground to then weave in and out of little valleys and rises, eventually arriving at the Brêche du Brévent, from where a wide track leads up to the **summit** (2525m). The path to the hut goes off right just before the top but it would be a shame to miss the highpoint – the panorama is fantastic.

Return to the junction for the Bel Lachat hut and follow a good rocky path which descends at a very gentle angle towards the deep dark waters of the Lac du Brévent. In bad weather I have seen herds of ibex here but usually the crowds ensure they are not around in daylight. However, marmots are often heard shrieking.

Well before the lake the path heads left, south, keeping altitude to contour around the hillside before taking to the ridge that overlooks the Chamonix valley. The walking is superb and quite unusually exciting as you have views in all directions, those down to the left being quite precipitous. Keep your eyes open and you'll spot the hut perched above the valley. The path swings rightwards then heads left again to reach the **Refuge de Bel Lachat** (2136m), by a small flight of steps.

From here, signs indicate the way to **Chamonix**. Prepare your knees as the path is quite steep and unrelenting. However, the views make up for this (in the first part at least). Later, the shade of the forest will be welcome on hot days. Just keep following 'Chamonix' and you'll finally pop out at Les Mottieux, where a left turn leads to the bottom of the Brévent cable car and the car park.

WALK 20

Grand Balcon Sud –
La Flégère to Planpraz

This is one of the classic walks of the Chamonix valley, a real must. It can be lengthened in various ways but, just as it is, will occupy you for a couple of hours or the whole day, depending on how long you want to savour the views. These are certainly superb: the whole of the Mont Blanc massif from the Aiguille Verte, Les Drus, the Mer de Glace, the Aiguilles de Chamonix, Mont Blanc du Tacul, Mont Maudit just behind, then the rounded snowy dome of Mont Blanc and the Goûter ridge leading down to the Aiguille du Goûter.

Avoid the last Sunday of June as this is usually the day of the Chamonix Marathon trail running event which finishes along this path – check with the tourist office.

The walk starts from the top of La Flégère cable car and more or less follows the 2000m contour line all the way around to the Planpraz cable car. There are odd undulations from time to time, but this certainly counts as one of the less hilly walks hereabouts.

At times in amongst the alpenrose bushes, at others emerging onto open scree slopes, the terrain is always changing and the views come and go intriguingly.

Car park	La Flégère cable car
Starting point	Chalet de la Flégère 1871m
Finishing point	Planpraz 2000m
Highpoint	Planpraz 2000m
Altitude gain	200m
Maps	IGN Top 25 3630 OT Chamonix Massif du Mont Blanc
Distance	5km (3.1 miles)
Time	2hr (if you don't stop for long)
Grade/difficulties	1. Good trail all the way
Public transport	Chamonix Bus or SNCF train to Les Praz
Tip	The cable cars normally open from mid-June to late September. This route is best done in the direction described (even though in reverse it would be slightly in descent) as the views of Mont Blanc are directly ahead.

In autumn the pink willowherb provides a perfect foreground for Mont Blanc, seen from the Balcon Sud

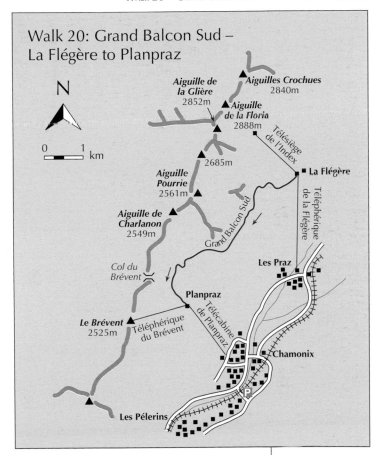

Walk 20: Grand Balcon Sud – La Flégère to Planpraz

N

0 — 1 km

Aiguilles Crochues
2840m

Aiguille de la Glière
2852m

Aiguille de la Floria
2888m

Télésiège de l'Index

■ La Flégère

2685m

Aiguille Pourrie
2561m

Grand Balcon Sud

Téléphérique de la Flégère

Aiguille de Charlanon
2549m

Les Praz

Col du Brévent

Planpraz

Télécabine de Planpraz

Le Brévent
2525m

Téléphérique du Brévent

Chamonix

P

Les Pélerins

Route
Take the cable car up to **La Flégère**. From the lift, walk down to the Refuge de La Flégère then turn right (south-west) and follow the path signed to Planpraz (do not descend to Les Praz). This is the **Grand Balcon Sud** trail. The path leads along the hillside, past the lovely open glade of Charlanon where there is a water source, and

135

climbs gently to reach the rather ugly ski trails of Le Brévent. From here traverse easily to the restaurant above the **Planpraz** cable car. Check out the paragliders taking off from here – probably the most popular take-off point in the valley – before getting the Planpraz lift down to Chamonix.

If you need to retrieve a car from La Flégère, the back road from the bottom of the cable car leads to Les Praz via Les Plans and Les Nants.

WALK 21
Lac Blanc

Avoid this walk on a high summer weekend. The quietest time is usually the evening, and a night spent at Lac Blanc enables you to savour the views and perhaps spot ibex roaming the rocky slopes.

Lac Blanc has to be a contender for 'most famous walking destination' in the Chamonix valley. Justifiably perhaps, for not only are the views unsurpassable, it is also very easy to get to, being just a 1hr 30min walk from the top of the La Flégère cable car. The fact that there is also an upmarket mountain hut and restaurant there is really just the icing on the cake.

Check out the postcards sold in town and you'll soon see that many of them feature, in some form or other, the panorama as seen from Lac Blanc: usually a foreground of rocks decorated with brightly coloured alpine flowers, against a background of the snowy slopes of the Aiguille Verte and to its right the soaring spire of Les Drus, seen to its best advantage from here. Right again is the grey, streaky Mer de Glace snaking down towards the valley, flanked by the spiky Chamonix Aiguilles and the rounded dome of Mont Blanc. The view is faultless and whilst this is not usually a solitary walk where you can reflect on the whys and wherefores of the world, it's nevertheless a must-do at some point in any alpine walker's career.

There are different ways to get to Lac Blanc. Here we take the regular motorway track up but come back by a less-frequented route to the top of the Index cable car, then on the descent we visit the café at La Floria, which is a delight.

Leaving Lac Blanc early in the season

Car park	La Flégère cable car in Les Praz
Starting point	Top of La Flégère 1877m
Finishing point	La Flégère car park 1060m
Highpoint	Col de l'Index 2385m
Altitude gain	510m
Map	IGN Top 25 3630 OT Chamonix Massif du Mont Blanc
Distance	10.5km (6.5 miles)
Time	4hr, could be a lot more if time is spent at Lac Blanc
Grade/difficulties	2. Good paths, but quite stony from Lac Blanc to the Col de l'Index
Public transport	Chamonix Bus or SNCF train to Les Praz
Accommodation	Refuge du Lac Blanc open mid-June to late September, 04 50 53 49 14
Tip	The slopes from Lac Blanc to the Col de l'Index can remain snowy well into the summer, so then the traverse across becomes more difficult and could be dangerous. In this case it may be best to return to La Flégère along the ascent route, then descend to La Floria. A grade 1/2 route would be Lac Blanc from the cable car, return by the same route, and take the cable car back down again or descend via La Floria.

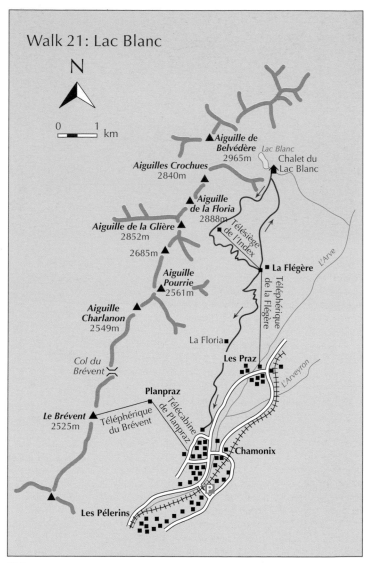

Walk 21: Lac Blanc

N

0   1 km

▲ Aiguille de
Belvédère
2965m

Lac Blanc

Chalet du
Lac Blanc ▲

Aiguilles Crochues
2840m ▲

▲ Aiguille
de la Floria
2888m

Aiguille de la Glière
2852m ▲

Télésiège
de l'Index

2685m ▲

L'Arve

■ La Flégère

Aiguille
Pourrie
2561m ▲

Téléphérique
de la Flégère

Aiguille
Charlanon
2549m ▲

La Floria ■

Col du
Brévent ✕

Les Praz ■

L'Arveyron

Planpraz ■

Télécabine
de Planpraz

Le Brévent ▲
2525m

Téléphérique
du Brévent

■ Chamonix

P

▲

Les Pélerins

Route

From the cable car Lac Blanc is signed – just follow everyone else (there is a short cut across the bouldery slope just after leaving the lift which avoids descending to reascend.) Listen out for the insistent screeching of marmots.

Refuge Lac Blanc in early morning light

A wide track leads up past a junction with the Grand Balcon Sud (also the TMB trail) which goes off right, but our route stays on the higher well-made path which rises gently. A small lake at 2171m provides a good resting place and an opportunity to get a fix on the mountains opposite, before the final climb to the **Chalet du Lac Blanc** (2352m). The first building to be seen is an old shack, the original hut until it was largely destroyed by avalanche. The new refuge occupies a much safer perch on rocks just beyond. The main building is beautifully made, inside and out, with paintings and huge crystals decorating the interior, whilst the annexe, long a shell for lack of funds, is finally being completed.

To descend, return to the old shack and begin to descend the hairpins. Very shortly, take a path that goes off to the right (southwest), signed to the Index.

It's waymarked in red all the way as it undulates around the hillside, in and out of the rocky cwm of Courbe des Aiguilles Crochues. Keep your eyes open as the cliffs above are the playground of climbers and becoming increasingly popular.

The top of the **Index chairlift** cannot be missed, and if time is short this could be used for the descent. If not, continue on to the ridge just beyond the lift and follow the narrow path down to the Col du Fouet. A path heads off right to the Col Cornu, but our destination is straight ahead. Soon the path joins the ugly bulldozed ski pistes of La Flégère but every so often a footpath short-cuts so look out for these and take the most comfortable route down to the top of the cable car. There is a café here, but save some thirst for La Floria.

Descend the track to the Refuge de la Flégère just below the cable car station. The route to Chamonix is signed from here, heading southwest then in wide zig-zags down through the forest. There are several junctions but if you follow the signs to **La Floria** you won't miss it as the footpath goes right through it – one of the floweri-est cafés around. The path goes on and down to the road linking Les Praz to Chamonix. Turn left to go back to the cable car car park.

WALK 22
Tête de Villy (2 days)

The Col d'Anterne has been used for passage for many centuries – in the past for shepherds taking their animals to graze the nutritious high pastures on Anterne and more recently by hikers, especially those embarked on long-distance treks such as the amazing GR5 which makes its way from the flatlands of the Netherlands to the foothills of the Alps then past the Mont Blanc massif, continuing south alongside several alpine massifs to finish on the shores of the Mediterranean.

This col is justifiably a very popular place with hik-ers, the views are wonderful and the contrast in scenery and terrain quite unique. So, definitely worth a visit. Yet sometimes it's a great pleasure to sneak away from the crowds in search of solitude and a chance to savour the landscape alone. The Tête de Villy is just what's needed when you've taken in the Col d'Anterne but need a little more.

Easily accessed from the col, it's just a question of turning right (east) and climbing up the rounded shoulder to the Tête de Moëde, and then the Frêtes de Moëde ridge leads all the way with hardly any more height gain to the summit. Unless you want to climb all the way back up to the Brévent it's best to descend to Servoz after and take the train back to Chamonix.

This walk can be done in a day from Plaine Joux, but it's better to take two days, going to the Col d'Anterne hut on the first day, the summit the second. This allows time to fully appreciate the scenery (and maybe take a dip in the Anterne Lake on the way back – if you're really brave).

Car park	Le Brévent cable car
Starting point	Le Brévent 2525m
Finishing point	Servoz 814m
Highpoint	Tête de Villy 2481m
Altitude gain	Day 1: 415m; day 2: 479m
Map	IGN Top 25 3530 ET Samoëns Haut-Giffre
Distance	Day 1: 7.4km (4.6 miles); day 2: 17.1km (10.6 miles)
Time	Day 1: 3-4hr; day 2: 7–8hr
Grade/difficulties	2. Good paths to the hut and up to the Col d'Anterne. More vague on the ridge, but the way is obvious. Not to be done too early in the season when snow remains
Public transport	SNCF train Servoz–Chamonix
Accommodation	Refuge Col d'Anterne (Moëde d'Anterne), 04 50 93 60 43
Tip	The first day could be lengthened by starting at Plan Praz and going to the Col du Brévent from there. NB The Refuge du Col d'Anterne is more commonly known as the Refuge Chalet Moëde d'Anterne, but the map refers to it as the Refuge du Col d'Anterne.

Route

From the top of the Brévent cable car station follow the waymarked path down the wide piste and northwards, though narrow rocky valleys along ridges to the **Col du Brévent** (2368m), from where the trail heads off down into the Diosaz valley. It is waymarked for the GR5 trek

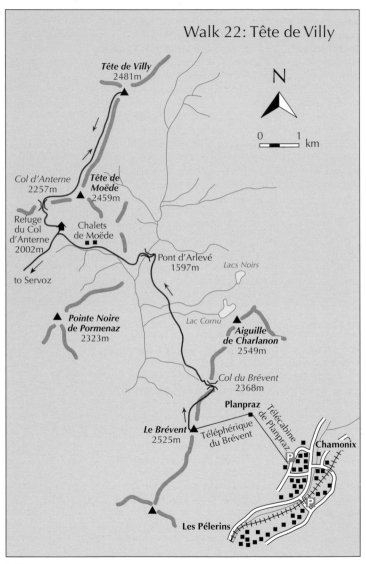

Walk 22: Tête de Villy

N

0   1
╟──■─■─■──╢ km

Tête de Villy
2481m
▲

Col d'Anterne
2257m

Tête de Moëde
2459m
▲

Refuge
du Col
d'Anterne
2002m
▲

Chalets
de Moëde
■ ■

Pont d'Arlevé
1597m

Lacs Noirs

to Servoz

▲ *Pointe Noire
de Pormenaz*
2323m

Lac Cornu

*Aiguille
de Charlanon*
2549m
▲

Col du Brévent
2368m

Planpraz

*Téléphérique
de Planpraz*

Le Brévent
2525m
▲

*Téléphérique
du Brévent*

P

Chamonix

P

▲

Les Pélerins

and provides a delightful descent along an alpenrose-bordered trail, past the ruined Chalets d'Arlevé to the **Pont d'Arlevé** (1587m).Take a coffee break in this sheltered sun trap before girding your loins for the lengthy ascent to the Refuge du Col d'Anterne. The trail is good and takes you past the **Chalets de Moëde** just before arriving at the hut.

Behind the hut the trail to the **Col d'Anterne** is impossible to miss as it winds up the hillside to the pass at 2257m, definitely a place to sit and enjoy those far-off snowy mountains before turning your thoughts to the way onwards. The rounded shoulder up to the **Tête de Moëde** (2459m) is easy to follow: the path flirts with the ridge and in places you can take your pick between the very edge or taking a less exposed version just below. The summit features a good-sized cairn and provides a nice resting place before you continue along the crest all the way to the Tête de Villy.

This is a considerable distance, so only go if you have plenty of time. The path winds along interestingly, sometimes following the ridge, sometimes traversing easy slopes on the west side. The **Tête de Villy** defines the very end of the ridge. Return by the same route or, if you like going off piste and the visibility allows, descend from here to the Lac d'Anterne then follow the main trail back up to the Col d'Anterne.

From the Col d'Anterne descend towards the hut until a well-signed trail goes off right (southwest). This path traverses all the way under the huge cliffs of the Fiz and makes for some impressive scenery. The way to Servoz is signed – take the left junction down through Le Souay and at 1522m, just before Ayères du Milieu, keep your eyes open for the path down through the woods into Le Mont. Once on the road the quickest way into Servoz is waymarked. The railway station is on the far side of town, over the river, and there is a good bar just before you get there.

On the Col du Brévent, looking back to Mont Blanc

WALK 23

Col de Salenton

The Col de Salenton forms one of the few amenable passes from the west to the east side of the Aiguilles Rouges. The area is principally composed of rocky summits creating a rugged landscape where it's almost impossible to see any sign of feasible walking routes.

The Col de Salenton (2526m) has been used for liaison from the Bérard valley to the Villy alpages for many centuries but, due to the altitude and shady slopes, névé stays late around this col and this, added to the bouldery nature of the terrain, means that near the pass there is only a very indistinct trail.

The route through the Villy alpages and onward to the col is one of wild walking through alpenrose and meadows, then scree slopes and boulderfields, far away from the busy valleys and bustling towns; as height is gained the views are far-reaching away southwest towards the ephemeral mists of the lower Arve valley. Up ahead to

The route to the Refuge du Col d'Anterne must be done quickly to complete this walk in a day. If in doubt, spend a night at the hut and go on to the col the next day.

Bad weather clearing over the Aiguilles Rouges during the descent from the Col de Salenton

Walk 23: Col de Salenton

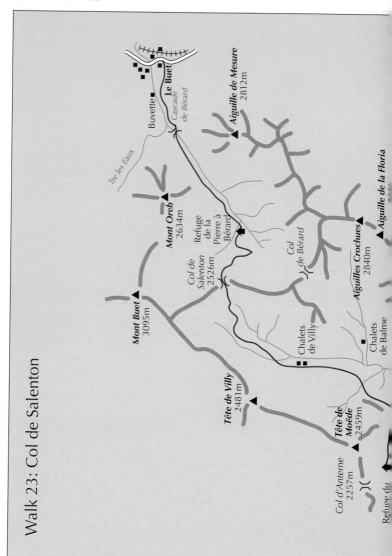

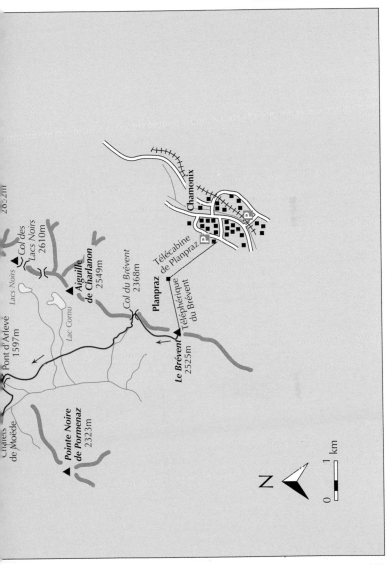

Car park	Le Brévent cable car
Starting point	Top of Le Brévent cable car 2525m
Finishing point	Le Buet 1350m
Highpoint	Col de Salenton 2526m
Altitude gain	Day 1: 415m; day 2: 650m
Map	IGN Top 25 3530 ET Samoëns Haut Vallée du Giffre; IGN Top 25 3630 OT Chamonix Massif du Mont Blanc
Distance	Day 1: 8km (5 miles); day 2: 12.2km (7.5 miles)
Time	Day 1: 3hr; day 2: 6hr
Grade/difficulties	2/3. Névé remains on both sides of the col well into the summer. For this reason the path is vague in places. This route should not be done in bad weather or early in the season
Accommodation	Refuge du Col d'Anterne, 04 50 93 60 43; Refuge de la Pierre à Bérard, 04 50 54 62 08
Public transport	SNCF train Chamonix–Le Buet
Tip	I strongly recommend taking two days over this trip. A night at the Refuge du Col d'Anterne will allow you to enjoy the Villy slopes and have time to linger at the Bérard hut. Alternatively stay at the Pierre à Bérard hut and do Mont Buet the next day. NB The Refuge du Col d'Anterne is more commonly known as the Refuge Chalet Moëde d'Anterne but the map refers to it as the Refuge du Col d'Anterne.

the east are the Aiguilles of this range: Bérard, Belvedère, Crochues...

Once over the col a whole new arena awaits, leading down the Bérard valley, with snowy peaks shimmering in the distance. Up to the left are the intricate slopes of Mont Buet.

The pleasant valley walk alongside the Bérard river provides a most pleasant finale to this walk.

Route
Follow directions for Walk 22 to the **Refuge du Col d'Anterne** (2002m). Staying here allows for a lazy after-noon sampling all the various refreshment options whilst sunning on the terrace or, for the more energetic, a dip in the Pormenaz lake.

The path for Salenton is signed and heads off east from the hut. It soon splits into a high and low version. The high one is signed to 'Buet Villy' and the low one 'par le bas'. The latter is the easiest to follow, even though some height is lost before it climbs up the valley to the **Chalets de Villy**. The higher one requires more concentration: follow it straight along and up and over a rounded shoulder. You can see the col straight ahead, so go towards it and do not be tempted to follow a path that breaks off left to go up to the ridge above. The path stays above the valley and does not go down to the Chalets de Villy as shown on the map. It continues along above the river, finally crossing it to join the path coming up from Villy as it begins to zigzag up towards the col.

This valley is quite a committing place as the only way out is up. The Diosaz valley cannot be descended on foot and has trapped its fair share of hikers looking for an escape route from this area. The trail continues around a shoulder and into the cwm leading up to the col, where it more or less disappears in scree. Don't panic: it's just a question of following your nose eastwards. Many people have been here before, and traces of a path do appear from time to time. The **Col de Salenton** is soon reached and below on the other side the path to Mont Buet is obvious, probably adorned with toiling would-be ascentionists. Take in the views, especially those away to the Rochers des Fiz and beyond, before leaving this vantage point to set off down. The path is more obvious now as it shares the Normal Route for Mont Buet and it winds down, often waymarked, to grassy zigzags above the **Refuge de la Pierre à Bérard**.

A cold beer is obviously called for here before following the easy trail all the way down the valley, first on the left bank of the Bérard, then the right. This finally brings you out at **Le Buet** where the Hotel du Buet will provide drinks whilst you wait for the train back to Chamonix.

WALK 24

Lac Cornu and Lacs Noirs

These lakes are wonderful places to spend a couple of hours on a hot day, swimming or bronzing on the beach. A longer variation is possible, passing both lakes and taking in a scrambly highpoint.

Whilst the south side of the Aiguilles Rouges is incredibly and justifiably popular, once over to the north side you enter a wilderness area where rocky buttresses shield hidden lakes and cwms, and all around are mountains and deep valleys.

Lacs Cornu and Noirs give the best of both worlds, being accessible from either the Planpraz lift system or that of La Flégère, but situated on the wild side of the range. The best way to envisage this walk is to start from one lift and finish at the other.

Car park	La Flegère cable car
Starting point	Index 2385m
Finishing point	Planpraz 2000m
Highpoint	Lacs Noirs 2500m
Altitude gain	Approximately 200m, more if you descend to Lac Cornu and/or the lower Lac Noir
Maps	IGN Top 25 3630 OT Chamonix Massif du Mont Blanc
Distance	6.3km (3.9 miles)
Time	3hr 30min–4hr. This does not include the descent to the lower Lac Noir or to Lac Cornu
Grade/difficulties	2. Paths all the way, sometimes bouldery, and a short section of very easy cable
Public transport	Chamonix Bus; SNCF train station at Les Praz
Tip	The cable cars will normally be open mid-June to late September. For a longer hike, from the higher Lac Noir head north to a small col on the ridge above the lake. From here the south face of the Aiguille du Pouce can be admired, and on any sunny day in the holiday season there will be several climbing teams on the excellent rock routes. A sparsely cairned route leads up right, east, to the highpoint (2685m). A little scrambling is involved, but then cairns can be followed down via the Col des Lacs Noirs to emerge at the first lake again. This extension is grade 3.

The walk is described from the top of the La Flegère–Index system finishing at Planpraz, but it's pretty much the same in reverse.

Lac Cornu seen from the Col Cornu

Route

Take the cable car to La Flégère, then the old chairlift to the Index. Head left, southwest, along a path that takes you to the edge of the large cwm formed by the **Aiguille de la Glière** and the Aiguille Pourrie. This path goes south down a rounded ridge to the small Col de Fouet (2361m). Here the Col de la Glière is signed off to the right. A well-made path traverses the cwm and heads up in about 1hr to the **Col de la Glière** (2461m). A small section of cable assists as the col is reached.

From here the path continues south above the Lac Cornu, but it would be a great shame to miss out the Lacs Noirs: follow the yellow waymarks up right, north, along a rocky ridge (Lac Cornu can be seen below) to the first **Lac Noir** (2500m) which is reached in about 20min. There are several perfect places to sit next to

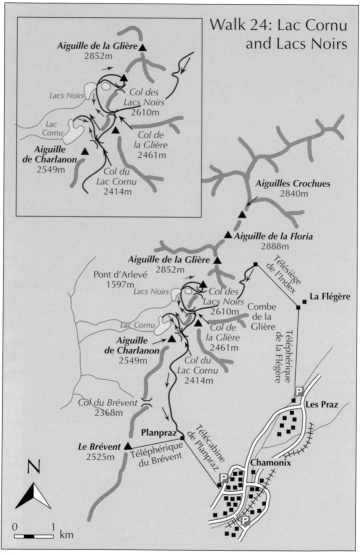

Walk 24: Lac Cornu
and Lacs Noirs

Aiguille de la Glière
2852m

Lacs Noirs

Col des
Lacs Noirs
2610m

Lac
Cornu

Col de
la Glière
2461m

Aiguille
de Charlanon
2549m

Col du
Lac Cornu
2414m

Aiguilles Crochues
2840m

Aiguille de la Floria
2888m

Aiguille de la Glière
2852m

Pont d'Arlevé
1597m

Lacs Noirs

Col des
Lacs Noirs
2610m

Télésiège
de l'Index

La Flégère

Combe
de la
Glière

Lac Cornu

Col de
la Glière
2461m

Téléphérique
de la Flégère

Aiguille
de Charlanon
2549m

Col du
Lac Cornu
2414m

P

Les Praz

Col du Brévent
2368m

Planpraz

Le Brévent
2525m

Téléphérique
du Brévent

Télécabine
de Planpraz

Chamonix

P

N

0   1
km

P

the water. Continue with the yellow marks and the second lake soon reveals itself further down on the left. Go on down or not, depending on time and energy levels.

To continue with the route to **Lac Cornu**, take the yellow waymarks back to the Col de la Glière then follow the path south to the **Col du Lac Cornu** (2414m). The going is bouldery and rocky but nowhere difficult. Views down to Lac Cornu and beyond to the stratified Rochers des Fiz are spectacular.

At the col a red waymarked path heads right (west) to the Lac Cornu and if there's time it's fun to descend to the shores of this deep lake. However, be careful not to miss the last lift down – from the col a good path goes south around to the Planpraz cable car, taking about 1hr.

Lac Noir is one of the most popular walks from Chamonix

CHAPTER 5

ARGENTIÈRE

The name Argentière is a derivation of the word argent, meaning silver – legend talks of a silver mine here, but the idea most probably comes from the silvery tinges and lights in the rocks of the mountains above Argentière, or perhaps in the glacial Arve river.

The Argentière that most people see, certainly from the road, is a ribbon development stretching ever further down the main road, lined with large apartment blocks, all in a sort of alpine style, some more genuine than others. Argentière has become the big construction companies' darling, and the holidaymakers lap it up. For a week away nothing could be more convenient – a modern flat in a small town with all necessary facilities, on both bus and train lines for Chamonix; fantastic views and lots of bars and restaurants where English is fast becoming the first language. There is certainly everything you need here, and the town is lively throughout the summer.

The views to the east are dominated by the Argentière glacier that wends down from under the north slopes of the Aiguille Verte. Even in its diminished condition (compared to a century ago) the glacier still towers above town, and the moraine slopes at its snout provide some great trails both for walking and biking.

The double cable car to the Grands Montets enables height to be quickly gained for both trail walking and glacier mountaineering, as well as providing a good view.

THE OLD VILLAGE

This is attractive, hidden along the side road which goes past the large and elaborate church. Old wooden barns nestle up to traditional chalets, with huge sunny balconies reaching out towards the Mont Blanc massif. The views are splendid and there are some superb examples of both ancient and modern alpine chalets, many of them typical of this region, with comfortable living accommodation for traditional extended families.

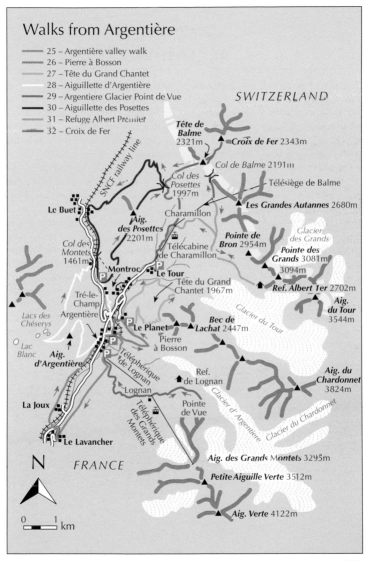

Walks from Argentière

- 25 – Argentière valley walk
- 26 – Pierre à Bosson
- 27 – Tête du Grand Chantet
- 28 – Aiguillette d'Argentière
- 29 – Argentiere Glacier Point de Vue
- 30 – Aiguillette des Posettes
- 31 – Refuge Albert Premier
- 32 – Croix de Fer

WALK 25

Argentière Valley Walk

There are lots of things to see in the valley, and a day wandering among the chalets and meadows can be a welcome change from the more demanding hills above.

Whilst the main street of Argentière has been invaded by sports and souvenir shops, the old part of the village is attractive, with its traditional elaborately decorated church and flower-bedecked balconies and walls. There are old barns with tiny wooden doors, traditional houses crammed one against the other, walls adorned with ancient farming tools and paintings depicting alpine scenes.

The back road leads around to the far more austere Protestant chapel, then becomes a track going under the railway, and this is where several walks begin.

The walk described here takes as its route the Petit Balcon, which has a higher twin, the Grand Balcon, which traverses the hillside above the tree-line. The Petit version stays low down near the base of the valley and serves as a good low-level walking trail.

The Balcons each have a north and south version and it's perhaps worth noting that the Petit and Grand Balcon Nord take the **south** side of the valley and the Petit and Grand Balcon Sud the **north** side – they are named according to their aspect. We'll take both aspects of the Petit Balcon for this walk. Despite being in the forest,

Car park	Argentière, near the church
Starting point	Argentière Catholic church 1250m
Finishing point	Argentière Catholic church 1250m
Highpoint	Petit Balcon Nord 1285m
Altitude gain	100m
Map	IGN Top 25 3630 OT Chamonix Mont Blanc Massif
Distance	7.9km (4.9 miles)
Time	2hr+, but more time could be taken to linger
Grade/difficulties	1. Excellent trails
Public transport	Chamonix Bus or SNCF train to Argentière
Tip	This walk could be combined with the Chamonix Valley Walk (Walk 13) for a full day out.

Argentière church

there are often clearings, and at these points not only are the views magnificent but also the sunshine is welcome.

Route

Leave the church to walk east through the village. The road swings round to the chapel and a track goes straight on under the railway bridge. It continues up to a junction of tracks. Take the one on the right, signed Petit Balcon Nord, and follow this over the river to another junction, where the left turn goes up to Lognan. Continue straight on here, under the cables of the **Grand Montets cable car**, towards La Rosière, then onwards again just above the children's winter ski area (the Panda Club). Now the trail is clear and goes on though the forest, coming out into a beautiful open area of grass just before the village of **Le Lavancher**. Ahead there are views of the Mont Blanc massif and this is a good place to savour. The village too

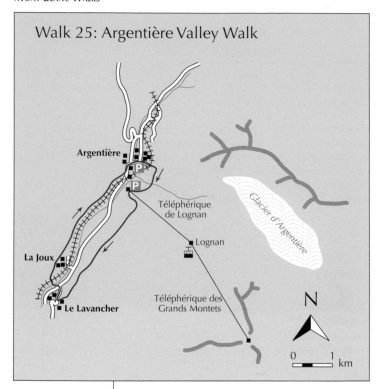

Walk 25: Argentière Valley Walk

Argentière

P
P

Téléphérique
de Lognan

Lognan

Glacier d'Argentière

La Joux

Le Lavancher

Téléphérique des
Grands Montets

N

0   1 km

is attractive – head down the road, taking a short-cut path as the road swings rightwards, to come out on the main road just below the paravalanche tunnel.

Go across the road and the bridge over the river. On the other side the trail zigzags up to rejoin the Petit Balcon – Sud this time – and heads (right) northeast above the idyllic hamlet of **La Joux**. The forest is relatively sparse and there are plenty of glimpses of the surrounding peaks.

Stay on the trail, above the railway line, until it meets the main road just beyond the railway tunnel. Walk up into town to the church.

WALK 26

Pierre à Bosson

This is a short walk, but there's nothing wrong with that. It can either be started and finished in Argentière or, for a real quickie, in Le Planet.

The Pierre à Bosson doesn't seem to be there anymore (if indeed it ever was), but the view of the Argentière glacier is good, even if it's less impressive than it must have been some years ago. It is best after fresh snow, or at least early in the season. Later on it tends to be rather grey with accumulated surface silt. The crevasses are still awe-inspiring, with their twisted shapes and scary depths.

A good walk for a half day or the first day of a holiday when the legs need breaking in gently.

Car park	Argentière, at the top of the village
Starting point	Argentière Catholic church 1250m
Finishing point	Argentière Catholic church 1250m
Highpoint	Viewpoint 1670m
Altitude gain	420m
Map	IGN Top 25 3630 OT Chamonix Massif du Mont Blanc
Distance	4.8km (3 miles)
Time	2hr 30min–3hr
Grade/difficulties	1. Good paths all the way
Public transport	SNCF train or Chamonix Bus to Argentière. SNCF train to Montroc is the nearest transport for Le Planet
Tip	The best viewpoint is actually just beyond the 'Danger' sign.

Alpine villages are always decked out in flowers

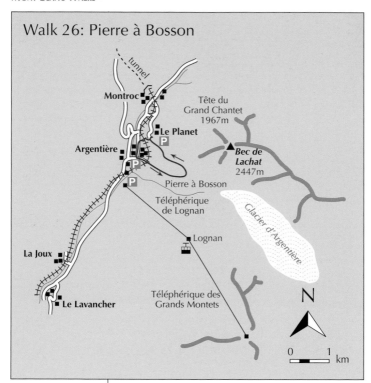

Walk 26: Pierre à Bosson

(map labels)
tunnel
Montroc
Tête du Grand Chantet 1967m
Le Planet
Bec de Lachat 2447m
Argentière
Pierre à Bosson
Téléphérique de Lognan
Glacier d'Argentière
Lognan
La Joux
Téléphérique des Grands Montets
Le Lavancher
N
0   1 km

Route

From the Catholic church find your way along the road east to the Protestant chapel. Go under the railway on the Chemin de la Moraine and then follow the Chemin des Rambles (an appropriate name from the English standpoint!) for a minute or two to a sign next to a big clean boulder. The sign points left to the Petit Balcon Nord and Le Grand Chantet. This way leads to another junction soon after, signed one way to Pierre à Bosson and the other to Le Planet. Go upwards towards **Pierre à Bosson**. The path goes gently towards the glacier, then in a series of hairpins up to join the path coming in from Le Planet.

The Aiguille Verte in high winds

Onwards and upwards, amongst larch and spruce forest with the odd birch and alder. The path is good and you can't get lost. Just after an area of granite slabs on the left, you reach the end of the path. A sign warns of 'Danger' and on the right is a lookout platform. Dogs and children should be kept on the lead as they could fall off the edge here.

Return by the same route, going straight on at the turn off to Argentière. Further, at Les Auges (1457m), there is a different path down to Argentière. This could be taken or, better, go right down to **Le Planet** to see the attractive cottages and the avalanche deflector wall protecting the big old white building. Previously an impressive hotel this now houses some of the most sought-after apartments in the valley, having lost its hotel licence due to its dangerous position right under the Grand Chantet avalanche couloir.

Turn left at the hamlet and go down through the woods into **Argentière**, coming out on the back road down from Montroc. This returns to the village at the Catholic church.

WALK 27
Tête du Grand Chantet

This is a walk that could be done in a half day, but could also occupy a full day if the weather is warm enough to linger.

The Tête du Grand Chantet is more of a bulge than a summit, situated on the long ridge leading up to the Bec de Lachat and beyond. It is an interesting and unusual viewpoint, and a less-frequented destination than some in this area. The Tête du Grand Chantet is named as such on the maps but signposts now refer to Le Pecleret.

To be seen from here are the Chamonix Aiguilles, with their soaring rocky buttresses and deep gullies, whilst nearby is the stately whaleback summit of the Aiguillettes des Posettes. Beyond the highpoint, the path remains elevated enough to give wide views of the Tour glacier. As it stands, the walk is a pleasant circuit from Le Planet, returning via the Petit Balcon Nord which comes from Le Tour. Le Planet is an attractive hamlet and the walk could be extended to visit Le Tour, Montroc and Les Frasserands, all of which feature charming old and modern chalets framed against stunning picture-postcard backdrops – enough to excite the most jaded photographer.

Car park	Le Planet, at the end of the road
Starting point	Le Planet, at the old hotel 1383m
Finishing point	Le Planet 1383m
Highpoint	Tête du Grand Chantet 1967m
Altitude gain	585m
Map	IGN Top 25 3630 OT Chamonix Mont Blanc Massif
Distance	6km (3.7 miles)
Time	3hr 30min
Grade/difficulties	2. The paths are good but the climb is quite stiff
Public transport	Chamonix Bus or SNCF train to Montroc
Tip	The Bec de Lachat can be climbed as a continuation to this route and gives great views of the Argentière glacier and surrounding peaks (see box).

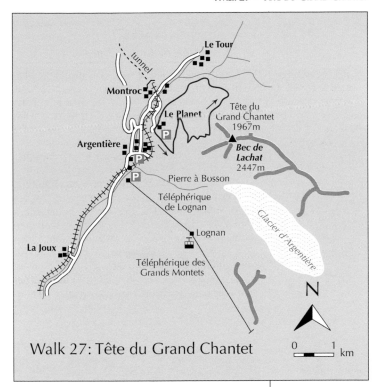

Walk 27: Tête du Grand Chantet

Route

Start from the big white building at **Le Planet** (that used to be a hotel – see Walk 26).

The path goes off southeast into the forest and soon reaches a junction with the Petit Balcon Nord coming from Le Tour. At the next junction go left through the forest and across the Grand Chantet couloir to a spot height (1608m) near a spring where the route swings back right again. Now comes the difficult bit as a long series of tight hairpins gains about 300m in a short distance – whilst it's quite arduous, at least it's above the tree-line so you can look around from time to time. Once this hurdle is overcome our objective is not far away, over to the left (north), and a shelter can be seen under the bulge of the Tête. Straight above is the Bec de Lachat summit.

DETOUR TO CLIMB THE BEC DE LACHAT

A very vague path goes up where the Grand Chantet path swings north after the hard climb. The start of this path is after the last zigzag, where the path goes off left. There are red arrows signalling the leftwards direction and a faded blue paint mark. The route is indistinct and takes a couple of hours from this junction. Do not follow the old trail that goes south around the hillside across the southern slopes of the Bec de Lachat as this is dangerously precipitous. Take the path that goes straight up. It is steep and in places exposed. Not a route for foggy days, rain, or for those with delicate knees.

The traverse to the **Grand Chantet** is easy and the pleasant grassy terrain imposes a break.

Still heading north the path goes around the hillside above the Tour glacier to then descend towards the village of **Le Tour**. At the junction with the Petit Balcon Nord trail turn left for a gentle finish to the walk, following this path (and not taking a left fork) all the way to Le Planet.

Most people in the Alps use wood as fuel to heat their houses

WALK 28
Aiguillette d'Argentière – Les Chéserys

High above the village of Argentière is the striking pinnacle known as the 'Aiguillette' – the 'needle-ette'. Behind are the cliffs of Les Chéserys, long used as a training ground for aspirant alpinists, now a popular rock-climbing spot. But it's the Aiguillette that is most impressive, even though it's only about 20m high: viewed from a certain angle it is seen in profile with Mont Blanc behind, which makes for rather fine photos.

It's worthwhile going up to see the Aiguillette, but the rocks of Les Chéserys would block further progress (for those not equipped with rock-climbing gear) if it weren't for the small but useful via ferrata (no equipment necessary) that leads through the end of this barrier. A couple of ladders and some iron rungs make it a fairly easy proposition, allowing access to the higher slopes and the flat wide ledge of La Remuaz which runs under the cliffs of the Aiguilles de la Perseverance and Encrenaz, both part of the Aiguilles Rouges.

Although this is popular walking country, there are marmots aplenty and ibex have been seen, both descending the via ferrata and also well up one of the grade 5 climbing routes on Les Chéserys cliffs!

Car park	Argentière, at the top end of the village on the right
Starting point	Argentière car park 1250m
Finishing point	Argentière car park 1250m
Highpoint	Lacs des Chéserys 2169m
Altitude gain	920m
Maps	IGN Top 25 3630 OT Chamonix Massif du Mont Blanc
Distance	8.5km (5.3 miles)
Time	6hr
Grade/difficulties	2/3. The paths are generally good. The short aided section, although technically not difficult, may cause a few heart flutters for those not at ease with heights. The path from the Lacs des Chéserys along La Remuaz can remain snowy well into the summer
Public transport	SNCF train and Chamonix Bus: both go to Argentière
Tip	It would be feasible to include a visit to Lac Blanc in this walk.

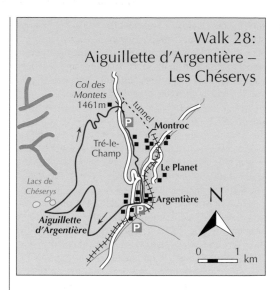

Walk 28:
Aiguillette d'Argentière –
Les Chéserys

Col des
Montets
1461m

tunnel

Montroc

Tré-le-
Champ

Le Planet

Lacs de
Chéserys

Argentière

N

**Aiguillette
d'Argentière**

0   1
km

A good day out can be had watching the climbers
then going on to the Lacs des Chéserys before following
the Grand Balcon Sud along La Remuaz then down interminable zigzags to the Col des Montets.

Route
Head down the main road from the car park and go past
the Hotel Couronne into another car park, just next to
the hairdresser's on the right. In the far corner the path
is signed and heads up next to a house, then on into
the woods past several large boulders. At the first main
junction be sure to go right – signed to the 'Aiguillette'
this path doubles back right and meets the path coming
in from Tré-le-Champ where it zigzags back left again,
always rising gently. Every so often there are very good
viewpoints in clearings in the trees and Mont Blanc and
its associated summits can be enjoyed.

Soon you'll see the rocky pinnacle, the **Aiguillette**,
and when you get there this is a good place to take a break
before tackling the exciting bit. The first ladder is quite

friendly, then there are rungs and cables before a second steeper ladder. After that it seems to be all over but there is a short third ladder somewhat further on. ▸ There just remain some quite steep hairpins to reach a very large cemented cairn at the aptly named Tête aux Vents – when it is windy you can usually get some shelter behind the cairn.

You can go left, right or straight on – take this last option to hit a bigger trail which goes up to Lac Blanc. The **Lacs de Chéserys** are just on the right and can provide a great swimming location in hot weather (or any weather for the very brave). This is certainly an attractive place to rest and picnic, and much less frequented than Lac Blanc, with almost equally good views.

After lunch head northeast along the big trail (the Grand Balcon Sud) away from Lac Blanc. This weaves pleasantly through rocks, past patches of cotton grass and alpenrose and, being quite flat and easy, allows full enjoyment of the fine panorama from this elevated position.

However, that ends when you start the descent to the Col des Montets, which is a bit rough and potentially ankle-turning – eyes down here. Steep it may be, but better to go down than up – it's quite a grind in the other direction.

At the **Col des Montets** turn left and take the time to check out the *Sentier Botanique* and the nature reserve building before continuing on the path which leaves the col on the far side of the road towards **Tré-le-Champ**. Go into this hamlet and continue on the small road to a path that heads off on the left just before the main road is regained. This path descends in zigzags to the River Arve. Join the main road very briefly, cross the river via the road bridge at the junction of the road going up to Montroc, and after the bridge turn right to go down the back road coming into **Argentière** by the cemetery. A right turn leads past the church and the post office to reach the main road. Another right and there's the car park.

This short aided section needs no equipment and should present no difficulty for most walkers. Small children and those with severe vertigo may be safer roped up.

Rock climbers in action on the Aiguillette d'Argentière

WALK 29
Argentière Glacier Pointe de Vue

Although the general retreat of the glaciers means that nowadays these viewpoints tend to be high above the ice, they are still good objectives for a walk.

Until the 20th century, the majority of the tourists who visited the Mont Blanc region were drawn there to see the glaciers, and there were plenty of well-documented places from which to view these incredible rivers of ice. The Argentière glacier Pointe de Vue is still impressive, and in addition to the glacier views there are also many fine high peaks to admire nearby.

There are several ways of doing this walk. The Lognan cable car allows the height to be gained painlessly – if it's open this is to be recommended. The return can be made by the forest footpath which descends to Les Chosalets.

Car park	Lognan, Grands Montets cable car
Starting point	Top of the Lognan cable car 1973m
Finishing point	Car park of Lognan cable car 1240m
Highpoint	Viewpoint 2168m
Altitude gain	200m
Maps	IGN Top 25 3630 Chamonix Massif du Mont Blanc
Distance	7.25km (4.5 miles)
Time	2hr 30min–3hr
Grade/difficulties	1. Good paths all the way
Public transport	SNCF train or Chamonix Bus to Argentière
Tip	Don't be too alarmed when you arrive at Lognan – a fine example of the delights of a ski resort in summer – all the arguments you need against bulldozed ski trails are to be found here. However, the glacier well makes up for this.

Route
From the cable car take the very obvious track which goes left (east) around the hillside, above the **Refuge de Lognan**. Views become increasingly spectacular, both of the glacier below and the nearby peaks – notably the Aiguilles de Chardonnet and d'Argentière. The glacier is most impressive as its angle steepens in its final descent causing the crevasses and seracs to form in a jumbled chaos. Where

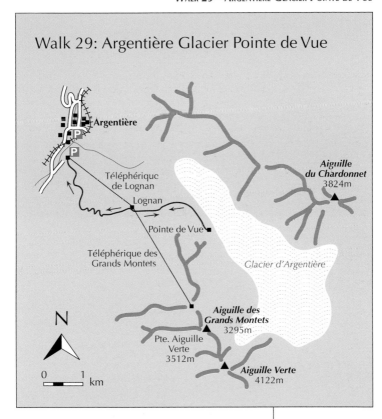

Walk 29: Argentière Glacier Pointe de Vue

the track reaches the abrupt edge of the cliff you will find a tunnel entrance. Immediately above this is a moraine with a path on its crest. Take this, steep at first then gradually easing (the wide track you were following zigzags up to the west of the moraine). Ignore a waymarked path which heads off left about half way up the moraine – this goes to the Argentière hut – and continue to the highpoint: this is the viewpoint (**Pointe de Vue**).

Return to the lift but continue along the same track past the lifts and restaurant at Plan Roujon (named 'Joran'

Sunset view of the Aiguilles de Chamonix

at the restaurant). Soon after there is a junction where the right branch descends steeply. This path can be taken, but for a more gentle descent it's best to continue along the main track for about 1km to where a path doubles back right. Take this to descend in forest all the way to Les Chosalets. At a junction with a wide track go right, then follow the road down through La Rosière and back to the car park.

WALK 30
Aiguillette des Posettes

Perfection is rare in this world, but the Aiguillette des Posettes comes pretty close.

The only downside to this summit is the proximity of the lift systems of Le Tour and Vallorcine which, since they do not aid the ascent in any way, are rather an eyesore. But it's not difficult to ignore the cables as the view from here is so breathtaking. Many's the time I've reached the top and just sat and stared: it's a summit to savour, a place you don't want to leave. Starting with the Chardonnet and the Verte, past Les Drus and the Aiguilles de Chamonix, all the way to Mont Blanc on the eastern side of the valley; then to the west there are the Aiguilles Rouges, Mont Buet, rarely seen so well, and the Lac d'Emosson.

A PERFECT SUMMIT

Such a place should, by definition, have an obvious top, ideally marked by a cross or a large cairn; uninterrupted 360-degree views, preferably ranging from snowy peaks, glaciers and rocky mountains to valleys and distant hazy plains; the route up should be interesting, ideally involving a ridge, not too long but long enough to make you feel achievement on arrival; and there should be a different way to go down. The Aiguillette des Posettes has it all.

Far away are the Dent de Morcles and the Rhône valley stretching all the way to the Bernese Alps.

The walk is a joy, up the Crete des Frettes with its winding path flitting from one side of the rounded ridge to the other, before finally reaching the top. The way down from the Col des Posettes is a delight once you get onto the footpath in the larch forest down to Le Buet. Sadly the

Car park	South side of the Col des Montets, on the right just after Tré-le-Champ, coming from Chamonix
Starting point	Car park just before the Col des Montets 1430m
Finishing point	Car park just before the Col des Montets 1430m
Highpoint	Aiguillette des Posettes 2201m
Altitude gain	930m
Maps	IGN Top 25 3630 OT Chamonix Massif du Mont Blanc
Distance	10.2km (6.3 miles)
Time	5hr 30min–6hr
Grade/difficulties	2. Good paths
Public transport	Chamonix Bus serves the Col des Montets in the summer season. SNCF train to Montroc nearby
Tip	In the summer season the route could be shortened by heading across to the Le Tour lift system from the Col des Posettes and taking the lift down to Le Tour. In this case start the walk from Montroc. Similarly the train can be taken from Le Buet back to Montroc, again best to start the walk here in this case. NB There is now a cable car from Vallorcine to the Col des Posettes. Assuming the cable car is open in the summer, this could be taken to descend to Vallorcine.

The Aiguillette des Posettes provides a fine climb to its summit

commune of Vallorcine – in its wisdom – seems intent on gradually eroding away its pristine mountainside, adding lifts, here, snow canons there...

Route

From the car park the path heads east into the forest and wends its way up northeast. All junctions are signed to the Aiguillette des Posettes. This part of the walk is delightfully shady in hot weather. At an obvious clearing, above the tree-line there is a junction where left goes to the **Aiguillette** via the *crête* – take this. The path zigzags up to a rockier section where steep steps are interspersed with flat grassy ledges. There are several false summits, but the true one is obvious with its huge cairn. On the Vallorcine side there is a large cross. Choose your view and take a break.

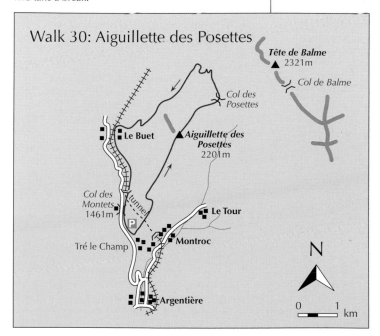

Walk 30: Aiguillette des Posettes

Tête de Balme
▲ 2321m

Col de Balme

Col des Posettes

Le Buet

▲ Aiguillette des Posettes
2201m

Col des Montets
1461m

tunnel

P

Le Tour

Tré le Champ

Montroc

N

Argentière

0   1
km

On the summit of the Aiguillette des Posettes, with the Argentière peaks behind. Aiguille Verte on the right.

The continuation of the route to the **Col des Posettes** follows a very well-made trail through alpenrose and bilberry bushes. At the col head down left (north) on a rather ugly wide track until a T-junction with an equally big piste where you go left and round a hairpin to some paved drainage channels. Just after these look out for a footpath heading off left to Vallorcine and Le Buet, which is followed all the way down through the forest.

The path brings you out at **Le Buet**, the main feature of which is the hotel of the same name where a stop is obligatory. To return to the **Col des Montets** stay on (or return to) the far side of the railway from the road and follow the well-made trail, which is the old road from the days of horse-drawn carriages, uphill to the col. The *Sentier Botanique* goes back to the car park.

WALK 31

Refuge Albert Premier

King Albert Premier was Belgian, and a very keen alpinist, killed in 1934 whilst abseiling: hence the hut is named for him.

This is a very popular route, especially with British walkers. One reason is that it gives a base from which to climb the Aiguilles du Tour, one of the most moderate alpine peaks in the Chamonix area. Guides flock there with their clients, and most nights during the summer season the hut is bursting at the seams. Unless you enjoy trying to sleep crammed in with lots of other sweaty bodies, this is not the place to go for that magical night out in the mountains.

The hut is easily accessed by using the Le Tour cable car and chairlift which gets you painlessly to 2100m. From there the walking is really enjoyable, undulating around the hillside. The views of Mont Blanc and associated peaks are exceptional.

People also seem drawn to the Albert Premier hut as an objective for a day's walk because of its proximity to the Le Tour glacier. This must have been most impressive in the glory days of the glaciers, when the huge seracs and deep crevasses gave ample cause to stop and stare. Whilst today the lower part of the Tour glacier is in a rather sorry state, higher up the crevasses and seracs are still spectacular, as are the views as you round the bend on the high trail to the hut, especially with the beautiful Chardonnet peak and its sculpted snowy ridges. Sitting on the hut terrace you won't be disappointed – choose a

Car park	Le Tour
Starting point	Top of Le Tour lift system 2100m
Finishing point	Le Tour 1450m
Highpoint	Refuge Albert Premier 2702m
Altitude gain	600m
Map	IGN Top 25 3630 OT Chamonix Massif du Mont Blanc
Distance	8.5km (5.3 miles)
Time	4hr
Grade/difficulties	1/2. Good paths all the way. Early in the season there could be névé, but the terrain is neither steep nor difficult and the popularity of the hut ensures that there will almost always be a good track across any snow
Public transport	Chamonix Bus to Le Tour
Tip	From the hut a further extension of the walk is possible, but at a much harder grade as scrambling is involved. Taking a direct line northeast a way can be found up to the Col des Grands and then upwards to the summit of the Pointe des Grands (3102m). This should only be done in good visibility and snowfree conditions, by those who are at ease on pathless rocky terrain. A rope is generally used.

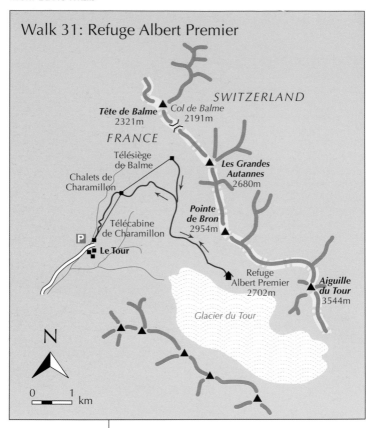

Walk 31: Refuge Albert Premier

SWITZERLAND

Tête de Balme 2321m
Col de Balme 2191m

FRANCE

Télésiège de Balme

Chalets de Charamillon

Télécabine de Charamillon

P

Le Tour

Les Grandes Autannes 2680m

Pointe de Bron 2954m

Refuge Albert Premier 2702m

Aiguille du Tour 3544m

Glacier du Tour

N

0   1   km

nice sunny day and the nearby snowy peaks (as well as those further away – especially the Aiguilles Rouges, Le Buet and the Emosson peaks) will make for some good viewing. Looking up to the Aiguilles du Tour, see if you can spot the characteristic 'table',a perched rock, from which one of the popular summit routes takes its name (Table de Roc Ridge).

Another good reason to go up to the hut during the day is for lunch, in which they do a booming trade.

On the return there is a direct route down from the moraine to Le Tour, but this trail is steep and not in good repair – it is particularly unpleasant after rain. It's much better to continue along the ascent route to a turning where you can go down to the middle station of the Le Tour lift system.

Walking around the hillside in the Aiguilles Rouges

Route

From the top of the chairlift take the very obvious trail heading around the hillside southwards, to the often dried-up Lac de Charamillon, which is a nice calm spot just off the beaten track. Continuing on, the path rises gradually to turn the ridge and here the views are impressive – the Tour glacier with the Aiguille du Chardonnet beyond.

After a short section on rocky ground the good trail resumes. The **Refuge Albert Premier** is obvious, perched on the hillside above the glacier, and is soon reached along the moraine path which has been remade. (The direct route from Le Tour joins the main trail, having come up the lower part of this moraine.) This excellent trail goes all the way to the hut, finishing with a few well-graded zigzags which bring you out next to the attractive old hut building, which is now the winter quarters.

Return by the same route all the way around the shoulder to a junction just before the Lac de Charamillon, and here go left and down to the **Chalets de Charamillon** where there is a café. From here there are two possibilities – either take the cable car, or follow the well-marked trail under the lift to Le Tour.

WALK 32
Croix de Fer

Three summits in the space of a couple of hours – a fourth if you include the Aiguillette des Posettes (Walk 30) – and a walk in two countries, within sight of a third: Italy. A Grand Day Out!

The Croix de Fer – the 'iron cross' – is an appropriate name for this summit, which has a rather fine wrought-iron cross on the top, dated 1984.This is a lovely summit, just far enough away from the lift system of Le Tour to feel mountainous, yet well placed so as use the cable car and chairlift to aid ascent if required.

The walk is a circuit, and can be done in either direction. I've described it using the Le Tour uplift for the ascent then walking down via the Col des Posettes. The Croix de Fer is in Switzerland, and the views from the summit stretch all the way to and along the unbelievably flat Rhône valley, towards the distant Bernese Oberland peaks. After enjoying this peak, the other two hills are the unnamed Pt 2333 and the Tête de Blame, on the top of which is an old frontier borne (stone) marked with the year 1783. Both are easy but fun, and a three-summit day is not to be sniffed at!

The Tête de Balme, with the Aiguilles Rouges behind

Car park	Le Tour
Starting point	Top of Le Tour chairlift 2200m
Finishing point	Le Tour 1450m
Highpoint	Croix de Fer 2324m
Altitude gain	150m
Map	IGN Top 25 3630 OT Chamonix Massif du Mont Blanc
Distance	7.6km (4.7 miles)
Time	3hr
Grade/difficulties	2. The paths are all good, if sometimes narrow, except the last part to the Croix de Fer. This path is exposed and a bit rocky, and in wet conditions should not be attempted
Public transport	Chamonix Bus
Tip	Instead of descending to Le Tour you could go down the Catogne hillside to La Grand Jeur, then on down to Vallorcine. A path to Catogne leaves the col between the Croix de Fer and Pt 2333.

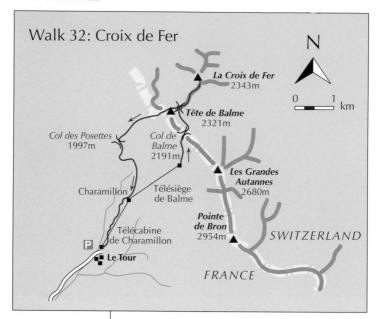

Walk 32: Croix de Fer

N

▲ *La Croix de Fer*
2343m

0   1
⊢━━━━━┥ km

▲ *Tête de Balme*
2321m

Col des Posettes
1997m

Col de Balme
2191m

▲ *Les Grandes Autannes*
2680m

Charamillon

Télésiège de Balme

Pointe de Bron
2954m ▲

SWITZERLAND

Télécabine de Charamillon

P

⊞ Le Tour

FRANCE

Route

Take the good track from the chairlift to the Col de Balme, the border with Switzerland. Behind is the Mont Blanc massif – seen at its best from here – and ahead the grassy flat of the Col de la Forclaz can be made out, the road passage to the Rhône valley. Directly ahead is the ridge with the Croix de Fer clearly visible along to the right.

Follow the broad track along north, across several shaly streams, to a small and unnamed **col** (2260m) where there is a sign warning that the route to the Croix de Fer is a 'dangerous way' and that 'to have access to point of view a good equipment is recommended' [sic]. And they are right – so if it's snowy or wet give this a miss.

The path beckons you on along the ridge, but after some time it leaves the edge to traverse the left (north-west) slopes and this is where it's a bit precipitous. A few rocky steps then you regain the ridge and go along to the

Croix de Fer. This is the end of the line – sadly it doesn't go beyond – so enjoy these views. To the northeast you can distinguish the Fenêtre d'Arpette, famous for the TMB variant that comes through there.

The Croix de Fer summit cross, with views stretching along the Rhône valley

Retrace your steps to the col, then continue on over the very obvious next grassy hill (Pt 2333) and on up a small path to the **Tête de Balme**. On top of the Tête enjoy great views over to Mont Buet, above and behind the Vallorcine valley, and to the north the characteristic curving wall of the Emosson dam.

You can descend directly from the Tête de Balme, down a small winding path to the top of the Esserts chairlift. From here you can cut down to the big path coming around from the **Col des Posettes**.

Various possibilities present themselves now for the descent to Le Tour. The simplest is to follow the path which heads across to **Charamillon** and then down near the cable car to **Le Tour**. Alternatively take the path that traverses the east face of the **Aiguillette des Posettes**, then take a left turn down to the village.

CHAPTER 6

VALLORCINE

Legend has it that the name Vallorcine comes from Vallée des Ours – 'valley of the bears'. The bears are long gone now (if indeed they were ever here – photographic evidence is scarce), but the valley retains an atmosphere of tranquillity and harmony with nature, a definite divergence from the main Chamonix valley. This village has yet to really see the influx of tourists and the consequent effects that have been experienced just over the other side of the Col des Montets. Change is, however, on the way, and it will be interesting – but hopefully not too distressing – to see how Vallorcine evolves during the next decade.

A major reason for the segregation of this village from the Chamonix conglomerations is the presence of the Col des Montets. Geographically it would seem to make sense to have the Franco–Swiss frontier on this pass, but in fact it is 4km further down the road in the apparently insignificant gloomy depths of Châtelard. The reasons for this anomaly have been lost in the mists of time, but the results are evident.

This col is threatened in the winter from avalanches on the steep slopes on either side, and until relatively recently Vallorcine was frequently cut off from the Chamonix valley for six months of the year. The only way out was to head north towards the Swiss villages of Trient and Finhaut and onwards to Martigny (in the days before motorised transport the route to Martigny did not take the Col de

The valley paths often make for beautiful strolls

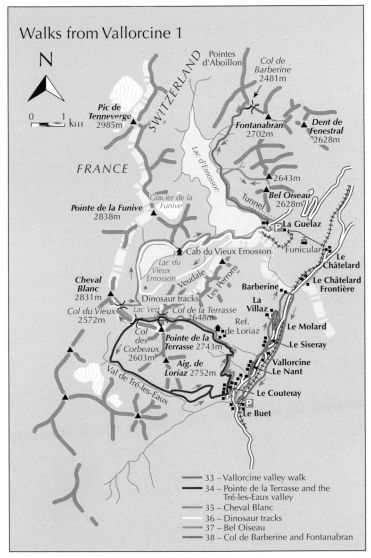

Walks from Vallorcine 1

N

0   1
         km

SWITZERLAND

FRANCE

Pointes
d'Aboillon

Col de
Barberine
2481m

Pic de
Tenneverge
2985m

Fontanabran
2702m

Dent de
Fenestral
2628m

Lac d'Emosson

2643m

Pointe de la Funive
2838m

Glacier de la
Funive

Bel Oiseau
2628m

Tunnel

La Guelaz

Funicular

Le
Châtelard

Cab du Vieux Emosson

Lac du
Vieux
Emosson

Le Châtelard
Frontière

Cheval
Blanc
2831m

Veudale

Les Perrons

Barberine

Col du Vieux
2572m

Dinosaur tracks

Lac Vert

Col de la Terrasse
2648m

La
Villaz

Ref.
de Loriaz

Le Molard

Col
des
Corbeaux
2603m

Pointe de la
Terrasse 2743m

Le Siseray

Vallorcine
Le Nant

Aig. de
Loriaz 2752m

Val de Tré-les-Eaux

Le Couteray

P

Le Buet

33 – Vallorcine valley walk
34 – Pointe de la Terrasse and the
       Tré-les-Eaux valley
35 – Cheval Blanc
36 – Dinosaur tracks
37 – Bel Oiseau
38 – Col de Barberine and Fontanabran

183

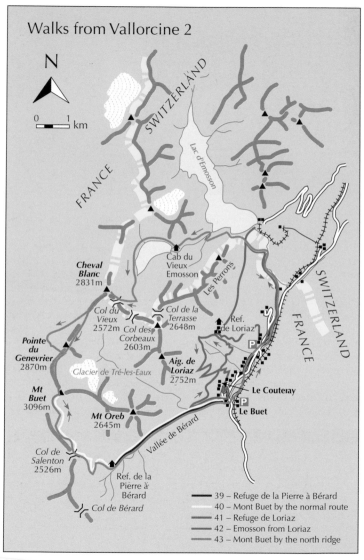

Walks from Vallorcine 2

N

0   1
━━━━━ km

SWITZERLAND

FRANCE

Lac d'Emosson

SWITZERLAND

FRANCE

Cab du Vieux Emosson

Cheval Blanc
2831m

Les Perrons

Col du Vieux
2572m

Col de la Terrasse
2648m

Ref. de Loriaz

P

Col des Corbeaux
2603m

Pointe du Genevrier
2870m

Glacier de Tré-les-Eaux

Aig. de Loriaz
2752m

Mt Buet
3096m

Le Couteray

Mt Oreb
2645m

Vallée de Bérard

P

Le Buet

Col de Salenton
2526m

Ref. de la Pierre à Bérard

Col de Bérard

━━━	39 – Refuge de la Pierre à Bérard
━━━	40 – Mont Buet by the normal route
━━━	41 – Refuge de Loriaz
━━━	42 – Emosson from Loriaz
━━━	43 – Mont Buet by the north ridge

Ibex enjoying the first rays of sun in the Aiguilles Rouges massif

la Forclaz but headed down the Trient Gorge to the Rhône valley).

The villagers would routinely seek seasonal work down in Valais, and consequently formed strong ties with the Swiss population. In Chamonix, Vallorcine is still referred to as le bout du monde – 'the end of the world'. However, since the arrival of the train in 1908, Vallorcine has been far more accessible to the outside world. In addition, security techniques have developed and now only rarely is the col closed, but even if it is cars can still drive through the train tunnel, between trains (only under strict surveillance!).

Nevertheless, Vallorcine does remain very French. This is the place to go if you want to feel you really are in France, you don't need a choice of grocery shops and nightlife is way down the list, below peace and quiet, beautiful surroundings and good walking right on the doorstep.

The Martigny–Chamonix railway, rather inappropriately named the Mont Blanc Express, stops both in the centre of Vallorcine and further south at Le Buet, but there is no bus service.

A WORD OF WARNING

Summer 2004 saw a cable car being built to link into the Tour system, but the rest of the hillsides remain lift-tree. However, this will lead to the inevitable bulldozing of ski pistes on the hillsides of the Aiguillette des Posettes. At the time of writing the lift is complete and the work seems to be finished. However, this should be taken into account when walking in this area – IGN maps could be incorrect as far as footpaths are concerned.

WALK 33
Vallorcine Valley Walk

A start and finish at Le Buet gives the option at the end of taking the train up from Vallorcine if you're tired (or the café in the village has proved too appealing!)

When I first came to live in Vallorcine my favourite local event used to take place every Sunday of Pentecost when the famous Foulées de Vallorcine (Vallorcine Fun Run) took place. Sadly, this is no more, but the route it took makes for a fascinating low-level walk for a day of bad weather, or – better – in hot sunshine to give the legs a break from grinding uphill.

This walk is a fine opportunity to discover the nooks and crannies of the small hamlets encountered all along the way. Many of the houses are traditionally built from stone and beautiful red larch. Check out the different roofs, all equipped with one means or another of keeping the snow from avalanching on visitors' heads; the small wooded mazot chalets in the gardens – these were traditionally used for storing the family valuables, such as best clothes, jewellery and so on, in case the main chalet went up in flames. Nowadays they are much in demand as a showpiece, along with vegetable plots which will stun you with their huge leeks (the secret of which I have yet to uncover), and multi-coloured flower boxes, bedecked with geraniums, petunias and marigolds.

Much of the walk skirts the edge of the larch forest which adds so much colour and elegance to the slopes of this valley. For some of the way we follow the chemin

CATTLE BATLES

During late spring and early autumn the cows will be grazing the fields along the valley. As well as the regular brown ones there will be a herd of sturdy black Herens cows whose natural fighting tendency is well known. Leadership of such herds is decided in an annual stand-off, and these cows also take part in transnational events – Combat des Reines – when farmers bring their best Herens cows to fight for supremacy. Currently Vallorcine's star goes by the unexpected name of 'Marmot'.

des diligences – the old road from the Col des Montets to Martigny, travelled by horse-drawn carriages hundreds of years ago.

Vallorcine church with its avalanche deflector wall

Car park	Le Buet
Starting point	Le Buet 1350m
Finishing point	Le Buet 1350m
Highpoint	Le Buet 1350m
Altitude gain	200m
Maps	IGN Top 25 3630 OT Chamonix Massif du Mont Blanc
Distance	9.2km (5.7 miles)
Time	3–4hr
Grade/difficulties	1. Good paths all the way
Public transport	SNCF train Le Buet or Vallorcine
Tip	From Le Buet the Col des Montets makes a good extension to this walk, for the beauty of the views and the botanical path at the col itself. Add on another 1hr 30min.

Route

From the car park, looking towards the station, take the small road which goes left in front of the houses which were formerly the station building. This road heads northeast.

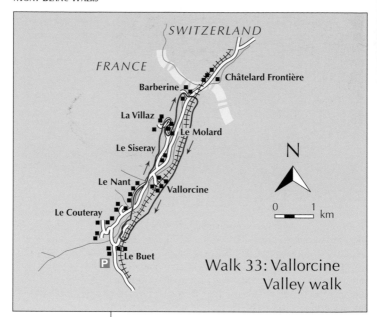

N

0   1 km

Walk 33: Vallorcine
Valley walk

After passing, but not taking, a tunnel under the railway line there is a sign to the left 'chemin des diligences'. Follow this down through the small hamlet of Les Montets, past the tennis courts and keep the same direction to come out, over the bridge, onto the main road at **Le Nant**.

On the other side of the road take the back road through Le Morzay and continue on the track above the main road. This leads to Le Crot. Just as you enter Le Crot look left. A tiny unmarked footpath sneaks up past a cottage and turns right (be sure not to go straight uphill) to then contour above the main track, through the fields to **La Villaz**. Follow the road down towards the church and just before reaching it take the road left into the charming hamlet of **Le Molard**. There is a welcome fountain here for a drink.

The road becomes a beckoning grassy path leading into the forest. At the bridge over the stream go right for the pleasant descent to Barberine. Ahead are the huge cliffs of

Typical Vallorcine house and scenery

Barberine and up left the Emosson dam on the Swiss frontier. The path emerges from the forest on the road, next to a red cable car, used by the electricity company.

Take the road down through the village of **Barberine** and up onto the main road, which is crossed. Go right up the road for a few metres and nip through a tiny tunnel under the railway. (NB. This tunnel is not the tiniest around; it is walking height. Apparently since the first copy of this guide appeared at least one person has tried to squeeze through a minuscule tunnel nearby!). Pick up a good path; turn right on this track, which parallels the train line all the way to Vallorcine. Views ahead now include the summits of Praz Torrent and Mont Oreb.

Arriving at **Vallorcine** you will doubtless be ready for a break, so check out La Bougnette café next to the station, known for its regional specialities. Thus refreshed you can then tackle the only real climb on this route: cross back over the railway line towards the big old hotel buildings (east side of the line) and take the path which leads through the meadows near to slabby cliffs which will probably be adorned with climbers. A short pull is soon over and the campsite of Les Montets is reached. Stay on the left of the railway on a lovely green path to a group of houses at Les Mayens des Biolles, then head under the bridge to the small back road and the car park at **Le Buet**.

WALK 34
Pointe de la Terrasse and Tré-les-Eaux Valley

This walk can be done in a day, but a dawn start from the Refuge de Loriaz means that the grind to the Col de la Terrasse (2648m) can be dealt with in the early morning cool.

The region to the northwest of Vallorcine, stretching across towards Emosson, is a veritable paradise for those searching for solitude, wild back country and space. Summits and cols can be linked to provide exciting explorations, far away from the trodden trails of the more famous hikes around Chamonix. Here you can almost feel like a pioneer, figuring out the way ahead more by the lie of the land than joining together the painted waymarks.

Whether done as a two-day trek or in one long day, it's a treat to leave rucksacks at the col and to go unburdened

Car park	Le Buet, opposite the Hotel du Buet
Starting point	Le Buet 1350m
Finishing point	Le Buet 1350m
Highpoint	Pointe de la Terrasse 2734m
Altitude gain	1450m
Map	IGN Top 25 3630 OT Chamonix Massif du Mont Blanc
Distance	13.5km (8.4 miles)
Time	8hr
Grade/difficulties	3. The paths are variable and good visibility is essential for the section from the Col de la Terrasse onwards. The via ferrata in the Tré-les-Eaux valley is well equipped and requires no special equipment but does require a certain ease on rock. Doing this walk over two days with a night at the Refuge de Loriaz certainly makes it less arduous, but the grade would still be 3 for the nature of the terrain and paths
Public transport	SNCF train to Le Buet
Accommodation	Refuge de Loriaz open mid-June to late September, 04 50 54 06 45 or 04 50 54 23 35
Tip	The slopes above Loriaz are steep and consequently can be dangerous when névé remains, especially early in the day when the snow is still hard; similarly much of the area from the Col de la Terrasse to the Col des Corbeaux and down into the Tré-les-Eaux valley will often be snowy until at least late July. This is not a walk for early summer, nor for anything but good weather conditions.

along the cairned ridge to the Pointe de la Terrasse (2734m). The omnipresent electricity pylons of the Loriaz Emosson hillsides can be forgotten here. It's a brilliant vantage point: the Mont Blanc massif (of course), with notably all the north faces of the Argentière basin, their shady walls sombre and cold; the Bérard valley dark and mysterious far below; to the north the Lac du Vieux Emosson, framed by intricate and enticing summits – the Cheval Blanc, Tête de Grenairon, Pointe de Finive. Further south and west – but very near – Mont Buet, presenting its sinister west face adorned with icy grey remnants of its glacier.

After the summit, from the Col de la Terrasse we head around by the glacial waters of Lac Vert (which usually keeps a few green icebergs until late into the summer months). At the Col des Corbeaux we leave this grandiose scene to descend into the wild and committing Tré-les-Eaux valley – committing because of its depth and the towering walls of Mont Buet just above. The valley yields its secrets little by little, and a via ferrata (no equipment necessary) adds excitement towards the end of the walk before finishing in Le Buet.

The north faces of the Argentière peaks, seen from the Col de la Terrasse

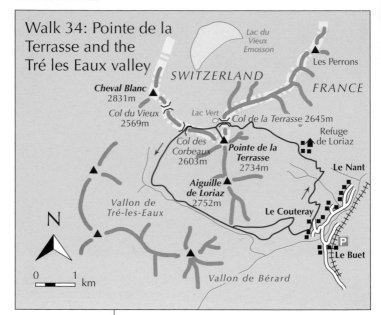

Walk 34: Pointe de la Terrasse and the Tré les Eaux valley

SWITZERLAND

FRANCE

Lac du Vieux Emosson

Les Perrons

Cheval Blanc
2831m

Col du Vieux
2569m

Lac Vert

Col de la Terrasse 2645m

Refuge de Loriaz

Col des Corbeaux
2603m

Pointe de la Terrasse
2734m

Le Nant

Aiguille de Loriaz
2752m

Le Couteray

Vallon de Tré-les-Eaux

N

Le Buet

0   1 km

Vallon de Bérard

Route

The quickest way to the Refuge de Loriaz is to go down the main road and turn left to the hamlet of **Le Couteray**. Loriaz is signed from the top of the village along a forest track. At a junction of track and footpath, near a barrier, take the footpath (right) which rises pleasantly in the forest, over the usually fast-flowing torrent of the Nant de Loriaz, then zigzagging up to the Loriaz meadows above. Just beyond a big boulder sporting a fine cross, the triangular roofs of the Loriaz outbuildings can be seen, with the **hut** itself just behind.

Continue northwest into the attractive cwm under the Pointe de la Terrasse, the beauty only marred by the pylons – presumably it would have been a prohibitively expensive undertaking to reroute these cables. The trail is good at first but does get rather steep, rocky and broken near the top – the result of yearly avalanches on these

slopes. There are waymarks to keep you on the trail, but beware of rockfall from people above.

At the **Col de la Terrasse** there is a signpost and a good flat area to rest. It's quite a different world up here, dotted with green lakes and surrounded by striated peaks and grassy slopes.

Cairns lead south past a pylon to the summit of the **Pointe de la Terrasse** and it's definitely worth including this, unless time is short. Only the last part is slightly exposed.

The via ferrata used to ascend or descend the Tré-les-Eaux valley

Returning to the col, head southwest across the slopes just above Lac Vert, then swing northwest to reach the **Col des Corbeaux**. There are waymarks and cairns, but often this section can be snowy. A path comes up to this second col from the **Lac du Vieux Emosson** below. The direction now is southwest and again there are waymarks, cairns and the vestiges of a trail but this is not a place to lose concentration – once off the trail there are few landmarks by which to navigate and it's important to avoid descending too low into the valley.

Keep your eyes open and follow the path down and through a sort of small ravine, before then traversing around a rocky shoulder to come out above the Gouille du Bouc, where the concrete waterworks are a bit of a shock in this otherwise unspoilt haven. Now the trail is very obvious as it wends alongside the river bed until a short climb aided in places by chains.

At a junction of paths there is a **choice**: those not at ease descending via ferratas should opt for the **left-hand version** which ascends to then descend steeply (but without difficulty) to Les Granges, Le Couteray and Le Buet. On the latest 1:25,000 map this is the only path shown as a major way, but in fact the **right-hand version** is the main trail down the valley and takes an audacious route down rocky slabs, making use of a chimney on the edge of the rock face, and equipped with a good cable and various rungs and footholds. ◄ Once this hurdle is overcome, the delightful **Vallon de Tré-les-Eaux** is followed along an attractive riverside path. This path is shown as a very vague black dotted path on the map, but in reality it's all there.

At the bottom of the valley it's best to take the signed path right to the unexpected houses at Sur le Rocher, then down the steep path behind to come out at **Le Couteray**. Follow the road down to the main road, turn right and there is **Le Buet**.

Note Although no equipment is necessary here for adults, those with severe vertigo and children may be better roped up for this descent. Dogs should **not** be taken on this route.

WALK 35

Cheval Blanc (2 days)

Quite why the Cheval Blanc ('white horse') is so named I have been unable to establish. Suffice to say it's a fitting highpoint for a walk that is not just about getting to the summit: this hike takes such an interesting route in such wild and remote surroundings that reaching the top of the mountain is really just the icing on the cake.

After a night spent at the Refuge de Loriaz, the ascent to the Col de la Terrasse is steep but otherwise not too complicated, and very enjoyable in the early morning cool. From here on there are plenty of surprises. The traverse around to the Col des Corbeaux is beautiful among small lakes, their jewel-like azure depths belying their glacial temperature.

The Cheval Blanc is an absolute dream: an all-round panorama, a feeling of remoteness seldom experienced in these parts, and the possibility of seeing ibex and chamois.

Car park	Le Buet, opposite the Hotel du Buet
Starting point	Le Buet 1350m
Finishing point	Lac d'Emosson 1960m
Highpoint	Cheval Blanc 2831m
Altitude gain	Day 1 to Loriaz hut 670m; day 2 to Emosson 811m
Map	IGN Top 25 3630 OT Chamonix Massif du Mont Blanc
Distance	Day 1: 3.8km (2.4 miles); day 2: 12.4km (7.7 miles)
Time	Day 1:1hr 30min; day 2: 6hr
Grade/difficulties	Day 1: 1; day 2: 3. The paths are somewhat indistinct in parts on the second day, and any remaining névé could seriously increase the difficulties. Short easy via ferrata section on Cheval Blanc – to ascend and descend
Public transport	SNCF train to Le Buet. Cable car/funicular combination from Emosson to Le Châtelard or bus to Finhaut. Train Finhaut–Le Châtelard–Vallorcine–Chamonix
Accommodation	Refuge de Loriaz open mid-June to late September, 04 50 54 06 45 or 04 50 54 23 35; Cabane du Vieux Emosson open end June to late September, 079 342 9566 or 027 768 1421
Tip	This is not a walk for early summer, as there will be too much névé.

ONE DAY OR TWO?

This hike can be envisaged in one long day if your legs and lungs are will-
ing. But why miss out on the pleasures of a night at Loriaz and a dawn start,
with the valley still in darkness and the first rays just kissing the summits of
the massif. We spend enough time in the lowlands so make the most of this
opportunity to maximise the time spent in the mountains. From the Cabane
du Vieux Emosson summits such as Bel Oiseau (Walk 37) and Fontanabran
(Walk 38) are perfectly feasible.

From the col the path is really quite délicat, as the
French would say. You need to wait till the névé has gone,
but then the ground is often wet and slippery – avoid
it unless you're sure-footed. Once the Col du Vieux is
reached the terrain becomes a little more regular – at least
the path is better, even if the way is steep and protected at
times by chains and cables (no equipment required).

The route doesn't end here, and the descent via the
Lac du Vieux Emosson continues to provide plenty of
entertainment, including the chance to view the well-
preserved dinosaur tracks. The Vieux Emosson hut tempts
you with its fantastic position: if you can stay there, then
do so, and go on to explore the peaks around the Lac
d'Emosson the next day.

Route

From Le Buet take the main road downhill to the hamlet
of **Le Couteray**. Walk up into this hamlet and follow signs
for Loriaz leading up into the larch and spruce forest. The
track is signed all the way, and at the forest barrier the
best bet is to take the footpath indicated to the right. This
crosses the Nant de Loriaz torrent and continues around
and up to the *alpages* of Loriaz and the **hut** (2020m).

From the hut take the small path northwest into the
cwm behind. The **Col de la Terrasse** (2648m) is fairly evident, and if the slopes up to it are snowy then alarm bells
should ring for the rest of this route. The path is steep but
is good until very near the top. For the last 100m of so
of ascent care should be taken not to dislodge rocks on

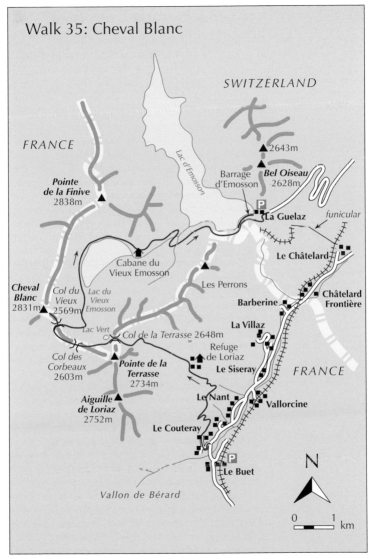

Walk 35: Cheval Blanc

SWITZERLAND

FRANCE

2643m

Bel Oiseau
2628m

Barrage
d'Emosson

Pointe
de la Finive
2838m

Lac d'Emosson

P

La Guelaz

funicular

Le Châtelard

Cabane du
Vieux Emosson

Les Perrons

Barberine

Châtelard
Frontière

Cheval
Blanc
2831m

Col du
Vieux
2569m

Lac du
Vieux
Emosson

La Villaz

Lac Vert

Col de la Terrasse 2648m

Refuge
de Loriaz

FRANCE

Col des
Corbeaux
2603m

Pointe de la
Terrasse
2734m

Le Siseray

Le Nant

Aiguille
de Loriaz
2752m

Vallorcine

Le Couteray

P

Le Buet

Vallon de Bérard

N

0   1
km

anyone below. There are waymarks and to reach the col the trail goes right amongst perched boulders.

There is a yellow signpost at the col but you'll need to spot the cairns too to find the next part of the route. In bad visibility you do not want to be here as it would be very simple to become disorientated (although the huge pylon is a good landmark).

Maintaining height, traverse above Lac Vert to the **Col des Corbeaux** (2602m). Ahead is the prominent tower of the Pointe à Corbeaux and this is turned on the left (southeast). You have to have some imagination to spot the path for the next part, although there are red way-marks. The narrow trail undulates around the rocky summit, and then takes a slippery line across slopes of shale where a determined and speedy approach will be more effective than a cautious tentative one. Once across this though you can breathe again. The **Col du Vieux** (2572m) is a friendly spot from which to assess the next section of the route. An easier option from the Col des Corbeaux is to descend (north) to a signpost then take the path to the Col du Vieux.

The hairpins are regular and numerous to allow the **Cheval Blanc** summit to be gained. Near the top the odd chain provides welcome security on slabby ground and very soon you'll pop out on top of the world – at least that's how it feels. Take it all in, from the Anterne plateau framed by the unmistakable Rochers des Fiz to the slopes of Le Buet against an unforgettable background of the Mont Blanc massif to the Lac du Vieux Emosson far below.

Tear yourself away and head back down to the Col du Vieux. Luckily the 'slippery traverse' does not have to be reversed as we take a different path, a traverse again but shorter and usually easier; under the Col du Vieux to go down towards the **Lac du Vieux Emosson**. This path is not on the 1:25,000 map but it's there, trust me! Head down towards a signpost where the path joins that coming up from the lake to the Col des Corbeaux. Unless it's night-time, there will almost certainly be people visiting the dinosaur tracks and this is next on your agenda (Walk

The summit of Cheval Blanc

36). In the middle of the summer there is usually a geologist on hand to explain what you're looking at, but even if not this site is definitely worth the 5min detour.

Afterwards, amble along the northwest side of the lake, through a short tunnel to meet a road and the **Vieux Emosson hut** below. This is also a café open during the day, so take time to sample some Swiss specialities before continuing down the narrow road, through a couple of tunnels, to the bigger **Lac d'Emosson**. Turn right and take the road around the lake to the dam and up to the information buildings and another café. The red monorail cabin joins up with a miniature railway and then a funicular, allegedly the steepest in the world with a section at 87 degrees, which arrives at **Le Châtelard**. Alternatively there is a bus service which goes down to Finhaut.

Note: See box on page 204 'Probable closures for construction work'.

WALK 36
Dinosaur Tracks

The creatures that left their prints above Lac d'Emosson were quite small compared to most people's image of dinosaurs, and the footprints are about the size of a human hand.

The dinosaur tracks above Lac d'Emosson were first discovered in 1976 by a French geologist. They date from the Triassic period, some 230 million years ago, when dinosaurs were relatively new on the earth. It's really incredible to imagine that so long ago all the region was flat and mostly under the sea. The dinosaur prints happened to set in the wet sand and then hardened to form a layer in the sea bottom.

When the Alps were formed, much more recently, these ocean layers were thrust upwards via the colliding of continental plates and finally came to rest here, tilted to angle of 45 degrees, perfectly placed for viewing. Very exciting to see, especially as there are also waveprints from the beach.

It's a testament to the wilderness of this area that the prints remained unknown for so long, and until the mid-1990s were just there to be found, or not, by hikers. Since this northwest-facing slope at 2400m often remains

Car park	Emosson Dam
Starting point	Emosson 1960m
Finishing point	Emosson 1960m
Highpoint	Top of the Veudale gorge 2500m
Altitude gain	550m
Map	IGN Top 25 3630 OT Chamonix Mont Blanc Massif
Distance	12.3km (7.6 miles)
Time	4hr 30min
Grade/difficulties	2, given no névé in the Veudale gorge. Beware because the upper slopes of the gorge hold snow and are steep. If in doubt use the descent route for the ascent
Public transport	SNCF train from Chamonix to the Swiss border at Le Châtelard; funicular railway and monorail to Emosson
Tip	Another good access route for the tracks is via the Refuge de Loriaz hut and the Col de la Terrasse (Walk 34)
Note	See page 204 'Probable closures for construction work'.

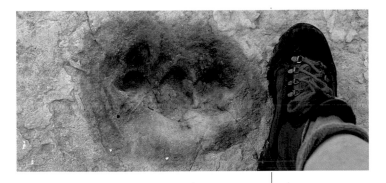

A dinosaur track near
Vieux Emosson

snow covered until well into August, many would-be
trackers came away with the impression that the dinosaurs did not come out in the snow!

Sadly, in a way, the spirit of discovery has gone now
as the tracks are signed, chained off and the snow is dug
out early in July so that they can be part of the attraction of the lake. In the height of the season a geologist
is on hand to provide additional information. However,
if this means that the tracks will still be there for future
generations of walkers to enjoy then so much the better.

The way most people reach the tracks is by the road
around the dam and up to Lac du Vieux Emosson. This for
us is the descent route, and a more remote and adventurous approach route is described up the Veudale gorge.
Views of the Cheval Blanc and neighbouring summits are
really fine.

Route

From the car park a road leads down to and over the dam.
Follow this and continue onwards around the lake past the
staircase path up to the Col du Passet. Find a small path
which goes into the **Veudale** gorge above an slight inlet,
just before the road goes around the small Tête du Largey
(this path goes off well before the obvious deep inlet further along). The path ambles up amongst alpenrose and
bilberry bushes, slowly gaining height as the gorge narrows and becomes more defined. This area is favoured by

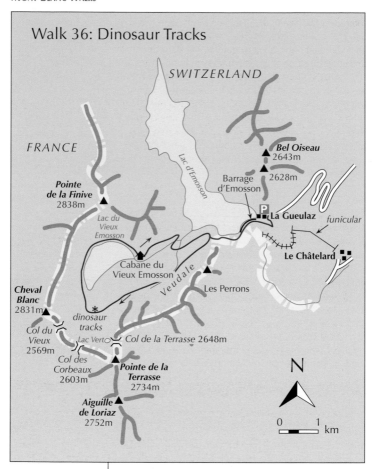

Walk 36: Dinosaur Tracks

SWITZERLAND

FRANCE

Bel Oiseau
2643m

2628m

Barrage
d'Emosson

Lac d'Emosson

**Pointe
de la Finive**
2838m

P La Gueulaz

funicular

*Lac du
Vieux
Emosson*

Le Châtelard

Cabane du
Vieux Emosson

Veudale

Les Perrons

**Cheval
Blanc**
2831m

Col du
Vieux
2569m

*dinosaur
tracks*

Lac Vert

Col de la Terrasse 2648m

Col des
Corbeaux
2603m

**Pointe de la
Terrasse**
2734m

**Aiguille
de Loriaz**
2752m

N

0   1
km

marmots, and you're sure to hear their screeches and probably see them scurrying away at your approach.

Towards the head of the gorge the slopes steepen up
for the final climb out onto the barren rocks way above
Lac du Vieux Emosson. Suddenly the views open up in
all directions, from the dark and forbidding peaks that

loom over the lake to the glaciated Mont Ruan and Tour Sallière. Cairns and a discreet trail lead along a vague shoulder then down a grassy gully to the slabs of orange and grey limestone where the **tracks** are to be found.

From the footprints it's easy to see the way down and around the north side of Lac du Vieux Emosson, through a tunnel and down past the **Vieux Emosson hut** where, if time permits, it's worth stopping for a drink. Follow the small road through a couple of tunnels down to the lakeside, then along, over the dam and back to the car.

WALK 37
Bel Oiseau

This conical summit is prominent from Vallorcine and fascinated me for several years before I climbed it. On the map no path is shown, but one day whilst exploring Lac d'Emosson I saw a cairn, and then another, and headed off up. There is indeed a small path all the way to the top.

Whilst this walk starts in the bustling car park of Emosson, it soon enters a much more remote region – rocks and rough grass, scree, shiny schist and often patches of snow. Several times I have encountered ibex on these slopes, on one memorable occasion a whole herd of huge males chilling out on the summit.

Why Bel Oiseau (beautiful bird)? From certain angles – particularly the Emosson dam – to my mind the huge scree on the southwestern slopes resembles a bird of prey in flight. That's good enough for me.

A COUPLE OF ANOMALIES

Note that the summit the path goes to is not the highest point of the mountain, but the point named Bel Oiseau. Presumably this is the summit visible from below, and hence became known as the highpoint of the mountain. However, the true highpoint is 20m higher and about 300m to the north. Another anomaly on the map concerns the Col du Bel Oiseau. Anyone who has visited this area on skis in winter will know that the col used to access Bel Oiseau is not the Col du Bel Oiseau as on the map, but a col further north. However, there is a very steep and indistinct path descending from the true Col Bel Oiseau to Fenestral – presumably dating from the days of Barberine alpage, but it seems the farmers had little cause to use it.

Car park	La Gueulaz at Emosson
Starting point	La Gueulaz, Emosson 1965m
Finishing point	La Gueulaz, Emosson 1965m
Highpoint	Bel Oiseau 2628m
Altitude gain	663m
Maps	IGN Top 25 3630 OT Chamonix Massif du Mont Blanc
Distance	5km (3.1 miles)
Time	4hr
Grade/difficulties	2/3; in good weather the cairns and small trail are fairly easy to follow, but bad weather would make it quite difficult to find the way. Be very careful, when descending, to head west rather than south from the summit
Public transport	SNCF train from Chamonix to the Swiss border at Le Châtelard; funicular, railway and monorail to Emosson
Tip	For a longer day Bel Oiseau could be a round trip from Vallorcine.

The views throughout the walk are fabulous, with the nearby neighbouring summits of the Pic de Tenneverge, the Pointe de la Finive and the Cheval Blanc, against a background of the Mont Blanc massif. Once at the top, the vista opens up over the Swiss Rhône valley with the

PROBABLE CLOSURES FOR CONSTRUCTION WORK

Starting in 2009 and planned to take at least six years, a new tunnel and pump storage system are being constructed for the Emosson and Vieux Emosson dams. This entails major construction work. Most of it will be underground, but it will affect access to the Vieux Emosson dam, and the Cabane du Vieux Emosson. At this time (February 2010) it is unclear how much disruption will be caused in that area, but be prepared for the small road to the hut and to the higher lake to be closed. A new path has been constructed from the Veudale Valley across to the hut. This is well signed but quite exposed in places. A bus service should operate in high season.

There have already been restrictions on access to the main Emosson dam and this could continue. For information ask at Finhaut Tourist Office, Tel : 027 768 12 78, Fax : 027 768 18 08, info@finhaut.ch.

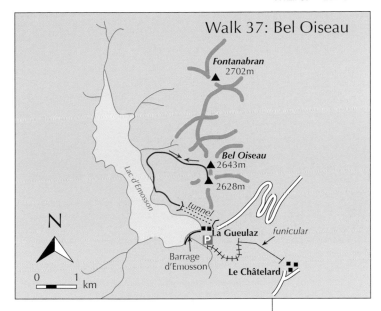

Walk 37: Bel Oiseau

Fontanabran
2702m ▲

Bel Oiseau
▲ 2643m
▲
2628m

tunnel

Lac d'Emosson

N

0   1   km

La Gueulaz   *funicular*

P

Barrage
d'Emosson

Le Châtelard

Dents du Midi and Morcles to the north and, amongst,
many others the Grand Combin to the south.

Route

Just before the **Col de la Gueulaz**, on the right at the first
parking area, is a **tunnel** with a barrier across and a yellow footpath signpost. Go into this tunnel, which is lit
dimly but just adequately once your eyes adapt to the
gloom. This provides an unusual start to the walk, and
also some welcome cool on hot days, especially for
the return. Rather oddly there are boats and a caravan
stored in niches hewn out of the rocks at the edge of the
tunnel. Emerging briefly into the sunlight, you'll plunge
once again into the dark, briefly this time as the tunnel
is short.

Once out of this a road leads along the side of
the hillside high above the lake. This accesses the one
remaining farm in the Emosson alpages – a poignant

The summit of Bel Oiseau with Mont Blanc beyond

reminder that long ago this was a thriving summer farming region before the needs of modern civilisation caused those lush meadows to be flooded. At the far end of the lake are the slopes of Mont Ruan, the mountain where Jacques Balmat, one of the first ascentionists of Mont Blanc, was lost searching for gold. Follow the road for about 20min. At a small bend, where a stream descends from the hillside, a cairn and 'Bel Oiseau' painted on the rock indicate the start of the ascent.

Cairns mark the path (although sometimes you need to search for them), and it winds up, heading northeast/east. The steep bits always alternate with pleasant flatter areas where you can rest and savour the views. At one of these old metal and concrete installations still remain, dating from the construction of the dam. Towards the top the path takes you to the left (north) of the summit from where it winds through rocks to reach the cairn on the top of **Bel Oiseau**. Descend by the same route to the lake.

WALK 38
Col de Barberine and Fontanabran

Starting from the magnificent Emosson dam, the walk heads around the lake and then up through meadows. The grass gives way to scree near the Col de Barberine and although the final slope is a little steep, the effort is well rewarded at the pass by the stunning views – behind of Mont Blanc and ahead down into the Emaney valley.

However, good though it is, it's about to get a whole lot better. A tiny path runs along right from the col and up the rounded shoulder to the summit of Fontanabran. From here there is a 360-degree panorama which will delight even the most seasoned of alpine walkers. From the Mont Blanc massif to the Grand Combin, to the Matterhorn and Monte Rosa, it's all there. The Rhône valley stretches away far below and on its left the double-summitted

Fontanabran is one of those little gems, lost among its more renowned neighbours, yet fulfilling all the criteria of a good peak: great views, a varied walk and a real summit feel.

Car park	Emosson dam – car park just before the dam at the Col de la Gueulaz
Starting point	Col de la Gueulaz 1965m
Finishing point	Col de la Gueulaz 1965m
Highpoint	Fontanabran 2702m
Altitude gain	737m
Grade/difficulties	2/3. Good paths, getting rougher towards the col. Small path up Fontanabran. To be avoided early in the season when névé remains under the col
Distance	10.5km (6.5 miles)
Time	6hr
Map	Carte Nationale de la Suisse 1324 Barberine
Public transport	SNCF train from Chamonix to the Swiss border at Le Châtelard; funicular, railway and monorail to Emosson
Tip	From the Col de Barberine a good path leads down northeast to the alpage of Emaney and then on down to Les Marecottes which is on the railway line from Martigny to Chamonix. However, the slopes down from the Col de Barberine on this northern side hold snow well into the summer.

Wildhorn, then further left the green hills of the Chablais. Much nearer, the dark slopes of Le Buet loom, and up close the glaciated Mont Ruan.

Route

From the car park head into the dimly lit tunnel (see Walk 37), emerging briefly before going through another much shorter tunnel. The flat track continues round the hillside well above the lake to a farm. Before the dam was built there were several summer farms in the meadows of the Barberine alpage. In low-water conditions the old Barberine dam, built in the 1920s, will be visible.

Go past the farm, then soon after find a red and white waymarked path heading up right, signed to the **Col de Barberine**. This is followed steeply at first into a meadow area, criss-crossed by gushing streams. The path is fairly obvious and, after the level area, heads again uphill over several streams to another flat respite before the final

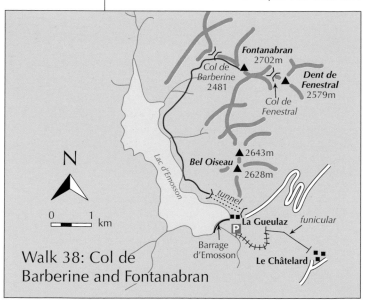

Walk 38: Col de Barberine and Fontanabran

climb to the col. There is a reasonable track over the scree but nevertheless it's quite steep, so watch your footing. Arriving at the col, head right and over a small mound then up towards **Fontanabran**. The path is very vague at first but cairns mark the way and it soon improves. After two false summits the real one is gained.

Return by the same route.

Approaching the summit of Fontanabran, with Emosson below

WALK 39
Refuge de la Pierre à Bérard

Not a major hike, but an outing that should nevertheless be on any walker's list for a semi-rest day.

There is nothing more idyllic than the Bérard valley on a hot summer's afternoon. Find yourself a nice large, flat rock, next to the babbling stream, just within reach so you can dangle your toes in the water from time to time, stretch out and relax – alpine walking at its best. Of course to merit this decadence you have to have a little exercise first, so a visit to the hut at the head of the valley provides just the right length of walk – not too long, but far enough so you feel the effort – and refreshments as a reward in beautiful surroundings.

The Pierre à Bérard hut is old and tiny. In winter it's almost impossible to find as it is squeezed into the protection of a huge boulder and consequently under metres of snow. There is a guardian from late June to late September and it's definitely worth a visit.

The Normal Route up Mont Buet goes by the Bérard valley and hut, so the really tired-looking hikers that

Car park	Le Buet, opposite the Hotel du Buet
Starting point	Le Buet 1350m
Finishing point	Le Buet 1350m
Highpoint	Pierre à Bérard hut 1924m
Altitude gain	580m
Map	IGN Top 25 3630 Chamonix Massif du Mont Blanc
Distance	8.5km (5.3 miles)
Time	3hr
Grade/difficulties	1. Good path
Public transport	SNCF train to Le Buet
Tip	Coming back you could take a variation at the second bridge (at about 1500m marked as Font Froide on the map – the one after the one used coming down to cross the river). Here a bridge goes across the river and there is a sign to Tré-les-Eaux and Sur le Rocher. This path can be taken to Sur le Rocher, then the descent path from there to Le Couteray. Walk down though the village to the main road, then back right to Le Buet.

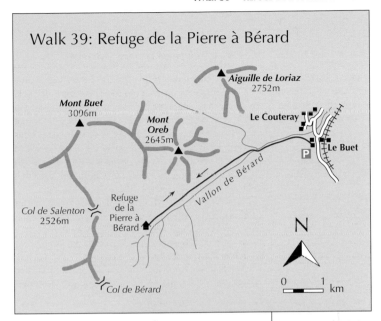

Walk 39: Refuge de la Pierre à Bérard

you'll see staggering down in a haze of sweat and pride are usually Mont Buet ascentionists.

The hut is in a cirque formed by several of the Aiguilles Rouges summits, notably the Aiguille de Bérard and the Aiguille

Réserve Naturelle du Vallon de Bérard

de Salenton which guard the head of the valley. The slopes of Mont Buet can be seen up to the right (north) and to the left (south) are the dying glaciers – Bérard, Ameuley and Beugeant – after recent warm years there's precious little left of these.

The Bérard river is a perfect place to take a break

Route

Cross the road and take the path just above the Hotel du Buet which goes across the little winter ski area and into the trees. It meets a bigger track and there are signs to the Cascade de Bérard. Follow this to the cascade and the café next to it. It's worth taking the time to go down and look at the waterfall – nip round the back of the café and down a chimney formed by a huge boulder.

After this diversion head on up the valley. You can't go wrong as there is a good path all the way. At the first bridge stay on the true right bank of the river, but cross over at the second one, La Vordette, and continue following the trail which rises in rocky steps to gain the flat valley above the tree-line.

Here a whole vista of this wild and barren cirque opens up. The valley is closed in by smooth rocky walls, whilst ahead the only weaknesses are the obvious cols of Bérard and Salenton, themselves formed of scree and seemingly impenetrable. The clear rushing water of the river is a welcome contrast to this harsh environment.

The **Pierre à Bérard hut** will be seen further up the valley and the path leads there with a climb at the end. Enjoy lunch before heading off down, but be sure to leave time to sunbathe on the way back.

WALK 40

Mont Buet by the Normal Route (2 days)

Mont Buet, at 3096m, is the highest peak in the Aiguilles Rouges massif. It is without doubt a beautiful mountain, a superb grandstand from which to view the whole area, and a wonderful and challenging walk. Its so-called 'Normal Route' should not be underestimated – it is long and varied and will provide any hiker with a well-deserved sense of fulfilment.

It can certainly be done in a day from Le Buet, but this is very long and the descent will probably not be a pleasure for most people. It's much better – unless you're looking for a humdinger of a day out – to spend a night at

Known locally as Mont Blanc des Dames this is an arduous undertaking and used to be considered an essential part of a Mont Blanc training programme, and the ultimate objective for any lady.

Car park	Le Buet, opposite the Hotel du Buet
Starting point	Le Buet 1350m
Finishing point	Le Buet 1350m
Highpoint	Day1: Pierre à Bérard hut 1926m; day 2: Mont Buet 3096m
Altitude gain	Day 1: 580m; day 2: 1170m
Map	IGN Top 25 3630 Chamonix Massif du Mont Blanc
Distance	Day 1: 4.25km (2.6 miles); ; day 2: 11.25km (7 miles)
Time	Day 1: 1hr 30min; day 2: 8hr
Grade/difficulties	Day 1: 1; day 2: 2/3. The path to the hut is excellent. The path onwards to Mont Buet is at times indistinct, although there are always cairns and waymarks, but it can hold the snow long into the summer. This does not always pose a problem but can make route-finding a bit tortuous. The ascent should not be undertaken early in the summer as too much névé will make it difficult and slow
Accommodation	Refuge de la Pierre à Bérard open late June to late September, 04 50 54 62 08
Public transport	SNCF train to Le Buet
Tip	The first day could be lengthened a little by going via Le Couteray and Sur le Rocher. The map shows an abri (shelter) on the Arête de la Mortine, just southwest of the Mont Buet summit. Do not search for this as it isn't there.

the Pierre à Bérard hut, then go on in the cool of the early morning and have time to savour the whole experience. Many are those who have set off to do Mont Buet and not succeeded first time around, so give yourself the best chance.

Route

See Walk 39 for the route to the Pierre à Bérard hut.

From the Pierre à Bérard hut the path is signed and heads off to the right up a series of good zigzags up a grassy and rocky hillside. The way tends round to the left and up into orange rocks under the **Col de Salenton**. Look out for waymarks as it's easy to miss the way. The trail traverses under the Aiguille de Salenton and arrives eventually at a small col under the Table au Chantre. You can see the route from here and so hope is restored.

The final weary steps before the summit of Mont Buet, with Mont Blanc behind

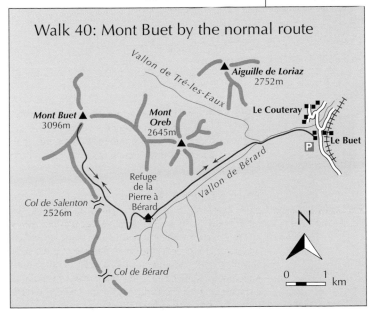

Walk 40: Mont Buet by the normal route

Vallon de Tré-les-Eaux

Aiguille de Loriaz
2752m

Le Couteray

Le Buet

Mont Buet ▲
3096m

Mont Oreb
2645m

P

Col de Salenton
2526m

Refuge de la Pierre à Bérard

Vallon de Bérard

Col de Bérard

N

0   1 km

Continue onwards in zigzags until a traverse right leads across under a small summit to finally reach the very welcome Arête de la Mortine. This rounded shoulder forms the best part of the route – so long as you're not too tired to appreciate it – as the angle is kind and the panorama quite special. To the north and west are the Giffre valley and the Anterne plateau, to the east and south the Mont Blanc massif and the Aravis; and, just up ahead, the summit of **Mont Buet**.

Return by the same route, but don't leave too soon – this is a place to linger and store it all up for those grey rainy days back home.

WALK 41
Refuge de Loriaz

There are lots of different ways to get to Loriaz from Vallorcine. This version also includes a short stroll up the idyllic Bérard valley.

Although the wild hillsides of the east side of the Vallorcine valley are gradually being eroded away by the slow-but-sure development of the Vallorcine ski area, the west side remains lift-free and hopefully will do forever. This is great walking country, starting in the larch forest so characteristic hereabouts, then emerging above the tree-line onto rugged slopes of scree and rock; beyond rise sharp summits separated by enticing cols.

There are lots of exciting hiking possibilities here, some verging on mountaineering, to reach the summits of Mont Oreb or the Corne de Loriaz for example, but equally there are very amenable walks, none more so than that to the Refuge de Loriaz.

Whichever way is chosen, the views will be fabulous. Whilst still in the trees, glimpses of the snowy peaks of the Mont Blanc massif provide a good excuse for a breather. Once out of the trees, the higher you go, the better it gets: from Mont Blanc to Les Drus to the Aiguille Verte to the nearer Aiguillette des Posettes to the Chardonnet to the Aiguille du Tour. The climb is quite sustained and as fatigue sets in a boulder topped with a cross signals that there is not too far to go. Those with keen eyes will spot a strange line of triangles – the roofs of the outbuildings of what was Loriaz farm, and is now the hut.

The effort is more than worthwhile. Assuming the hut is open a wide variety of food is available, including the omnipresent *tarte aux myrtilles*.

THE CHARM OF LORIAZ

The hut is owned by the commune of Vallorcine and local cattle are brought up for summer grazing. It is a typical alpage, being in a flat area above the tree-line, and whilst the hut has been renovated, the interior still retains a traditional ambience. The guardians are local and will be happy to tell you all about the area. If you can be here for the evening you may be lucky to see chamois roaming nearby and if you have the chance to spend the night you'll really savour the special atmosphere.

Car park	Le Buet, opposite the Hotel du Buet
Starting point	Le Buet 1350m
Finishing point	Le Buet 1350m
Highpoint	Loriaz hut 2020m
Altitude gain	670m
Map	IGN Top 25 3630 OT Chamonix Massif du Mont Blanc
Distance	8.6km (5.3 miles)
Time	4hr
Grade/difficulties	1/2. Good paths all the way
Public transport	SNCF train to Le Buet
Tip	To reach Loriaz from Les Granges it is possible to take the forest track and then descend the footpath, but it's much pleasanter to go the way described here – up the footpath and down the track.

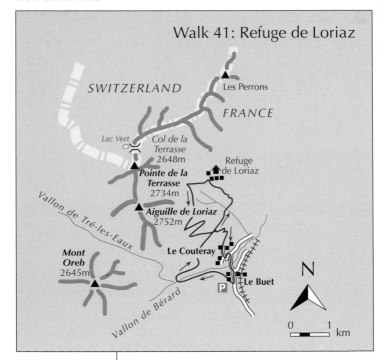

Route

Cross the road and take the footpath heading west. This goes uphill to meet several wide forest tracks all heading to the 'Cascade de Bérard'. This is soon reached, and it's worth taking 5min to check it out: behind the café a little path is directed under a boulder and down a dark gully. A short descent leads to a viewing platform. If there has been recent rain the waterfall can be quite impressive, but by far the most memorable sight for me is the old dilapidated walkway on the other side, dating from Victorian times... imagine walking along that, especially in crinoline and petticoats!

Back up to the café – you could have the first refreshment stop here. Then follow the path up the delightful

GROTTE DE FARINET

Above the cascade is the Grotte de Farinet. Monsieur Farinet was a sort of modern-day Robin Hood who hid out in the region in the 19th century forging money and giving it to the poor. The Vallorcine people let him use this cave whilst the Swiss police were chasing around looking for him. Not surprisingly he is said to have died later in mysterious circumstances. There's not much to see in the cave.

valley. Take time to enjoy this as it is exceptional. After about 20min at a bridge take a right over the river and head back on the other side of the valley in a rising traverse to the hamlet of Sur le Rocher. There is a good water source here, and next to it a path leading towards the Tré-les-Eaux valley. Take this, but be sure to take the right turn to Les Granges.

From here take the main track which climbs steadily. Just after a big bend there is a barrier, and on the right a footpath signed to Loriaz: take the footpath for the ascent (the forest track is the descent). For some way the footpath is quite flat, as far as the Nant de Loriaz torrent which is crossed by a bridge. Height is gained from here on in a series of hairpins, until a sign announces that Loriaz is just 20min away and that dogs should be kept on a lead. The time estimate is about right and after leaving the trees just follow the track up to the huts – the **Refuge de Loriaz** is behind the long row of buildings.

To return, from the hut go back down the footpath a little way until just above an obvious cross perched on a rock, then take the big track west which goes down and across a flat area under the Tete de la Chevrette before heading into the forest. Finally you'll arrive back at the barrier where you stay on the track, but, instead of returning to Les Granges, take the turn left (Le Nant), then at the next signed junction several zigzags below go right to **Le Couteray**.

Walk down through the village to the main road, then turn right to go back up to **Le Buet**. Watch out – there's no pavement and the cars go fast.

WALK 42
Emosson from Loriaz

Walking in the Alps tends to involve an awful lot of up and down, only to go back up again. Sometimes it's nice to stay high and follow the contour line for a while, way above the valley.

This route stays high, linking the beautiful Loriaz alpage with Lac d'Emosson, whilst undulating around the hillside. This is visual overload: the massif is spread out to the south, its sublime snowy summits glistening in the distance, whilst ahead are the grey and green walls of gneiss that form the Gietroz Barberine climbing area. Towering above are the jagged summits of the Perrons and the Aiguille du Van with their intricate rock faces, streaked orange and black.

There are various routes to Loriaz from Vallorcine and Le Buet – the route described starts from the far end of the village in Le Siseray. From the hallowed heights

Car park	Vallorcine tourist office, opposite the tabac
Starting point	Vallorcine tourist office 1256m
Finishing point	Vallorcine tourist office 1256m
Highpoint	Footpath 2075m
Altitude gain	900m
Map	IGN Top 25 3630 OT Chamonix Massif du Mont Blanc
Distance	10.75 km (6.7 miles)
Time	6hr
Grade/difficulties	2/3. The paths are all very good, despite the presence of a few rocky steps on the traverse from Loriaz to Emosson, some of which are aided by cables and iron rungs
Public transport	SNCF train to Vallorcine
Tip	The hillside of Loriaz is very sunny so it is easy to think that by May or early June there is no possibility of snow on the route. But from below you cannot see into all the gullies, and often snow will be hidden on the shady aspects of the couloirs that are traversed from Loriaz to Emosson. This can make the route very difficult and indeed dangerous, as a fall on snow slopes in these gullies could be much more serious than expected. Late June and onwards are the best time for this walk; even then if snow is encountered proceed very carefully, or turn back.

of Emosson we return to earth by the rather relentless, but nevertheless very pretty, path down from the Col du Passet to Barberine.

En route to Emosson from the Refuge de Loriaz in early morning light

Route

The tourist office is situated on the corner of the main road and a side road going to Le Siseray and the church. This side road leads almost straight away to another small road that goes into the hamlet of Le Crot. At its end this small road makes a T-junction with a track. Go more or less straight across and take a tiny footpath that sneaks round the edge of a house, then immediately doubles back right. Very soon another path heads off left. Take this and follow it.

When it meets a bigger trail coming in from the right go left again on this track which goes up in a series of zigzags. It emerges from the tree-line near a big boulder with a cross on top, and from here the **buildings** of Loriaz can be seen up above as a line of triangular roofs. The hut is out of sight behind these outbuildings. Be sure to take a break at the hut as they do a fine line in refreshments. Have a look inside as the building has retained its traditional atmosphere.

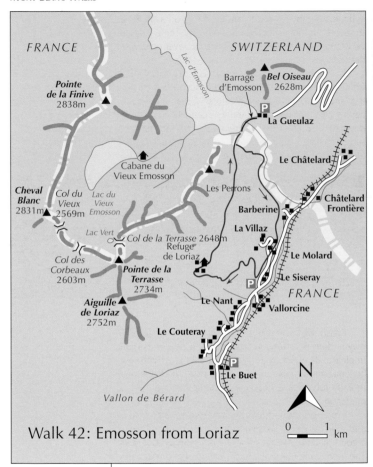

Walk 42: Emosson from Loriaz

0   1 km

    A good trail heads away from the hut north, and this
is our route. It is certainly not flat, but compared to most
alpine paths it's pretty gentle and so you will have plenty
of energy to appreciate the sights. It traverses under some
odd-looking cables which are used in winter when the
slopes are heavily loaded with snow – gas stored in huge

cylinders nearby is used to artificially set off avalanches to secure the slopes for the village below. There is also a very large pylon for the electricity cables, ever-present on these slopes.

Scrambly steps and via ferratas lead to a rocky climb followed by an equally awkward descent, but by now the Emosson dam (**Barrage d'Emosson**) seen up ahead is getting closer. If you have time it's definitely worth going down to the dam as the construction is very impressive. A short time later you'll arrive at the Col du Passet (2000m). Our descent path leaves from here.

This short aided section needs no equipment but small children and those with severe vertigo may be safer roped up.

LAC D'EMOSSON

The dam was completed in 1975. It is the third dam to be constructed here, the first being higher up the valley, clearly visible when the water is low earlier in the season, now flooded by the bigger lake. The other dam is the Vieux Emosson dam seen up to the west. This whole hydro-electric venture is a joint Franco-Swiss operation, and a free guided visit of the dam is offered several times daily in the summer season from the Emosson restaurant. (See box on page 204 for information on the latest developments at the dams.)

Returning to the Col du Passet, take the signed and waymarked path towards **Barberine**. It descends quite unpleasantly at first in a rocky gully, but the ground soon becomes more stable and the angle eases. If you're there in early July look out for one of the best-ever groups of martagon lilies.

Alpenrose and alder give way to raspberry bushes and soon the forest is reached; at a path junction there is a good place to rest on some smooth rounded boulders. The path continues down to a junction near the Cascade de Barberine where we go right, rather than descending all the way to the Barberine village. This path traverses across a scree slope then into forest again to reach the charming hamlet of **Le Molard** and then the road back past the church to the tourist office.

WALK 43
Mont Buet by the north ridge (2 days)

It goes without saying that this is a hike to save for later in the walking holiday rather than one for the first day!

I defy anyone to find a walk more beautiful than that from the Vieux Emosson hut to the summit of Mont Buet in good weather. A dawn start means the sun comes up just as you are walking around the Lac d'Emosson, and its rays blast through the gap formed by the Tête des Gouilles and La Veudale. Camera ready at exactly the right moment and you'll have a magnificent shot with reflections and star-burst – and the day has only just begun. At this time in the morning there are rarely any other walkers, so you have the fascinating dinosaur tracks all to yourself and then the wonderful ascent to Cheval Blanc with its stunning panorama of the Mont Blanc massif and the Chablais range.

From here a flattish, barren section leads to the unnamed col beyond the Pointe de Genévrier where the trail comes up from Grenairon. Here there will certainly be fellow hikers heading in the same direction, towards Mont Buet, but there won't be too many as the vast majority of Mont Buet ascentionists come up the Normal Route from the Bérard valley. The via ferrata (no equipment required) provides just enough excitement without being too alarming, then a pleasant rounded shoulder allows you to arrive at the summit looking suitably calm and relaxed.

The belvedere provided by Mont Buet makes it all worthwhile. Take the time to drink it all in – from Mont

MONT BUET

This summit was long regarded as a training route for Mont Blanc (or substitute for those who shouldn't aspire to the real thing!) if only in terms of the length of the ascent. This peak is sought-after, suffered-for, and not always attained first time round. Do not underestimate those who have come up the Normal Route – when you descend you'll realise how very long it is and be surprised how many people do make the journey to the top. On national holidays and religious festival days you are guaranteed a festive atmosphere on the summit.

Sunrise from the Cabane du Vieux Emosson

Car park	Le Buet
Starting point	Le Buet 1350m
Finishing point	Le Buet 1350m
Highpoint	Mont Buet 3096m
Altitude gain	Day 1: 1050m; day 2: 900m–1100m depending on the route taken
Map	IGN Top 25 3630 OT Chamonix Massif du Mont Blanc
Distance	Day 1: 9.4km (5.8 miles); day 2: 15.25km (9.5 miles)
Time	Day 1: 4hr; day 2: 6–7hr
Grade/difficulties	Day 1: 2; day 2: 3. Paths to the hut are good; the paths on the second day are all reasonable but névé remains on some slopes well into the summer and this route should not usually be envisaged until mid-July at the earliest, sometimes much later. The via ferrata is not too difficult, but requires concentration in places and is quite intimidating
Accommodation	Cabane du Vieux Emosson open end June to end September, 079 342 9566 or 027 768 1421
Public transport	SNCF train to Le Buet
Tip	Mont Buet can also be climbed by its north ridge from the Loriaz hut (see Walk 35), via the Col de la Terrasse. The path from the Col de la Terrasse to the Col des Corbeaux is good but from there the route behind the Pointe à Corbeaux to the Col du Vieux is quite exposed and often the shale slopes are slippery. Again névé often remains on shady aspects throughout the summer. The map shows an *abri* (shelter) just southwest of the summit, but it doesn't exist.

Heading up above the Lac du Vieux Emosson

Blanc all the way around past the Aravis, the Arve valley, the Rochers des Fiz, Mont Ruan, the Tour Sallière, and the rest of the Alps – what you don't see from here isn't worth seeing! Good fitness and plenty of stamina are essential criteria for any ascent of Mont Buet – getting to the top is only half the challenge, so prepare to be pretty weary by the time you reach the oasis of the Bérard hut. Beer is sold here, an important motivator before staggering off for the final part of the descent down the Bérard valley.

Route
From Le Buet take the *chemin des diligences* track which sets off near the railway then across the road to Le Nant. Follow this to the church, then continue through Le Molard to a bridge where there is a junction.

Take the left which goes around the hillside and meets a good trail coming up from **Barberine** (nearby is the Cascade de Barberine which is worth a look). Follow this good trail up and out of the trees, past several small cliffs. Sometimes steep, sometimes less so, this is certainly a hot and sweaty ascent and will require several breathers. Luckily the views are good. Ahead is the unmistakable looming wall of the Emosson dam so you can see exactly where you're headed. The final climb is a bit of

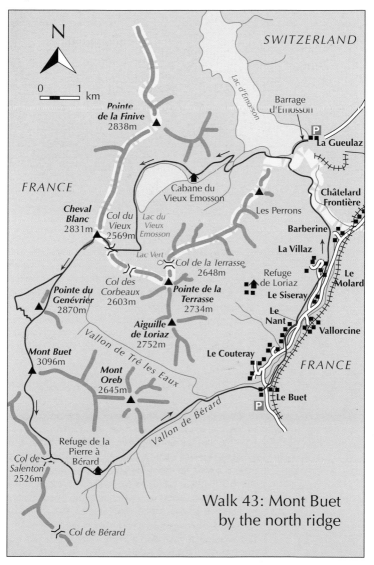

SWITZERLAND

Lac d'Emosson

Barrage
d'Emosson

P
La Gueulaz

*Pointe
de la Finive*
2838m

FRANCE

Cabane du
Vieux Emosson

Châtelard
Frontière

Les Perrons

Barberine

*Cheval
Blanc*
2831m

*Col du
Vieux*
2569m

Lac du
Vieux
Emosson

Lac Vert

Col de la Terrasse
2648m

La Villaz

Refuge
de Loriaz

Le Molard

Le Siseray

*Col des
Corbeaux*
2603m

*Pointe de la
Terrasse*
2734m

Le
Nant

*Pointe du
Genévrier*
2870m

*Aiguille
de Loriaz*
2752m

Vallorcine

Mont Buet
3096m

*Mont
Oreb*
2645m

Le Couteray

Vallon de Tré les Eaux

FRANCE

Le Buet

P

Vallon de Bérard

Refuge de la
Pierre à Bérard

*Col de
Salenton*
2526m

Walk 43: Mont Buet
by the north ridge

Col de Bérard

227

Getting to grips with the north ridge of Mont Blanc

a sting in the tail, but once the Col du Passet (2000m) is reached the views of the **lake** are superb. From the col descend by a rather smart staircase made of a tree trunk to the road (you may want to go along to the dam as it's very impressive when seen close up. There is a café beyond, but getting there involves a small ascent).

To continue, follow the road around the lake away from the dam. Up left the smaller Vieux Emosson dam is just visible and the hut is just in front of it. It is signed at a hairpin on the road that goes off left after about 30min and this leads to the hut through a couple of tunnels which on hot days give a brief respite from the heat.

Once at the **hut** – if it's hot – a dip in the higher lake may be in order. During the evening keep a look out for the herds of ibex that often roam the nearby hillsides.

Leave early the next morning so as to have plenty of time for all the joys of this day (and also for any hitches you may encounter en route). If the weather is bad don't go at all.

The road leads through a tunnel onto a path around the north side of the **Lac du Vieux Emosson**. At its end the dinosaur tracks are signed up and left and are not to be missed (see Walk 36) unless they are still covered by snow; if they are it is too snowy to do the rest of the route. Continue uphill until a junction where the path straight ahead goes to the Col des Corbeaux. Our route goes right and traverses around under the Pointe à Corbeaux to the **Col du Vieux** (2572m). (Neither of these paths is marked on the current 1:25,000 map.) From the Col du Vieux the route is fairly clear and goes across diagonally to the southeast slopes of the **Cheval Blanc** (2831m). A zigzag route goes all the way to the summit with a couple of sections of chain.

From the summit head southwest. The terrain descends a little but in general is fairly flat. Red paint marks and cairns mark the way but you need to concentrate and if the visibility is bad it's best to be satisfied with the Cheval Blanc and return to Emosson – it would be easy to get disorientated, and the consequences could be bad.

We are heading to the Col Genévrier (2691m) from where a decision must be made. We need to get beyond the next summit, the **Pointe du Genévrier**, to the unnamed col on the other side (2808m). If the east slopes of the Pointe Genévrier are snowfree then this is the way, and the waymarks and cairns lead across in a slightly rising line to the col beyond. However, if these slopes are snowy this is very dangerous and you must follow a descending path on the west side of the summit which goes all the way down to the Plan du Buet (2543m). Here you will pick up the good trail coming from Grenairon which goes up to the unnamed col. Whilst this adds 250m more of ascent there is no option if the east slopes are snowy – do not try to cross in the snow as a fall could be fatal.

From the col the north arête looks fairly intimidating, so enjoy the views to the south whilst you take a break. The way is obvious, along to the ridge then follow the cables. ◄ Whilst it is not difficult to climb this ridge a loss in concentration could easily lead to a slip. Poles should be attached to the sac as you need both hands in places.

This short aided section needs no equipment and should present no difficulty for most walkers. Small children and those with severe vertigo may be safer roped up.

At the top get your breath back and continue along the gentle narrow track. The summit cairn can be seen from afar, but more interesting for this section are the steep slopes of the east face of **Mont Buet**, adorned with remnants of the dying Tré-les-Eaux glacier, the summit of which is often overhung by old snow cornices.

Once on the top join the crowds and celebrate.

The descent route takes the broad southwest shoulder for about 500m before the path descends to the left around the hillside to a small col at 2700m, from where your gaze will stretch over to the Plateau d'Anterne and the Rochers des Fiz.

Continuing down, the sometimes indistinct trail leads around the north ridge of the Aiguille de Salenton and beneath the **Col de Salenton**, becoming increasingly rocky. Red flashes mark the way, along with the odd cairn, but a keen eye is needed not to miss the way here, especially if there are patches of snow.

Eventually the path improves and you'll spy the **hut** far below, with lots of lucky people sitting outside enjoying an ice-cold beer. As your mouth waters and your lips become unbearably dry you will finally exit from the interminable zigzags and find yourself in heaven.

Some time later take the big and very pleasant trail all the way down the **Bérard valley**. Just stay on the main trail, which meanders along next to the idyllic Bérard river all the way to the Hotel du Buet.

CHAPTER 7

COURMAYEUR

Often referred to as the Italian version of Chamonix, Courmayeur occupies a similar position on the south side of the massif and is certainly the main centre north of Aosta. However, to consider it as a slightly less renowned version of the French Mecca of mountaineering is to do disservice to this interesting and mostly attractive town.

The name Courmayeur comes from the Roman *Curtis Major*, designating Courmayeur the centre of this administrative system. The town was important in those times as it was on the route over the Col de la Seigne to what is now France. Its prosperity depended largely on its ecclesiastical status until the 13th century, when the Compte de Savoie began to exploit the iron mines situated in the Val Ferret, named after this mineral. Later the presence of iron and sulphur in the waters of Courmayeur was regarded as a cure. The town offered thermal

There are numerous possibilities around Courmayeur for enjoying the stunning massif

baths and prospered, thus creating the birth of tourism in the area.

Today Courmayeur is known far more for its mountains, but it also attracts an elegant Italian clientele which is lacking in its famous neighbour on the other side of the hill.

This side of the Mont Blanc – Monte Bianco in Italy – massif is quite different in many ways. Courmayeur is a much smaller town than Chamonix, having just over 3000 permanent residents (although the population muliplies several times in the holiday seasons, especially winter). The ambience is calmer than on the French side, not quite so centred around mountaineering (despite the fact that from this side the Mont Blanc massif is, if anything, more impressive than from the Chamonix valley); rather than being a base for alpinism, Courmayeur sees itself as a refined tourist resort. The centre features lots of shoe shops and few supermarkets, but enough nevertheless for hikers to stock up. The old church is worth a look, and the *gelati* is legendary.

A big cable car goes up to Plan Dolonne and gives access to Col Chécrouit from where the Monte Bianco massif is seen in all its glory. There are also regular buses serving the Val Ferret and the Val Veny. A twice-daily bus links Courmayeur to Chamonix by the Mont Blanc tunnel.

BEST NON-WALKING EXCURSION

This has to be a trip up the Helbronner cable car system (three cars, each one smaller and more ancient than the one before) which is linked to the Aiguille du Midi by a rather old-fashioned gondola lift. The whole spectacular journey can be done in a day, returning by bus to the start point.

Reflections of the Pyramides Calcaires in the lakes near Lac Caubal (walk 45)

WALK 44

Punta della Croce

The Colle San Carlo (from where this walks starts) is some way southwest of Courmayeur, but this only enhances the panorama from the summits: looking to the north the view is totally consumed by the massif of Monte Bianco – a monstrous mass of steep ice, snow and rock buttresses, interspersed with chaotic tumbling glaciers and gullies.

You're well off the long-distance treks here, but will be sharing the path with Italians of all descriptions – hardy hikers sweating it out at full speed, elegant ladies sporting the latest Milan fashions and weighed down by gold jewellery, *bambini* of all ages (each child with its entourage of extended family from parents to grandparents and beyond). Most people will have the Lac d'Arpy as their objective rather than the summit.

The Punta della Croce is an interesting peak, not difficult or long, and in addition to the views there is the

As its name suggests this is a summit with a cross, but it's far more than that. It's a summit with a view to die for!

Car park	Just before Colle San Carlo
Starting point	Just before Colle San Carlo 1941m
Finishing point	Just before Colle San Carlo 1941m
Highpoint	Punta della Croce 2478m
Altitude gain	550m
Map	IGC 1:25 000 107 Monte Bianco Courmayeur La Tuile Chamonix Mont Blanc
Distance	9.75km (6.1 miles)
Time	3–4hr
Grade/difficulties	The trails are good all the way to the Colle della Croce, then the path to the summit is slightly less used. Waymarks abound, but are not always comprehensible
Public transport	None
Tip	There is a path to return to Colle San Carlo around the other side of the peak, but taking this would miss out the lake (unless you went there first). Colle San Carlo is probably best avoided on high-season weekends and feast days (unless you particularly like crowds).

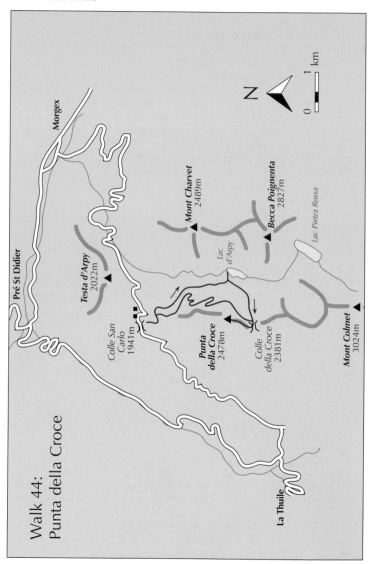

Walk 44:
Punta della Croce

old fort on the summit – certainly a good place from which to spot any would-be intruders. There are various options for walks to the summit and continuations thereafter. Here I've described the summit ascent followed by a foray to the lake as it is in a lovely position surrounded by peaks. A first visit to the Colle San Carlo will probably inspire a desire to explore the region further, especially as this area is unusual in that the road goes right up to almost 2000m. **Note**: the 1:25,000 map is Italian, and by reputation some Italian maps can be a little misleading. However, it's the French map that needs noting here as the col is named Col St Charles on the IGN 1:50,000 map.

Route
The trail leads into the trees from the car park and is signed to the Lac d'Arpy and Colle della Croce. After some distance there is a junction where the left branch is signed to the lake. Stay right and follow the waymarked trail uphill and then east and south around the mountainside in the trees. The route goes under the summit and heads across in a rising line to the **Colle della Croce** (2381m). The views are spectacular. To reach the summit turn right and go along the wide ridge all the way to the obvious highpoint.

Return to the col then take the path straight down (east) past ruined farm buildings to the lake. At the north end of the lake the trail heads back into forest and leads in about 3km back to the parking area.

WALK 45
Mont Fortin

This walk is circular and so can be done in either direction. The **anti-clockwise** route (shown by the arrows on the map) has a flat start along the Val Veny, then a gentle but long climb up to the Col de la Seigne. Afterwards the climbing continues across to the Col de Chavannes, with no really steep parts, and the final 150m stretch is really gentle all the way to the summit of Mont Fortin.

There are 1180m of ascent to be gained on this walk one way or the other.

Going **clockwise** the ascent starts straight off the ground. It is not too bad to begin with, alternating with flatter sections and a convenient ruined building that offers rocks to sit on, but the ascent from here to Mont Fortin (over about 10km in the first version) is crammed into 1km in this direction. Do not make your decision too impulsively: what goes up must generally come down, so if you opt for the gentle climb you'll be on for a knee-crunching descent. I think most folk will choose the anti-clockwise version.

The Col de la Seigne is well known as it's the passage on the TMB from France to Italy. TMBers who are doing the trek in the anticlockwise direction (that's an issue too, and rather more complicated) arrive at this col with only one thought – getting down to Courmayeur for a rest and the chance to devour all those Italian delicacies that have filled their dreams during their ascent to the pass. The TMB has a variant via Mont Fortin, but most people hit the col and head straight down towards the valley.

Car park	Val Veny, Cantine de la Visaille
Starting point	Val Veny, Cantine de la Visaille 1660m
Finishing point	Val Veny, Cantine de la Visaille 1660m
Highpoint	Mont Fortin 2753m
Altitude gain	1100m
Map	IGN Top 25 3531 ET St Gervais-les-Bains Massif du Mont Blanc
Distance	19.4km (12 miles)
Time	8–9hr
Grade/difficulties	Good paths but not a route for bad weather
Public transport	Bus from Courmayeur up to the Cantine de la Visaille
Tip	The ascent to the Col de Chavannes is described from the Col de la Seigne, but there is a path going up to the col before you reach the frontier. If standing on the international frontier is not a must this path can be taken instead. If you start late in the day a night spent at the Rifugio Elizabetta would give good views of the Glacier de la Lée Blanche behind, and also make this walk a friendlier length.

Martagon lilies are pollinated by one type of moth, which visits late afternoon

So Mont Fortin remains relatively unfrequented and hence a joy for a day walk. It just happens to be situated right opposite the steep and intricate Italian face of Mont Blanc, dominated by the Aiguille Noire de Peuterey. The terrain to the summit is pastoral walking at its best, and the Col de la Seigne, defining as it does the Franco–Italian border, is worth a visit in its own right.

Route
Follow the road up to the **Lac de Combal**, a mixture of blues where glacial water mingles with fresh. The road continues along the flat valley and this is followed past a couple of gushing streams to where it starts to climb. A

Heading up towards Alpe Vieille with alpenrose in the foreground

steep trail cutting the road here is useful in descent, but a bit masochistic in ascent. Continue up the road to reach some renovated farm buildings. The **Rifugio Elisabetta** can be seen above, and whilst a cappuccino is tempting bear in mind that there is a long way to go yet.

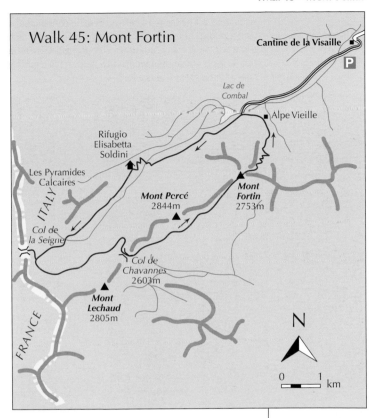

Walk 45: Mont Fortin

Cantine de la Visaille

Lac de Combal

Alpe Vieille

Rifugio Elisabetta Soldini

Les Pyramides Calcaires

ITALY

Col de la Seigne

Mont Percé
2844m

Mont Fortin
2753m

Col de Chavannes
2603m

Mont Lechaud
2805m

FRANCE

N

0   1
                  km

The trail wanders up the Vallon de la Lée Blanche, under the unusual limestone slabs of **Les Pyramides Calcaires**, to reach the **Col de la Seigne** (2516m), which has a big cairn, an orientation table and usually lots of walkers. Turn around and you'll see why – Monte Bianco presents itself in all its glory, the first view of the mountain from this side for those on the TMB anticlockwise version.

Walk across the flat col to the south to pick up the path which heads south and then east, at first contouring at 2500m to then climb up to the **Col de Chavannes** (2603m). From the col the views of the massif are even more spectacular and it's quite surprising to come upon an area of gentle meadows, pasture and farmland on the other side of the col, with imposing rocky buttresses and icy seracs nearby.

The trail winds its way along, past small lakes, without losing altitude, to make the final ascent to the summit of **Mont Fortin**. The contrast between the easy climb up and the precipitous descent on the other side is striking. After summit photos take a deep breath, put on your steady legs and solid knees, and set off carefully down this good trail, heading northeast. When you tentatively raise your eyes from the terrain immediately in front of your boots you'll see that the **Alpe Vieille** is not so far below and there are flowery meadows, a gushing stream and lots of picnic rocks just waiting for you. Once the worst of the descent is done you can relax and once again savour this truly fine situation. There are two separate alpages, and from the lower one the path descends very easily to the road and the car.

WALK 46
Mont Chétif

Situated high above the joining of Val Veny, Val Ferret and the main Aosta valley, the summit of Mont Chétif is a great vantage point, made even better by the proximity of the Mont Blanc massif and associated peaks. The summit is crowned by a most impressive Madonna.

Apart from splendid views there are other reasons for making this excursion, notably to spend some time at the Maison Vieille at the nearby Col Chécroui, where good food is offered in a wonderful location (complete with sun loungers!), and even the possibility to spend the night should you wish to combine this with Walk 45 (Mont Fortin), for example.

The walk can be done as described in a circuit from Courmayeur, or the Dolonne lift can be used to reach Plan Chécroui, making the ascent much shorter. You could even take the bus from Notre Dame de la Guerison back into town to avoid too much road walking. The main pleasure is the summit and the Col Chécroui, so what happens in between is less important.

Car park	Piazzale Monte Bianco in the centre of Courmayeur, next to the bus station
Starting point	Piazzale Monte Bianco 1220m
Finishing point	Piazzale Monte Bianco 1220m
Highpoint	Mont Chétif 2343m
Altitude gain	1123m
Map	IGN Top 25 3531 FT St Gervais les Bains Massif du Mont Blanc
Distance	13.5km (8.4 miles)
Time	6hr
Grade/difficulties	2. Good if rough and steep paths all the way.
Accommodation	Maison Vieille, 03 37 23 09 79
Public transport	Bus from Notre Dame de la Guerison to Courmayeur
Tip	I prefer to walk up from Dolonne, an ascent which is on a jeep track and footpaths, then tackle the short road section from Notre Dame de la Guerison to Courmayeur in descent.

However, it is worth taking time to wander through the old windy streets of Dolonne and admire the ancient stone houses and the fine slabs of the fountain, used in times past by the local women doing their laundry.

Route
From the main square in **Courmayeur** head out of town towards Dolonne. There is a signpost, and the first part is on a busy road, so watch out. Go under the main road and down to the river, which is crossed to then follow the road up left to the charming village of **Dolonne**. Take the right turn to go down the attractive narrow street which leads to the fountain where you turn left along the Via Della Vittoria, to then join the Strada Chécroui. Views are already stunning as the Dent de Géant dominates the head of the valley.

Take the TMB route which is signed off on the right into the trees. A nicely maintained trail climbs steeply in the forest and avoids much of the unpleasant ski piste

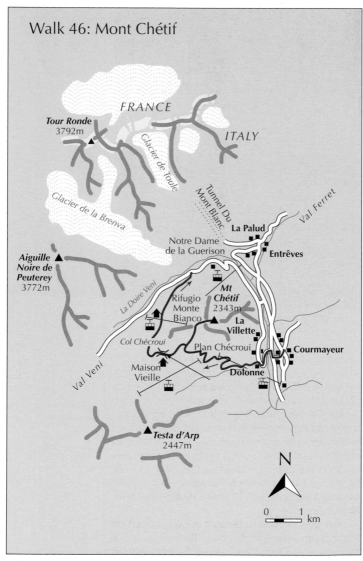

Walk 46: Mont Chétif

The summit of Mont Chétif is crowned by an impressive black Madonna. Here the sun is just rising on Monte Bianco behind.

which used to be the only option for this section. Sadly this still has to be taken eventually where the path pops out from the forest, to finally reach the houses at **Plan Chécroui**. In high summer a café is open here. To reach the **Col Chécroui** the TMB goes left (south) through this hamlet and follows a yellow waymarked path steeply up the meadows above. It is – thankfully – only about 30min and, once you put the ski lifts behind you, the beauty of the col makes it all worthwhile. The attractive stone building of **Maison Vieille** is framed by the imposing rocky flanks of the Aiguille Noire de Peutrey, with Mont Blanc hiding to its right.

You will doubtless be tempted by the sun loungers and buzzing scene of the café. Be warned: once ensconced it is difficult to muster up the enthusiasm to leave, so maybe it's best to do the summit first before fully committing to the joys of capuccinos and gelatis.

Descend the ski piste from the Col Chécroui (towards Plan Chécroui) taking the track left through Pra Neyron where there is a chairlift. The track goes under the chairlift and there is a signed path leading into the forest – it indicates path 5a and gives a time of 1h15 to the summit. The trail climbs steeply through the trees, before traversing left under some crags and heading up a scree slope. The Aosta peaks to the south and east look superb from here as does Courmayeur and the Val Veny far below.

A brief respite can be enjoyed at a flat area where the trail meanders through a tiny green valley before a final scrambly climb to the top, where there is a flat concrete square, an orientation table, and just a bit further on, an imposing Madonna. ◄

The views are beyond description - you just have to go see!

Return to the col by the same route and indulge your fancy before considering the descent.

Take the path behind the **Maison Vieille** which heads northwest then northeast down though forest to a ski lift in a clearing. Go down, then turn right onto a track running down to the **Rifugio Monte Bianco**. Here drinks can be had before continuing the descent down the road which goes into the Val Veny. The views are still wonderful, even if by now quite familiar. The British alpinist T Graham Brown chose to study the Brenva face of Mont Blanc (where he was extremely active in the 1920s and 30s) from this spot.

Once in the valley you join the main valley road. Keep right here to go down past the attractive chapel of **Notre Dame de la Guerison**. You can see the entrance to the Mont Blanc tunnel on the other side of the valley. In between, huge mounds of silt and gravel attest to the power of the Miage glacier as it grinds its way down from the summits.

The road enters the main Aosta valley. Here stay right as far as **La Villette**, where the road crosses the large Dora Baltéa river and continues down into Courmayeur.

WALK 47

Col and Lac Liconi

There are lots of places around Courmayeur from where you get great views, but one disadvantage is that often you have to hike up a long way. This walk is different. Whilst in its totality it's quite an undertaking, after only about 1hr the panorama of the Mont Blanc massif opens up.

But it's a tough one. You only have to look at the map to see that in places the path seems to go straight up steep hillside but – these being Italian maps – it's easy to convince yourself that the bends have just been left out. Unless you're of a masochistic tendency, or training for a steep trail race, you may not enjoy every bit of the way. The joys of reaching the top far outweigh the pain experienced en route, and the suffering will be instantly forgotten when you see the lake and all those snowy peaks behind.

This walk features some really cruel paths, clearly made before the invention of the zigzag.

Car park	Ermitage, up above Courmayeur, beyond Villair
Starting point	Ermitage 1433m
Finishing point	Ermitage 1433m
Highpoint	Col de Liconi 2674m
Altitude gain	1360m
Map	IGC 107 Monte Bianco Courmayeur La Tuile Chamonix Mont Blanc
Distance	10.6km (6.6 miles)
Time	6–7hr
Grade/difficulties	2/3. The paths are generally quite good, if a bit vague in places, but the climb is long and quite hard
Public transport	None beyond Villair
Tip	Being a circuit, the walk could be done in either direction. Having thought hard about whether one way is easier on the legs than the other I've decided to describe it the way I did it. Study the map and make up your own mind.

245

TAKE CARE

Throughout this walk there are many red and white paintmarks and numbers on trees and rocks. These are not footpath waymarks but rather denote ownership of land and forest. The waymarks are generally yellow, sometimes with numbers which do at the moment match the map, and there are some old red marks from time to time.

Route

From the **Ermitage** the footpath is signed right into the woods. After 2min take the track that goes up slightly left and it soon becomes a footpath with the odd yellow waymark. Ignore a sign going right to Tirecorne –this is the route down – and follow signs to **La Suche**, reached after about 45min. This small hamlet enjoys wonderful views – from the head of the Val Veny, capped by the Aiguille des Glaciers, to Mont Blanc and its defining Peutrey ridge, the Dent du Géant and the Grandes Jorasses.

From La Suche the path takes a long and undulating traverse across several stream beds which could become more difficult to cross after heavy rain. Eventually – when it stops going around – it heads straight up grassy slopes. Keep looking up, and finally a large yellow blodge announces that this section of zigzag-less terrain is done.

Traversing again leads to a small jutting shoulder where there are the remains of some sort of service lift. There is also a signpost which points left for the Col Sapin and right for the Col de Liconi. The 1hr 30min time indication given might be a little optimistic as the path from here on is unrelenting, so although height is gained quickly your legs cry out for a rest after about three steps. Play mind games, force yourself to go to the next waymark before stopping, anything to keep going. Do look behind frequently, as those views only get better.

At around 2450m a path leads right to Tirecorne, and is signed on the rocks just above the junction. This will be the way to go later on. For the moment we, of course, must go directly up.

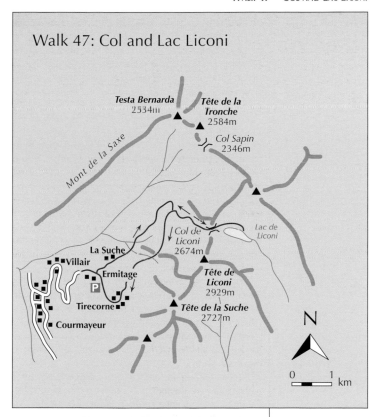

Walk 47: Col and Lac Liconi

Finally the **Col de Liconi** is reached and below, on the other side, is the lake. To go down or not is a decision that depends on time, weather, temperature, energy. The views are best from the col but the lake is worth visiting, especially on a still, clear day, for the beautiful reflections.

The other route to the lake comes up from the hamlet of Morge, above Morgex south of Courmayeur. This route is not shorter, although at first glance on the map it appears so. It is, however, quite popular so there may be a surprising number of fellow hikers around.

From the col redescend to the junction seen on the way up, then follow this at times vague path across the hillside. There are yellow waymarks, and some old faded red ones. Signs indicate the path when there is a choice, the direction being Tirecorne. For much of the way this path is less steep than the ascent route (but that is made up for near the end of the walk).

The hamlet of **Tirecorne**, whilst quite scruffy, to my mind boasts one of the best vistas ever. Imagine living here and having the Brenva face of Mont Blanc outside your front window. Be careful not to miss the path – there is some building work going on and the signpost for the paths is hidden among the buildings. If you miss it, be sure to turn right when you hit the stone wall beyond the houses.

Walk steeply down and into the forest where the path winds its descent to Ermitage, joining the ascent path about 20min from the car park.

WALK 48
Mont de la Saxe

If the massif of Mont Blanc – or Monte Bianco – is the theatre stage, then Mont de la Saxe is the circle.

Imagine a wide flat valley which runs under some of the highest peaks in the Mont Blanc massif. The steep faces are adorned with the tumbling chaos of glaciers and imposing rock slabs, whilst the summits form jagged peaks and snowy domes.

Imagine now being able to view this spectacular scene from a vantage point 1000m above the valley; not just a summit but a long whaleback ridge, nearly 3km long, the traverse of which gives plenty of time to feast your eyes on this visual treat. And there you have the Mont de la Saxe, high above the Val Ferret.

The route along the ridge is a variant on the TMB – the regular route being via the Col Sapin – which is used here for the return to Courmayeur. Many people on the TMB trek just walk up the Val Ferret, or even take the bus to the end of the road. Who can blame them – the trek is long – but if they knew what they were missing they would surely choose to include the Mont de la Saxe in their journey. Happily though, it remains relatively unknown, so does not get too busy except in high season when many people go up to the Rifugio Bertone for lunch. The hardy few who are still able to contemplate walking uphill after a full Italian midday gastronomic extravaganza continue on up to the first highpoint of the ridge for the view.

And what a view it is! From the Col de la Seigne far away beyond the mysterious mists of the Val Veny, past the fantastically spiky Peutrey ridge, the dark foreboding spire of the Aiguille Noire contrasting with the snowy peaked Aiguille Blanche, the two separated by the finely named Dames Anglaises, allegedly a cold and inhospitable place; next is Monte Bianco itself, then the aptly named Dent du Géant, and to its right the Grandes Jorasses presenting its rather more gentle, but nevertheless impressive, south

Car park	Villair, just on the outskirts of Courmayeur; the car park is at the end of the road
Starting point	Villair 1327m
Finishing point	Villair 1327m
Highpoint	Testa della Tronche 2584m
Altitude gain	1260m
Map	IGC 107 Monte Bianco Courmayeur La Tuile Chamonix Mont Blanc
Distance	12km (7.5 miles)
Time	7hr+
Grade/difficulties	2/3. The paths are good, although along the ridge and down to the Col Sapin the trail is quite narrow in places. The descent to the col is steep and after rain gets quite slippery
Public transport	Local bus to Villair
Accommodation	Rifugio Bertone open mid-June to late September, 0165 844612
Tip	This hike could be extended by continuing on from the Col Sapin across the Armina valley and up to the Pas Entre Deux Sauts, then onward to the Rifugio Bonatti (Walk 49).

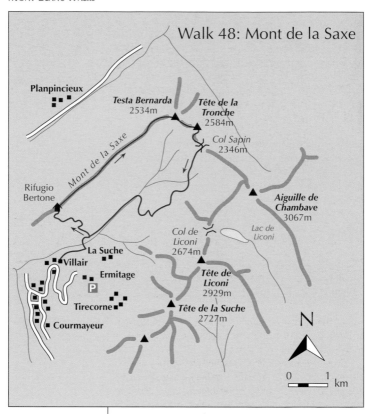

Walk 48: Mont de la Saxe

Planpincieux

Testa Bernarda
2534m

Tête de la
Tronche
2584m

Col Sapin
2346m

Mont de la Saxe

Rifugio
Bertone

Aiguille de
Chambave
3067m

Col de
Liconi
2674m

Lac de
Liconi

La Suche

Villair

Ermitage

Tête de
Liconi
2929m

P

Tirecorne

Courmayeur

Tête de la Suche
2727m

N

0   1
━━━━━━ km

face. Up at the head of the Val Ferret is Mont Dolent, a
unique summit where France, Switzerland and Italy all
meet up. It goes without saying that it would be a bit of a
shame to do this walk on a cloudy day...

Route
Head up into the forest on a wide track. The Rifugio
Bertone and the Col Sapin are signposted and the path
is marked in yellow TMB waymarks. After a short way do
not miss a turn off to the left to the **Bertone hut**. This very

Sunrise on Mont Blanc seen from Mont de la Saxe

well-made trail zigzags up at a perfect grade, but is nevertheless quite tiring, and fortunately there are some nice rocky seats on some of the bends.

Eventually the tree-line is reached and above you'll see the small hamlet of Le Pré where the hut is situated at nearly 2000m, amongst a cluster of beautifully renovated farm buildings. Only the most hardened walker would resist taking a break on the hut terrace, shaded by rowan trees, so this is definitely the time to have a cappuccino or antipasti. Bear in mind there's a way to go so don't get too chilled out.

The path behind the hut is a bit of shock as it dispenses with the next 125m of ascent in a fairly direct manner, but as the hammering of your heart just starts to reach red alert status you'll arrive on the ridge and all thoughts of abandoning hiking altogether will be forgotten as you lose yourself in visual ecstasy.

Having got over that, the way is pretty simple – just follow the rounded shoulder. There is a little path, dotted with yellow waymarks from time to time, but it wanders around a bit so if you want to hold the ridge line just make your own way.

Sooner or later you'll take to the path as you either feel saturated with the views or, after point 2548m as you head towards the **Testa Bernarda**, the path stays just under this summit, on the southern side.

The **Tête de la Tronche** (2584m) provides a final huff and puff but is a lovely highpoint and a good pace to refuel before heading down the rather steep zigzags to the **Col Sapin** (2436m). In muddy weather people with worn soles will regret it.

The col is wide and grassy and the way over to the wild Armina valley is tempting. However, our way takes the steep path to the south to gain the Val Sapin which we started up from Villair. We have 1100m of descent and a good 400m of it is lost in the first kilometre. Later the angle eases considerably as we traverse the south side of the Val Sapin, through the Curru alpage. The junction to Lac de Liconi is passed on the left and soon after our trail drops down to the Sapin valley. Cross the stream and follow the track which leads back to **Villair**.

WALK 49
Tête Entre Deux Sauts

Note that on Swiss maps of the area the summit is named Tête Entre Deux Sex.

Rather than list what you can see from the summit of this fine peak it's perhaps quicker to say what you can't: if we're talking the Mont Blanc massif there's little on the Italian side that's not included. The Chamonix peaks such as the Aiguille Verte and Les Drus are hidden from here, as well as the major Swiss summits, but Mont Dolent is there, representing all three countries. The Tête Entre Deux Sauts is a summit with a view.

This walk can be done comfortably in a day, but even if you don't stay the night at the hut do factor in time for lunch there – preferably on the way down (an Italian lunch tends to seriously compromise any subsequent physical activity). Hence the walk is described in

Car park	Pra Sec in the Val Ferret
Starting point	Pra Sec 1640m
Finishing point	Pra sec 1640m
Highpoint	Tête Entre Deux Sauts 2729m
Altitude gain	1100m
Map	IGC 107 Monte Bianco Courmayeur La Tuile Chamonix Mont Blanc
Distance	11.5km (7.1 miles)
Time	6–7hr
Grade/difficulties	2/3. Fairly good paths all the way, if in places indistinct. The summit path is narrow in places
Public transport	SAVDA bus from Courmayeur to Arnuva at the end of the road in the Val Ferret
Accommodation	Rifugio Bonatti open June to October, 0165 869055
Tip	This walk could be combined with the Mont de la Saxe (Walk 48) for a great two-day trek.

the direction that avoids any preprandial gastronomic temptation.

Route

From the hamlet of **Pra Sec** walk across the footbridge over the Doire du Val Ferret and follow the waymarked trail up through the woods. It is signed to Armina. Emerging from the woods you enter the beautiful remote Armina valley with fantastic views of the Mont Blanc massif opening behind you. At the ruins of **Armina** you meet a wide track; left is signed to the Rifugio Bonatti. However, do not go this way, but rather go right (southeast) and up into the higher pastures of Armina. Our trail wanders up into a delightful cwm, formed from rocky summits and steep slopes; at the ruined farm buildings of Alpe de Séchéron (2260m) look out for the yellow waymarks as they are quite difficult to spot here.

We are headed up to the Pas Entre Deux Sauts and the path goes across the slope under the col to the far right before zigzagging back left. It is joined by the TMB path coming from the Col Sapin to the west, and is better waymarked when the two routes coincide. This

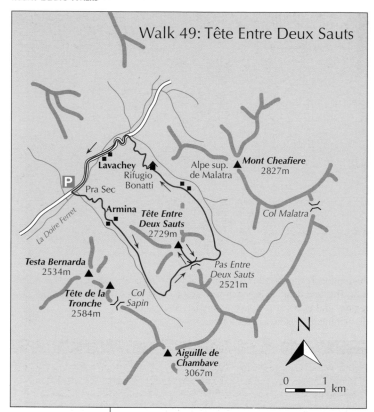

Walk 49: Tête Entre Deux Sauts

Lavachey
Rifugio Bonatti
Pra Sec
Armina
La Doire Ferret
Tête Entre Deux Sauts 2729m
Testa Bernarda 2534m
Tête de la Tronche 2584m
Col Sapin
Alpe sup. de Malatra
Mont Cheafiere 2827m
Col Malatra
Pas Entre Deux Sauts 2521m
Aiguille de Chambave 3067m

N

0   1 km

now good trail leads easily to the **Pas Entre Deux Sauts** (2521m).

Our route is up to the left and it's not difficult to spot the way up, past the small subsidiary summit then along to the main top where a spindly wooden cross adorns the summit cairn of **Tête Entre Deux Sauts** (2729m).

Return to the col, then go down into the Malatra valley and follow the path down through alpine meadows past the **upper Malatra alpage** and down to the lower farm buildings. The **hut** is not seen until the last minute

then suddenly is right below you, in all its gleaming new-ness. This fine building is one of several such huts in the region, and if this is your first alpine hut prepare to be disappointed frequently in the future.

At the Pas Entre Deux Sauts

RIFUGIO WALTER BONATTI

This walk is not just about bagging a peak. En route is the spectacular Rifugio Walter Bonatti, named after the alpinist himself, a mountaineering legend as well as an accomplished photographer. This is a rifugio in name only – inside it's more luxurious than many hotels, and is also a showcase for Bonatti's photos which document his extensive travels.

The track from the hut to the valley follows an old mule track in the forest, used for centuries to access the higher pastures for summer grazing.

On reaching the road turn left and follow it down to Lavachey where there are a couple of excellent cafés just in case you need another cappuccino fix before following the road for 1km or so back to **Pra Sec**.

WALK 50
Tête de Ferret

Standing like a proud sentinel on the Swiss–Italian frontier at the heads of both the Swiss and Italian Val Ferrets, the Tête de Ferret demands to be climbed.

Many hikers toil past the Tête de Ferret every day during the summer, some perhaps raising a tired head to consider the ascent but soon discounting any extra unnecessary upwards effort. The summit separates two passes, either of which can be taken by trekkers embarked on the TMB en route from Italy to Switzerland or vice versa. Those walkers have got things to do, places to go, so – as on many long-distance treks – end up forsaking such temptations. The great thing about a multi-day trek is that it takes you to places you may never have considered visiting otherwise, and which can be revisited later.

Car park	Arnuva at the end of the Italian Val Ferret road
Starting point	Arnuva 1769m
Finishing point	Arnuva 1769m
Highpoint	Tête de Ferret 2713m
Altitude gain	944m
Map	IGN Top 25 3630 OT Chamonix Massif du Mont Blanc
Distance	8.4km (5.2 miles)
Time	5hr 30min
Grade/difficulties	2. The path to the Grand Col Ferret is a major highway. From thereon to the summit it is much narrower but can't really be missed
Public transport	SAVDA bus from Courmayeur to Arnuva
Tip	From the summit it is possible to continue on and traverse the mountain and descend to the Petit Col Ferret and from there quite steeply down to Arnuva. However, this continuation is not as straightforward as the rest of the route – care is needed on several passages. Thea Tête de Ferret can also be done from the Swiss side, starting at the end of the road near Les Ars Dessus and ascending via La Peule – this is also the TMB trail. For the return, a good variation is to follow the Arête des Planfins over La Dotse and down to rejoin the main path.

I have found time on several occasions during the TMB to sprint up the Tête de Ferret but it's usually been a bit of a rush, with some people choosing to stay at the col and the worry that they are getting chilled. The real joy is to do the peak for its own sake and take the time to really enjoy it. For the views are fine indeed – from Mont Dolent (the crossroads of France, Italy and Switzerland) and the Aiguille du Triolet to the west, not to mention the Grandes Jorasses further down the Italian Val Ferret and, to the east, the St Bernard peaks with Mont Velan and the Grand Combin behind. Ahead the Swiss Val Ferret stretches away into the distance. I've said it often, but these relatively small peaks really do provide belvederes far out of proportion to their size. In addition there's the joy of escaping the rather social atmosphere that usually prevails on the Grand Col Ferret for a bit of peace and quiet.

Below the Grand Col Ferret; the rounded summit of the Tête de Ferret is directly above the hikers

Route
From the car park in **Arnuva** the wide track continues heading up the valley, with Mont Dolent standing guard at the end. On the left is the grey, rounded snout of the

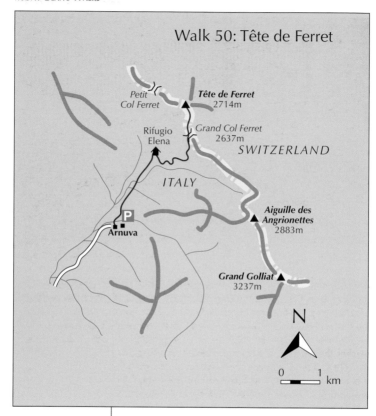

Walk 50: Tête de Ferret

Petit Col Ferret

Tête de Ferret 2714m

Grand Col Ferret 2637m

Rifugio Elena

SWITZERLAND

ITALY

P

Arnuva

Aiguille des Angrionettes 2883m

Grand Golliat 3237m

N

0   1 km

Pré de Bar glacier. Stay on the track as it winds uphill –
there are a couple of short-cut footpaths to take or not
depending on personal gradient preference. The **Rifugio
Elena** is one of the relatively new huts in the Aosta region,
the construction cost of which can only be guessed at.
It's certainly worth stopping there for a cappuccino – and
maybe again on the return.

The slopes above are soft and earthy and consequently the TMB has worn a deep trench in parts of the
path up to the **Grand Col Ferret** – come here on a rainy

day and you'll see why – mud city. In dry weather it's no problem except that with trekking poles your arms get tired being raised above the trench. At least you can't lose the way and the route takes well-graded zigzags up to a viewpoint at 2463m from where the way levels out as it reaches the col 2537m. Sacs could be left here to go to the **Tête de Ferret** but since this will be a quieter picnic spot it's maybe best to take them. Just head left and follow your nose – there are small paths going straight up to the top.

Return by the same route, doing full justice to the delights on offer at the Elena hut on the way down.

The Italian face of Mont Blanc provides a beautiful backdrop to the high-level paths above the Val Ferret

Ibex chilling out near Cheval Blanc, with Mont Blanc behind

CHAPTER 8

MULTI-DAY TREKS

Four multi day treks are briefly detailed here. With a little imagination many more can be invented. The idea of doing a journey across the mountains, staying each night in a mountain hut, is highly appealing. The fact is that most trekkers are attracted to the main well-documented treks, notably the Tour du Mont Blanc and the northern part of the GR5 in the Mont Blanc region. These treks are certainly wonderful, but it is really fulfilling to make up your own trek and just go where your instincts lead you.

It is advisable to book ahead at the mountain huts and plan to arrive by 6pm. A wardened hut will be equipped with bedding and will provide meals, so the only extra gear needed is a change of clothes and a toothbrush. Most huts in the area will provide a picnic if you ask the night before, which reduces still further the weight of your sac. So, look at the maps and follow your dreams!

The trek descriptions given here are short, with just map information, daily altitude gain, distance and route details. These are not intended to be full guides to these routes, rather a basic outline to be used in conjunction with the appropriate maps and complemented by

A paraglider taking off from the Plan Praz near the Brévent

walkers' previous experience of speed and fitness.

If these treks seem to be biased to the Aiguilles Rouges area that's because this is a great place for treks and there are plenty of refuge possibilities.

WALK 51

Vallorcine to Plaine Joux (3 days)

This trek could be done in the opposite direction. It is described from Vallorcine as there are more accommodation options there.

This high-level traverse of the Aiguilles Rouges keeps to the south-facing side for the first 1.5 days before crossing over to plunge into the wild depths of the Diosaz gorge. It provides a short trek which would give a great introduction to hut-to-hut touring in the Alps and a chance to explore the moyenne montagne of the Mont Blanc region.

Starting point	Vallorcine SNCF railway station 1250m
Finishing point	Plaine Joux 1360m
Time	3 days
Maps	IGN Top 25 3630 OT Chamonix Mont Blanc Massif; IGN Top 25 3530 ET Samoëns Haut Giffre
Accommodation	Refuge du Lac Blanc, 04 50 53 49 14; Refuge du Col d'Anterne, 04 50 93 60 43
Public transport	SAT bus Plaine Joux to Le Fayet; SNCF train Le Fayet–Vallorcine
Reference walks	28, 21, 20, 8
Tip	This walk can be planned for anytime during the summer (end of June onwards). There may be odd patches of névé around Lac Blanc and on the far side of the Col du Brévent but usually these slopes do not present any real problems.

DAY 1

Vallorcine to Lac Blanc

Altitude gain	1100m
Distance	8.5km (5.3 miles)
Time	4hr

A nice footpath leads from the far side of the railway line through meadows, under the famous climbing slabs of

Vallorcine. The path continues alongside the railway past the campsite at Les Montets and onwards to the **Col des Montets** (1461m). From here a well-made path heads up in switchbacks into the Aiguilles Rouges, steeply at first then flattening out at Le Remuaz. The Lacs des Chéserys (2133m) provide a tempting place to stop before carrying on up the trail to the **Refuge du Lac Blanc** (2352m). This hut is finely situated for superb evening views of Les Drus and the Verte.

DAY 2
Lac Blanc to the Refuge du Col d'Anterne

The Col des Montets, gateway to the Chamonix valley from Switzerland

Altitude gain	905m
Distance	14.25km (8.8 miles)
Time	6–7hr

The trail from Lac Blanc to La Flégère (1877m) cannot be missed. Once at the top of the cable car descend a little to pick up the Grand Balcon Sud that traverses across to Planpraz (2000m) – views of the massif are wonderful, as are the alpenrose bushes nearby.

Head up northwest to the **Col du Brévent** (2368m), then leave behind the frequented south-facing slopes and venture into the more remote hinterland of the Aiguilles Rouges. The path snakes down, still heading northwest.

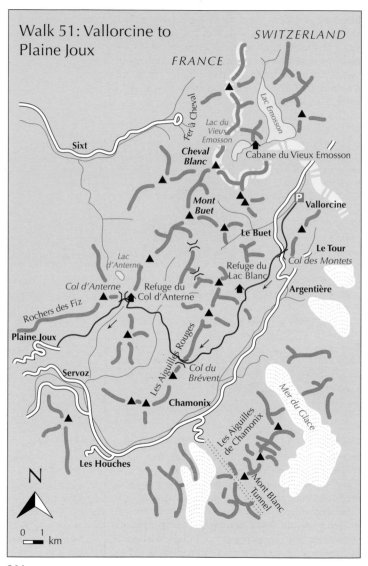

Walk 51: Vallorcine to
Plaine Joux

SWITZERLAND

FRANCE

Fer à Cheval

Sixt

Lac Emosson

Lac du
Vieux
Emosson

Cheval
Blanc

Cabane du Vieux Emosson

P Vallorcine

Mont
Buet

Le Buet

Le Tour

Col des Montets

Lac
d'Anterne

Refuge du
Lac Blanc

Argentière

Col d'Anterne

Refuge du
Col d'Anterne

Rochers des Fiz

Plaine Joux

Les Aiguilles Rouges

Servoz

Col du
Brévent

Mer du Glace

Chamonix

Les Aiguilles
de Chamonix

Les Houches

Mont Blanc
Tunnel

N

0   1
km

Below lie the dark depths of the Diosaz gorge and ahead are the impressive limestone walls of the Rochers des Fiz. The Pont d'Arlevé (1597m) marks the end of the descent, and now a gentle climb meanders up through meadows past the Chalets de Moëde to the **Refuge du Col d'Anterne** above, which at 2002m commands a superb view of the massif.

DAY 3
Refuge du Col d'Anterne to Plaine Joux

Altitude gain	None
Distance	6km
Time	2hr

From the hut take the jeep track that goes west then southwest in a descending traverse around the hillside under the mighty cliffs of Les Fiz, staying well above the Souay torrent all the way to the chalets at Ayères des Pierrières. Either stay on the high trail all the way past Barmus, or drop down through Le Châtelet to visit Lac Vert en route to **Plaine Joux**. Both ways are signed and of equal distance. The bus service runs regularly from Plaine Joux down to the Arve valley.

WALK 52
Tour of the Aiguilles Rouges (4–5 days)

Standing proud opposite the spectacular glaciated summits of the Mont Blanc massif, the Aiguilles Rouges are in no way diminished by proximity to these towering and forbidding peaks.

The tour is a circuit of this area, designated a nature reserve from the boundaries of the Col des Montets to its southwestern extremity at the Diosaz gorge. Whilst

The Mont Blanc massif forms a perfect backdrop for the orange-tinted rocky buttresses and grassy slopes of the Aiguilles Rouges range.

walking on the south-facing slopes the views are dominated by Mont Blanc and its neighbours; once the interior
of the range is penetrated the area is wild and remote,
surrounded on all sides by impregnable rock faces and
scree-filled cols.

Starting point	Le Buet 1350m, near Vallorcine
Finishing point	Le Buet 1350m
Time	4–5 days
Maps	IGN Top 25 3630 OT Chamonix Massif du Mont Blanc;
	IGN Top 25 3530 ET Samoëns Haut Giffre
Accommodation	Refuge du Lac Blanc, 04 50 53 49 14; Refuge du Col
	d'Anterne, 04 50 93 60 43; Refuge du Grenairon, 04 50
	34 47 31; Refuge de la Pierre à Bérard, 04 50 54 62 08
Public transport	SNCF train Chamonix–Le Buet
Reference walks	28, 21, 20, 22, 43, 40
Tip	This is a high-level trek so it shouldn't be envisaged
	before midsummer – August is usually the best time.
	The ascent of Mont Buet is described by its steep north
	ridge. However, this could be avoided by going over the
	Col de Salenton (Walk 23) on Day 3 and staying at the
	Refuge de la Pierre à Bérard then doing the summit by
	the Normal Route from there.

*This rather fine
cantilever is on the
route from Mont Buet
to the Bérard Valley.
Below can be seen
the Chalets de Villy
(walk 23)*

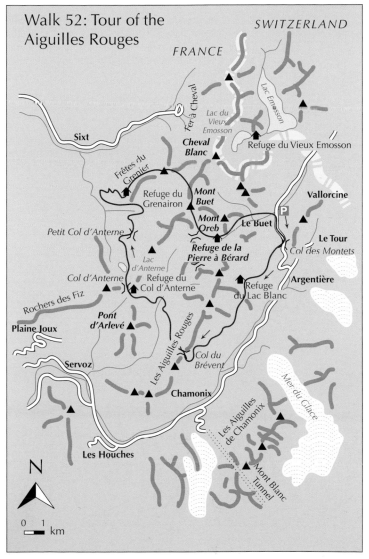

Walk 52: Tour of the
Aiguilles Rouges

SWITZERLAND

FRANCE

Lac Emosson

Sixt

Lac du
Vieux
Emosson

Fer à Cheval

*Cheval
Blanc*

Refuge du Vieux Emosson

Frêtes du Grenier

Refuge du
Grenairon

*Mont
Buet*

Vallorcine

P

*Mont
Orcb*

Le Buet

Le Tour

Petit Col d'Anterne

*Refuge de la
Pierre à Bérard*

Col des Montets

*Lac
d'Anterne*

Col d'Anterne

Refuge du
Col d'Anterne

Refuge
du Lac Blanc

Argentière

Rochers des Fiz

*Pont
d'Arlevé*

Les Aiguilles Rouges

Plaine Joux

Servoz

*Col du
Brévent*

Mer du Glace

Chamonix

Les Aiguilles
de Chamonix

Les Houches

Mont
Blanc
Tunnel

N

0   1
⊢——⊣ km

DAY 1
Le Buet to Lac Blanc

Altitude gain	1000m
Distance	8km (5 miles)
Time	3hr 30min

Take the good track that leads from the far side of the railway line at Le Buet to the **Col des Montets** (1461m). From here a well-made path heads up in switchbacks into the Aiguilles Rouges, steeply at first then flattening out at Le Remuaz. The Lacs des Cheserys (2133m) provide a tempting place to stop before carrying on up the trail to the **Refuge du Lac Blanc** (2352m). This hut is finely situated for superb evening views of Les Drus and the Verte.

DAY 2
Lac Blanc to the Refuge du Col d'Anterne

Altitude gain	905m
Distance	14.25km (8.8 miles)
Time	6–7hr

See Day 2 Walk 51.

DAY 3
Refuge du Col d'Anterne to the Refuge du Grenairon

Altitude gain	1150m
Distance	15km (9.3 miles)
Time	7–8hr

The Rochers d'Anterne and Col d'Anterne seen from the Frêtes du Grenier

Take the good trail up to the **Col d'Anterne** (2257m) then head down and across the delightful Plateau d'Anterne, past the lake and the Refuge Alfred Wills – named after a British alpinist (founder of the Alpine Club, who wrote prolifically about his exploits) – a good place for a coffee break.

Continue on to the **Petit Col d'Anterne** (2038m) where the scenery changes quite dramatically as you leave the idyllic pastoral meadows of the plateau and head down through steep forested slopes to the Refuge des Fonds (1368m). A late lunch here, then press on down the valley to a path junction. Our objective is the **Refuge du Grenairon** which involves a long climb back up to 1974m. However, the effort is worthwhile as Grenairon is a fine hut – good views, warm welcome and great food.

DAY 4
Refuge du Grenairon to the Refuge de la Pierre à Bérard

Altitude gain:	1125m
Distance:	10km (6.2 miles)
Time:	7hr

Set off early from the hut so as to allow plenty of time for the ascent of Mont Buet and the long descent down the Normal Route. The ascent should only be considered in good weather. The path from the hut is immediately rough as it clambers among slippery limestone boulders to reach the **Frêtes du Grenier** ridge. Wend in and out of rocky towers, past the distinctive tower of La Cathédrale, to reach easier ground across a scree slope heading for the Plan du Buet.

Up ahead the north ridge of Mont Buet looms menacingly – from here it looks quite improbable and this perception increases as you climb the zigzag trail across black shaly slopes to the unnamed col at 2808m, just southwest of the Point de Genevrier.

Follow the narrow trail up the Arête du Buet which is equipped in part with cables. Once the steep section is overcome a lovely rounded shoulder leads easily to the summit of **Mont Buet** (3096m), crowned with a huge cairn.

The descent is by the Normal Route and the path is generally good, waymarked in red, but in bad weather it would nevertheless be easy to lose your way. Be sure to head across south towards the Col de Salenton before going southeast to finally reach the **Refuge de la Pierre à Bérard** (1924m).

DAY 5
Refuge de la Pierre à Bérard to Le Buet

Altitude gain	None
Distance	5km (3.1 miles)
Time	1hr 30min

This day could be incorporated into Day 4, but a night spent at the refuge allows you to fully enjoy the stroll down the Bérard valley. Just follow the path – first on the true left bank, then switching to the right further down.

WALK 53
Vallorcine to Servoz (4 days)

This is a superb high-level trek goes from one end of the Aiguilles Rouges massif to the other: starting at the Franco–Swiss frontier, passing through the wild and remote area to the west of Emosson, emerging onto the Anterne plateau and finally descending to Servoz.

Vallorcine and Servoz are two of the most traditional villages in the French Mont Blanc region.

Starting point	Vallorcine railway station 1264m
Finishing point	Servoz railway station 814m
Time	4 days
Maps	IGN Top 25 3630 OT Chamonix Massif du Mont Blanc; IGN Top 25 3530 ET Samoëns Haut Giffre
Accommodation	Cabane du Vieux Emosson, 079 342 9566 or 027 768 1421; Refuge du Grenairon, 04 50 34 47 31; Refuge du Col d'Anterne, 04 50 93 60 43
Public transport	SNCF train Servoz to Vallorcine.
Reference walks	43, 35, 8
Tip	This is a high-level trek so it shouldn't be envisaged before midsummer – August is usually the best time.

DAY 1
Vallorcine to Refuge du Vieux Emosson

Altitude gain	920m
Distance	7km (4.3 miles)
Time	4hr

From Vallorcine take the back road to the church, then on through Le Molard towards Barberine. Do not descend to the village but rather pick up the path to go around the hillside and up to the Col du Passet (2000m), just above Lac d'Emosson. Follow the road westwards around the lake and then its continuation up through a couple of

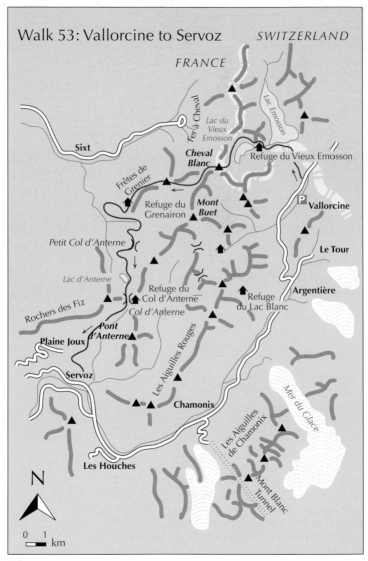

Walk 53: Vallorcine to Servoz

SWITZERLAND

FRANCE

Sixt

Fer à Cheval

Lac du Vieux Emosson

Lac Emosson

Cheval Blanc

Refuge du Vieux Emosson

Frêtes de Grenier

Refuge du Grenairon

Mont Buet

P **Vallorcine**

Petit Col d'Anterne

Le Tour

Lac d'Anterne

Refuge du Col d'Anterne

Refuge du Lac Blanc

Rochers des Fiz

Col d'Anterne

Argentière

Pont d'Anterne

Plaine Joux

Les Aiguilles Rouges

Servoz

Chamonix

Mer du Glace

Les Aiguilles de Chamonix

Les Houches

Mont Blanc Tunnel

N

0   1
▭▬ km

short tunnels to reach the **Refuge du Vieux Emosson** just before the higher lake (2181m).

DAY 2
*Refuge du Vieux Emosson to
Refuge du Grenairon*

Altitude gain	700m
Distance	11km (6.8 miles)
Time	6hr

Walk around the north side of **Lac du Vieux Emosson** to almost reach the dinosaur tracks. At a signpost head up southwest towards the Col des Corbeaux before taking the narrow path west to the Col du Vieux (2572m). From here a good path zigzags up the southern shoulder of the **Cheval Blanc**, with some well-placed chains to gain the summit (2831m).

The Refuge du Vieux Emosson in its splendid position high above Lac d'Emosson

Early light on Lac du Vieux Emosson

From the summit head southwest to the Col Genévrier (2691m). The terrain descends a little but in general it's fairly flat. Red paint marks and cairns mark the way but you need to concentrate– it would be easy to get disorientated. From the col take a descending path on the west side of the summit, underneath electricity cables, which goes down to the lake at the Plan du Buet at 2543m (this path is not shown on the IGN map but it is well marked by cairns, and the cables provide a good landmark.)

A signpost indicates the westerly route to Grenairon. Ignore the rather optimistic timing given – it's a good 2hr 30min from here. The trail traverses across scree to the defined rocky ridge, and the distinctive tower of La Cathédrale. Winding along the intricate ridge, the route eventually emerges at the top of a grassy slope. A gap in the rocks nearby gives access to the final descent to the **Refuge du Grenairon** (1974m).

DAY 3
Refuge du Grenairon to the Refuge du Col d'Anterne

Altitude gain	1450m
Distance	15km (9.3 miles)
Time	7hr

Take the path that heads steeply south, down into woods to the Fonts valley. Once next to the river head up the valley (east) to the Refuge des Fonts (1368m), situated in a small hamlet under the imposing west face of Mont Buet. The trail up to the **Petit Col d'Anterne** sets off south from the hut and makes its way up the hillside to finish steeply at the col (2038m). Ahead is the wild and beautiful Plateau d'Anterne, its western flank defined by the towering cliffs of the Rochers des Fiz. A gentle descent leads to the Refuge Alfred Wills, named after an English alpinist, and here a lunch stop cannot be resisted. The route takes you over flat grassy meadows past the **Lac d'Anterne**, its clear waters tempting but deceptively icy. The climb to the **Col d'Anterne** (2257m) is not difficult and the rewards are huge – the Mont Blanc massif appears in all its glory.

A short descent and the **Refuge du Col d'Anterne** (2002m) provides a perfect place to spend the last night.

DAY 4
Refuge du Col d'Anterne to Servoz

Altitude gain	Hardly any
Distance	8km (5 miles)
Time	2hr 30min

A well-signed trail goes off southwest from the hut and traverses all the way under the huge cliffs of the Fiz, providing impressive views in all directions. The way to Servoz is signed – take the left junction down through Le Souay and at 1522m, just before Ayères du Milieu, keep your eyes open for the path down through the woods into Le Mont. Once on the road the quickest way into **Servoz** is waymarked. The railway station is on the far side of town, over the river, and there is a good bar just before you get there.

WALK 54
Italian Val Ferret Circuit (3 days)

This trek encompasses all that is special about this area of northern Italy – the views, the food, and the quintessential Italian huts.

The Italian Val Ferret holds numerous delights for walkers, both along its beautiful river and also high up on the flanks of the mountains on the southwest side of the valley. This circuit described ventures into the midst of this walker's paradise for a short trek of three days, staying in two mountain huts which, although very different in character, both offer superlative views and situation.

Starting point	Planpincieux 1564m
Finishing point	Courmayeur town centre 1220m
Time	3 days
Map	IGC 107 Monte Bianco Courmayeur La Tuile Chamonix Mont Blanc
Accommodation	Rifugio Bonatti, 0165 86 90 55; Rifugio Bertone, 0165 84 46 12
Public transport	SAVDA bus from Courmayeur town centre to Planpincieux
Reference walks	49, 48
Tip	This trek could be done in two days, but who could pass up the chance to spend a night at the Rifugio Bertone, high above Courmayeur – why rush down!

DAY 1
Planpincieux to the Rifugio Bonatti

Altitude gain	550m
Distance	7km (4.3 miles)
Time	3hr

From Planpincieux walk down the road a few hundred metres to a bridge that crosses the river. A footpath then leads along the true left bank of the Ferret river to Neyron. The path rises up to the alpage of **Armina** where a wide

Walk 54: Italian Val Ferret Circuit

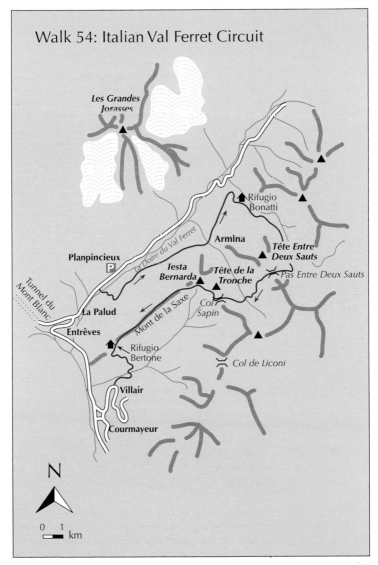

Les Grandes Jorasses

Rifugio Bonatti

La Doire du Val Ferret

Armina

Tête Entre Deux Sauts

Planpincieux

Testa Bernarda

Tête de la Tronche

Pas Entre Deux Sauts

Tunnel du Mont Blanc

La Palud

Mont de la Saxe

Col Sapin

Entrêves

Rifugio Bertone

Col de Liconi

Villair

Courmayeur

N

0   1
km

trail is signed around the hillside northeast to meet the forest rack coming up from La Vachey. Follow this on upwards to the **Rifugio Bonatti** (2056m).

DAY 2
Rifugio Bonatti to Rifugio Bertone

Altitude gain	990m
Distance	10km (6.2 miles)
Time	5–6hr

Take the meandering footpath up into the Malatra cwm and onwards up to the **Pas Entre Deux Sauts** (2524m) on the south side of the **Tête Entre Deux Sauts**. The summit is up to the right and it's not difficult to spot the way up, past the small subsidiary summit then along to the main top where a spindly wooden cross adorns the summit cairn at 2729m.

Return to the col and descend into the Armina valley. Opposite is the next objective, the **Col Sapin** (2436m). From here a small path winds up past the highpoint of the **Tête de la Tronche** (2584m) to give access to the rounded whaleback of Mont de la Saxe. Follow this to its far western end and the **Rifugio Bertone** is just below.

DAY 3
Rifugio Bertone to Courmayeur

Altitude gain:	None
Distance:	4.5km (2.8 miles)
Time:	1hr 45min

A delightful path wanders down south/southwest into larch and spruce forest to Villair. Take the back roads into town and enjoy a gelato.

APPENDIX A
Mont Blanc Region Tourist Offices

France
Chamonix Tourist Office
85, Place du Triangle de l'Amitió
74401 Chamonix Mt-Blanc
Tel: 04 50 53 00 24
Fax: 04 50 53 58 90
info@chamonix.com
www.chamonix.com

Argentière Tourist Office
24, route du village
74400 Argentière
Tel: 04 50 54 02 14
Fax: 04 50 54 06 39
accueil@argentiere.com

Les Houches Tourist Office
Place de l'Eglise
BP 9
74310 Les Houches
Tel: 04 50 55 50 62
Fax: 04 50 55 53 16
info@leshouches.com
www.leshouches.com

Servoz Tourist Office
Le Bouchet
74310 Servoz
Tel: 04 50 47 21 68
Fax: 04 50 47 27 06
info@servoz.com

Passy/Plateau d'Assy Tourist Office
1133 Ave Jacques Arnaud
Tel: 04 50 58 80 52
Fax: 04 50 93 83 74
info@ot-passy.com

Vallorcine Tourist Office
Chef Lieu
Vallorcine 74660
Tel: 04 50 54 60 71
Fax: 04 50 54 61 73
vallorcine@wanadoo.fr
www.vallorcine.com

Saint-Gervais Mont-Blanc Tourist Office
115 Ave Mont Paccard
St Gervais les Bains 74170
Tel: 04 50 47 76 08
Fax: 04 50 47 75 69
welcome@st-gervais.net
www.st-gervais.net

Les Contamines-Montjoie Tourist Office
BP 7 – F–74170
Les Contamines-Montjoie
Tel: 04 50 47 01 58
Fax: 04 50 47 09 54
info@lescontamines.com
www.lescontamines.com

Italy
Courmayeur Tourist Office
Apt Monte Bianco
P.Le Monte Bianco 13-CAP
11013 Courmayeur (AO)
Tel: 0165 842060
Fax: 0165 842072
apt.montebianco@psw.it
www.courmayeur.net

Switzerland
Martigny Tourist Office
Place Centrale 9
Martigny CH 1920
Tel: 027 721.22.20
Fax: 027 721.22.24
info@martignytourism.ch
www.martignytourism.ch

APPENDIX B
Useful Terms and Glossary

Vocabulary – Weather

English	French	Italian
weather	*temps*	*tempo*
forecast	*prévision*	*bolletino*
hot	*chaud*	*caldo*
cold	*froid*	*freddo*
sunny	*ensoleillé*	*soleggiato*
rainy	*pluvieux*	*piovoso*
windy	*venté*	*ventoso*
cloudy	*nuageux*	*nuvoloso*
foggy	*brouillard*	*nebbioso*
stormy	*orageux*	*temporalesco*
snowy	*enneigé*	*nevoso*
temperature	*température*	*temperatura*
changeable	*variable*	*variabile*
thunder	*tonnère*	*tuono*
lightning	*éclair*	*fulmine*
gusts/gales	*rafales*	*raffiche di vento*
white out	*jour blanc*	*luce abbacinante*
ice	*glace*	*ghiaccio*
verglace	*verglas*	*ghiaccio vivo,verglace*
hail	*grêle*	*grandine*
avalanche	*avalanche*	*valanga*
freezing	*glacial*	*congelamento*
starry	*étoillé*	*stellato*

Vocabulary – Emergency

English	French	Italian
Help!	*au secours!*	*aiuto!*
Accident	*accident*	*incidente*
Emergency	*urgence*	*emergenza*
Stop!	*halte*	*stop (alt)*
Quick	*vite*	*presto*
Be careful!	*faites attention*	*attenzione*
Rescue	*secours*	*soccorso*

Helicopter	*hélicoptère*	*elicottero*
Ambulance	*ambulance*	*ambulanza*
Hospital	*hôpital*	*ospedale*
Doctor	*medecin, docteur*	*dottore, medico*
SOS telephone	*téléphone d'urgence*	*telefono di soccorso*
Heart attack	*crise cardiaque*	*infarto, attacco di cuore*
Stroke	*hémiplégie*	*attacco*
Broken arm/leg	*bras/jambe cassé(e)*	*braccio rotto, gamba rotta*
Asthma attack	*crise d'asthma*	*attacco d'asma*

**The following terms may need some explanation.
They are used throughout the book.**

Alpage: A summer farm usually above the tree-line. The cattle are brought up here for the months of July and August to graze.

Col: A pass or a saddle. In Italian *colle* or *bocca*.

Cwm/corrie/combe: A basin formed around three sides by hills or mountains. It can be steep sided or more gently rounded. Often there is a lake in the basin and a stream flows out of the unenclosed side, down into the valley.

Moyenne montagne: Non-glaciated terrain, usually between 1500 and 3000m in the Mont Blanc region.

Névé: Snow that fell in the winter but has remained until well into the summer months.

APPENDIX C
Transport in the Chamonix and Courmayeur Valleys

NB Times and costs vary so do check beforehand. This information was valid in November 2009.

Lifts, trains and buses
In Chamonix all lifts are now run by the Compagnie du Mont Blanc (tel: 04 50 53 22 75).

NB When relying on lifts and trains to descend at the end of the day make sure you check the time of the last service before setting out.

Montenvers: The train runs year-round, every 20–30min from 09.00h until the end of the afternoon. The full visit costs €24.
Tramway du Mont Blanc: The tram opens mid-June until mid-September. Exact dates vary, as do opening hours.
Aiguille du Midi two-stage cable car: This is open almost year-round, but is usually closed for a short period in May and December. Opening times vary according to the time of year, but in summer it opens very early. The last trip up is usually around 17.00h. Return trip Chamonix–Aiguille du Midi costs €41; with Helbronner included the return trip costs €65.
Le Brévent, La Flégère, Le Tour: These lifts open mid-June until mid-September (the exact date varies, as do the opening hours). The last lift down is usually around 17.00h. Return trips to the top of these lift systems cost €24 for Le Brévent and La Flégère and €22 for Le Tour.
Grand Montets: This lift system opens early July. Closing date varies, but is usually early September. The return trip Argentière–Les Grands Montets costs €263.
Helbronner: This is normally open mid-June to mid-September, if not longer.

For information on the Chamonix Bus service, tel: 04 50 53 33 07. For the SNCF trains, tel: 04 50 53 07 02.

The buses that serve the Val Ferret and Val Veny from Courmayeur are fully operational from 1 July. The Val Ferret as a partial year-round service, tel: 0165 842031.

APPENDIX D

Rainy Day/Rest Day Activities

There are plenty of activities available to fill those days when either you do not want to walk or the weather dictates against it.

In **Chamonix** the Alpine Museum provides a haven of tranquillity and is filled with interesting displays about the history of the town, and the evolution of mountaineering. The museum is usually open every day from 14.00h to 19.00h, but it does close sometimes for several days (tel: 04 50 53 25 93).

The Espace Tairraz is an exhibition centre and is open 14.00h–19.00h (as well as 10.00h–12.00h in the school holidays). A combination ticket can be bought for this that allows access to the museum as well (tel: 04 50 55 53 93).

A Guide de Patrimoine provides weekly guided tours of Chamonix. The tourist office will provide further information (tel: 04 50 53 00 24).

The swimming pool is open every afternoon (tel: 04 50 53 23 70) and the skating rink is nearby (tel: 04 50 53 12 36). There are tennis courts (tel: 04 50 53 28 40) and the golf course (tel: 04 50 53 06 28). Advance reservation is advisable.

All visitors staying in any sort of accommodation in the Chamonix and Vallorcine valleys are eligible for a *Carte d'hôte* card, available from the person in charge of their accommodation. This entitles you to free travel on the Chamonix Bus as well as various discounts at many of the facilities in Chamonix.

The cinema in Chamonix has a full programme of films, including some in English (tel: 04 50 53 03 39).

Courmayeur offers many activities including horse riding (tel: 0165 551580) and fishing with the Val Ferret fishing club, permits sold at 4810 Sports (tel: 0165 844631).

The Forum Sports Centre offers, amongst other activities, ice skating, tennis, indoor golf and a climbing wall (tel: 0165 844096).

There is an Alpine Museum in Courmayeur, near the Guides Bureau in the centre of town (tel: 0165 842064).

Numerous restaurants in Courmayeur provide plenty of opportunity to sample the local specialities. Valdotain (Aosta valley) food tends to be based around cheese and cured meats, as well as the Italian staples of pasta and pizza.

Local markets can be a good diversion. Chamonix has its market on Saturday morning, Courmayeur on Wednesday morning.

APPENDIX E
Hut Etiquette

All huts are different, but the following applies to them all:

- It is advisable to book your stay in advance. It is not only a question of being sure of a place, it is also considered polite to warn the guardian that you will be coming. Outside the high season telephoning the night before will usually ensure you have a place. If you have special dietary requirements tell the guardian at this point. Bear in mind that huts offer a limited choice of meals, so only insist if yours really is a long-term special diet.
- Most huts provide hut shoes, but you cannot assume this to be the case. Ask when you reserve, or take a pair of very light flip flops or slippers.
- It is advisable (and compulsory in Italy) to take a sheet sleeping bag if you are sleeping in a hut. These can be bought (very lightweight ones are made of silk) or made by sewing up the sides of an old sheet.
- You are expected to leave the dormitories in the state you found them – blankets folded neatly on the beds.
- Dormitories are always mixed in alpine huts.
- Many huts do not accept credit cards. You should take cash to pay, preferably the local currency.
- When you arrive at a hut you must find the guardian to register your arrival. Usually you are expected to remove your boots before entering.
- People in huts are generally there to explore the mountains. You are expected to go to bed and to be quiet after 22.00h.
- Respect the rules – sometimes there is a special place to leave your rucksack; there may be a lot of people, necessitating two sittings at dinner; the guardian may want to tell you at which table to sit, and so on. Remember: you are a guest.
- If camping in the vicinity of a hut you must confirm with the guardian that this is acceptable. You will normally be expected to pay a nominal sum for using the facilities.

APPENDIX F
Climbing Peaks and Hiring Guides

You may decide during your walks in the Mont Blanc region that you would like to go on to more difficult things. There are several glaciated peaks that are well within the grasp of many fit hikers. Since travelling on glaciers is potentially dangerous it is advisable to hire a guide unless you are equipped with the necessary gear and techniques to do it safely. The only guides legally able to guide commercially in the Alps on glaciated terrain are high mountain guides, holding the UIAGM certificate.

You can find a guide at local Guides' Office – there are several in Chamonix and Courmayeur – or by searching the Internet. There are many companies offering holidays for a week or so, or you can find a guide for a couple of days to do a summit. There is an agreed local daily rate for guides, as well as an agreed guide:client ratio, and some summits (such as Mont Blanc) have their own tariff. Guides should adhere to these, so do not expect them to negotiate. The guide will also be able to advise on kit hire. Requirements are basic – you can go up a glaciated peak in your regular walking gear. You will need leather boots and gaiters, and will need to wear a climbing harness, crampons, and probably carry an ice axe.

You will be expected to pay for the guide's daily rate as well as his accommodation in huts and any lift costs incurred. Most peaks are done in two days – one day to walk up to a hut, the second to do the summit and descend. Any peaks above about 3500m require acclimatisation, so you would be expected to attain that height gradually – to climb Mont Blanc, for example, you would first do a peak less than 4000m, then one at around 4000m, before going for the 'Full Monty' at 4810m. If the weather is bad but you have reserved a guide you are expected to pay at least some of the guiding fee. The guide may well suggest an alternative lower-level activity such as rock climbing.

LISTING OF CICERONE GUIDES

**BRITISH ISLES CHALLENGES,
COLLECTIONS AND ACTIVITIES**
The End to End Trail
The Mountains of England and Wales
  Vol 1: Wales
  Vol 2: England
The National Trails
The Relative Hills of Britain
The Ridges of England, Wales and
  Ireland
The UK Trailwalker's Handbook
Three Peaks, Ten Tors

NORTHERN ENGLAND TRAILS
A Northern Coast to Coast Walk
Backpacker's Britain: Northern
  England
Hadrian's Wall Path
The Dales Way
The Pennine Way
The Spirit of Hadrian's Wall

LAKE DISTRICT
An Atlas of the English Lakes
Coniston Copper Mines
Great Mountain Days in the Lake
  District
Lake District Winter Climbs
Roads and Tracks of the Lake District
Rocky Rambler's Wild Walks
Scrambles in the Lake District
  North
  South
Short Walks in Lakeland
  Book 1: South Lakeland
  Book 2: North Lakeland
  Book 3: West Lakeland
The Central Fells
The Cumbria Coastal Way
The Cumbria Way and the Allerdale
  Ramble
The Lake District Anglers' Guide
The Mid-Western Fells
The Near Eastern Fells
The Southern Fells
The Tarns of Lakeland
  Vol 1: West
  Vol 2: East
Tour of the Lake District

**NORTH WEST ENGLAND AND THE
ISLE OF MAN**
A Walker's Guide to the Lancaster
  Canal
Historic Walks in Cheshire
Isle of Man Coastal Path
The Isle of Man
The Ribble Way
Walking in Lancashire
Walking in the Forest of Bowland
  and Pendle
Walking on the West Pennine Moors
Walks in Lancashire Witch Country
Walks in Ribble Country
Walks in Silverdale and Arnside
Walks in The Forest of Bowland

**NORTH EAST ENGLAND,
YORKSHIRE DALES AND PENNINES**
A Canoeist's Guide to the North East
Historic Walks in North Yorkshire
South Pennine Walks
The Cleveland Way and the Yorkshire
  Wolds Way
The North York Moors
The Reivers Way
The Teesdale Way
The Yorkshire Dales Angler's Guide
The Yorkshire Dales:
  North and East
  South and West
Walking in County Durham
Walking in Northumberland
Walking in the North Pennines
Walking in the Wolds
Walks in Dales Country
Walks in the Yorkshire Dales
Walks on the North York Moors
  Books 1 & 2

**DERBYSHIRE, PEAK DISTRICT AND
MIDLANDS**
High Peak Walks
Historic Walks in Derbyshire
The Star Family Walks
Walking in Derbyshire
White Peak Walks:
  The Northern Dales
  The Southern Dales

SOUTHERN ENGLAND
A Walker's Guide to the Isle of Wight
London: The Definitive Walking
  Guide
The Cotswold Way
The Greater Ridgeway
The Lea Valley Walk
The North Downs Way
The South Downs Way
The South West Coast Path
The Thames Path
Walking in Bedfordshire
Walking in Berkshire
Walking in Buckinghamshire
Walking in Kent
Walking in Sussex
Walking in the Isles of Scilly
Walking in the Thames Valley
Walking on Dartmoor

WALES AND WELSH BORDERS
Backpacker's Britain: Wales
Glyndwr's Way
Great Mountain Days in Snowdonia
Hillwalking in Snowdonia
Hillwalking in Wales
  Vols 1 & 2
Offa's Dyke Path
Ridges of Snowdonia
Scrambles in Snowdonia
The Ascent of Snowdon
The Lleyn Peninsula Coastal Path
The Pembrokeshire Coastal Path

The Shropshire Hills
The Spirit Paths of Wales
Walking in Pembrokeshire
Walking on the Brecon Beacons
Welsh Winter Climbs

SCOTLAND
Backpacker's Britain:
  Central and Southern Scottish
    Highlands
  Northern Scotland
Ben Nevis and Glen Coe
Border Pubs and Inns
North to the Cape
Scotland's Best Small Mountains
Scotland's Far West
Scotland's Mountain Ridges
Scrambles in Lochaber
The Border Country
The Central Highlands
The Great Glen Way
The Isle of Skye
The Pentland Hills: A Walker's Guide
The Scottish Glens
  2 The Atholl Glens
  3 The Glens of Rannoch
  4 The Glens of Trossach
  5 The Glens of Argyll
  6 The Great Glen
The Southern Upland Way
The West Highland Way
Walking in Scotland's Far North
Walking in the Cairngorms
Walking in the Hebrides
Walking in the Ochils, Campsie Fells
  and Lomond Hills
Walking in Torridon
Walking Loch Lomond and the
  Trossachs
Walking on Harris and Lewis
Walking on Jura, Islay and Colonsay
Walking on the Isle of Arran
Walking on the Orkney and Shetland
  Isles
Walking the Galloway Hills
Walking the Lowther Hills
Walking the Munros
  Vol 1: Southern, Central and
    Western Highlands
  Vol 2: Northern Highlands and the
    Cairngorms
Winter Climbs – Ben Nevis and
  Glencoe
Winter Climbs in the Cairngorms

UK CYCLING
Border Country Cycle Routes
Lands End to John O'Groats Cycle
  Guide
Rural Rides No 2: East Surrey
South Lakeland Cycle Rides
The Lancashire Cycleway

ALPS – CROSS BORDER ROUTES
100 Hut Walks in the Alps
Across the Eastern Alps: E5

Alpine Points of View
Alpine Ski Mountaineering
    Vol 1: Western Alps
    Vol 2: Central and Eastern Alps
Chamonix to Zermatt
Snowshoeing
Tour of Mont Blanc
Tour of Monte Rosa
Tour of the Matterhorn
Walking in the Alps
Walks and Treks in the Maritime Alps

FRANCE
Écrins National Park
GR20: Corsica
Mont Blanc Walks
The Cathar Way
The GR5 Trail
The Robert Louis Stevenson Trail
Tour of the Oisans: The GR54
Tour of the Queyras
Tour of the Vanoise
Trekking in the Vosges and Jura
Vanoise Ski Touring
Walking In Provence
Walking in the Cathar Region
Walking in the Cevennes
Walking in the Dordogne
Walking in the Haute Savoie
    North
    South
Walking in the Languedoc
Walking in the Tarentaise &
    Beaufortain Alps
Walking on Corsica
Walking the French Gorges
Walks in Volcano Country

**PYRENEES AND FRANCE/SPAIN
CROSS-BORDER ROUTES**
Rock Climbs In The Pyrenees
The GR10 Trail
The Mountains of Andorra
The Pyrenean Haute Route
The Way of St James
    France
    Spain
Through the Spanish Pyrenees: GR11
Walks and Climbs in the Pyrenees

SPAIN & PORTUGAL
Costa Blanca Walks
    Vol 1: West
    Vol 2: East
The Mountains of Central Spain
Trekking through Mallorca
Via de la Plata
Walking in Madeira
Walking in Mallorca
Walking in the Algarve
Walking in the Canary Islands:
    Vol 2: East
Walking in the Cordillera Cantabrica
Walking in the Sierra Nevada
Walking the GR7 in Andalucia
Walks and Climbs in the Picos de
    Europa

SWITZERLAND
Alpine Pass Route
Central Switzerland

The Bernese Alps
Tour of the Jungfrau Region
Walking in the Valais
Walking in Ticino
Walks in the Engadine

GERMANY
Germany's Romantic Road
King Ludwig Way
Walking in the Bavarian Alps
Walking in the Harz Mountains
Walking in the Salzkammergut
Walking the River Rhine Trail

EASTERN EUROPE
The High Tatras
The Mountains of Romania
Walking in Bulgaria's National Parks
Walking in Hungary

SCANDINAVIA
Walking in Norway

**SLOVENIA, CROATIA AND
MONTENEGRO**
The Julian Alps of Slovenia
The Mountains of Montenegro
Trekking in Slovenia
Walking in Croatia

ITALY
Central Apennines of Italy
Gran Paradiso
Italian Rock
Italy's Sibillini National Park
Shorter Walks in the Dolomites
Through the Italian Alps
Trekking in the Apennines
Treks in the Dolomites
Via Ferratas of the Italian Dolomites:
    Vols 1 & 2
Walking in Sicily
Walking in the Central Italian Alps
Walking in the Dolomites
Walking in Tuscany
Walking on the Amalfi Coast

MEDITERRANEAN
Jordan – Walks, Treks, Caves,
    Climbs and Canyons
The Ala Dag
The High Mountains of Crete
The Mountains of Greece
Treks & Climbs in Wadi Rum, Jordan
Walking in Malta
Western Crete

HIMALAYA
Annapurna: A Trekker's Guide
Bhutan
Everest: A Trekker's Guide
Garhwal & Kumaon: A Trekker's and
    Visitor's Guide
Kangchenjunga: A Trekker's Guide
Langtang with Gosainkund &
    Helambu: A Trekker's Guide
Manaslu: A Trekker's Guide
The Mount Kailash Trek

NORTH AMERICA
British Columbia
The Grand Canyon

SOUTH AMERICA
Aconcagua and the Southern Andes

AFRICA
Climbing in the Moroccan Anti-Atlas
Kilimanjaro: A Complete Trekker's
    Guide
Trekking in the Atlas Mountains
Walking in the Drakensberg

IRELAND
Irish Coastal Walks
The Irish Coast To Coast Walk
The Mountains of Ireland

EUROPEAN CYCLING
Cycle Touring in France
Cycle Touring in Ireland
Cycle Touring in Spain
Cycle Touring in Switzerland
Cycling in the French Alps
Cycling the Canal du Midi
Cycling the River Loire
The Danube Cycleway
The Grand Traverse of the Massif
    Central
The Way of St James

**INTERNATIONAL CHALLENGES,
COLLECTIONS AND ACTIVITIES**
Canyoning
Europe's High Points

AUSTRIA
Klettersteig – Scrambles in the
    Northern Limestone Alps
Trekking in Austria's Hohe Tauern
Trekking in the Stubai Alps
Trekking in the Zillertal Alps
Walking in Austria

TECHNIQUES
Indoor Climbing
Map and Compass
Mountain Weather
Moveable Feasts
Outdoor Photography
Rock Climbing
Snow and Ice Techniques
Sport Climbing
The Book of the Bivvy
The Hillwalker's Guide to
    Mountaineering
The Hillwalker's Manual

MINI GUIDES
Avalanche!
Navigating with a GPS
Navigation
Pocket First Aid and Wilderness
    Medicine
Snow

For full and up-to-date information
on our ever-expanding list of guides,
please visit our website:
www.cicerone.co.uk.

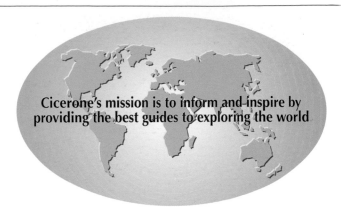

Cicerone's mission is to inform and inspire by providing the best guides to exploring the world

Since its foundation 40 years ago, Cicerone has specialised in publishing guidebooks and has built a reputation for quality and reliability. It now publishes nearly 300 guides to the major destinations for outdoor enthusiasts, including Europe, UK and the rest of the world.

Written by leading and committed specialists, Cicerone guides are recognised as the most authoritative. They are full of information, maps and illustrations so that the user can plan and complete a successful and safe trip or expedition – be it a long face climb, a walk over Lakeland fells, an alpine cycling tour, a Himalayan trek or a ramble in the countryside.

With a thorough introduction to assist planning, clear diagrams, maps and colour photographs to illustrate the terrain and route, and accurate and detailed text, Cicerone guides are designed for ease of use and access to the information.

If the facts on the ground change, or there is any aspect of a guide that you think we can improve, we are always delighted to hear from you.

Cicerone Press
2 Police Square Milnthorpe Cumbria LA7 7PY
Tel: 015395 62069 Fax: 015395 63417
info@cicerone.co.uk www.cicerone.co.uk